OXFORD MONOGRAPHS ON SOCIAL ANTHROPOLOGY

General Editors

Fetching water from the river — an Iban woman and girl in the Lemanak

THE IBAN
AND
THEIR RELIGION

BY

ERIK JENSEN

OXFORD
AT THE CLARENDON PRESS
1974

Oxford University Press, Ely House, London W. 1

GLASGOW NEW YORK TORONTO MELBOURNE WELLINGTON
CAPE TOWN IBADAN NAIROBI DAR ES SALAAM LUSAKA ADDIS ABABA
DELHI BOMBAY CALCUTTA MADRAS KARACHI LAHORE DACCA
KUALA LUMPUR SINGAPORE HONG KONG TOKYO

ISBN 0 19 823179 2

© *Oxford University Press 1974*

*Printed in Great Britain
at the University Press, Oxford
by Vivian Ridler
Printer to the University*

FOR PAMELA

PREFACE

A CHANCE meeting in Oxford with the Right Revd. Nigel Cornwall, of the Anglican Church of Borneo, first made me aware of Borneo and the Iban. The Revd. Jack Sparrow taught me something of their language and infected me with his real sympathy for the Iban (it is sad that he is not alive to see the results of an investigation in which he was so genuinely interested). I am grateful to them both and to the Anglican Church of Borneo for their interest and for making the preparatory stages of this study possible.

I sailed for Borneo in October 1959 and returned to Europe finally in August 1966. On arrival in Sarawak I spent nearly eighteen months in an Iban community in the Ulu Undup and the next three years living among the Iban of the Lemanak, both in the Second Division. For the remainder of my time in Sarawak, I was based at the Divisional headquarters in Simanggang but continued to visit and work with the Iban daily. The initial period was devoted to general research and to learning the Iban language, which I was able to speak quite fluently after the first year, and which I used in all conversation with Borneans for the rest of my time in Malaysia. From 1961 to 1965 my responsibilities, initially as a Community Development Officer, and subsequently as an Administrative Officer (Divisional Development Officer), not only enabled but actually obliged me to further my studies of Iban social organization and agricultural practice. In 1966 a grant from the Secretariat for Technical Co-operation with the Developing Countries of the Foreign Office of Denmark, for which I am most grateful, made it possible for me to return to Sarawak and undertake further research.

I received great kindness, hospitality, and encouragement from all the Second Division Residents in my time: Mr. and Mrs. Anthony Richards, Mr. and Mrs. Richard Morris, Mr. and Mrs. Julian Drake-Brockman, Mr. and Mrs. Terry Weekes, Mr. and Mrs. Graham Lloyd-Thomas. Anthony Richards, in particular, shared my enthusiasm for the Iban, and I am indebted to him for many insights which arose during our discussions both in Sarawak and, more recently, in Cambridge. Tom Harrisson and his successor as curator of the Sarawak Museum, Benedict Sandin, also stimulated my thinking in a variety of ways. My colleagues, District and Development Officers Tom Ainsworth, Martin Christie, H. A. L. Ferguson, Arni Haji Lampam, Jim Warburton, and many others both within and outside the Administration, but especially Dr. and Mrs. Colin Menzies-Kitchin and Major and Mrs. Ian St. Johnston, were unfailing friends and showed me more kindness that I can hope to repay.

In preparing this book, I am particularly indebted to Dr. Rodney Needham, of the Institute of Social Anthropology, who supervised my work at Oxford, and offered me continuing encouragement and perspicacious comment, to the late Professor Sir E. E. Evans-Pritchard for criticizing what I had written and urging me to publish, and to Dr. H. S. Morris of the London School of Economics for his constructive advice. I am grateful to the State Scientific Research Foundation of Denmark for its generous assistance and to Professor Nikolajsen of the University of Copenhagen for most helpful support during the period spent organizing my notes and for permission to republish material from *Folk*.

I also want to thank several of my friends for their assistance, direct and indirect, and those who worked long and painstakingly on the typescripts and index, my mother and sister for their tolerance when, on returning from Sarawak, I flooded their apartment with my material, and my father for his example.

Ultimately, however, it was the Iban who made this study possible. I can never express adequately much of what they taught me of themselves and their way of life, and equally about life in general. They made my years in Sarawak as happy as they were profitable. I cannot mention them all individually—the list would be too long—I owe hospitality to so many for many nights and days in different longhouses, but I must name Nulie and my fellow-workers during three years in the Lemanak, in particular, Nanyie, Klunchai, Dundang, and Jabah; rarely have I found equal qualities of helpfulness, love, and loyalty.

ERIK JENSEN

December 1973

CONTENTS

LIST OF ILLUSTRATIONS

LIST OF TABLES

I. INTRODUCTION

BORNEO has been the subject of many books. The country and its people fascinated European travellers from the time of their coming to South-East Asia and many recorded their experiences. Among the earliest voyages to South-East Asia were those of Magellan and Ludovico de Barthema. But the travellers' tales which deal specifically with Borneo and Sarawak date from the advent of James Brooke towards the middle of the nineteenth century. Keppel,[1] then Low (1848), Marryat (1848), and others produced lengthy descriptions of their journeys which contain important observations, and in the 1860s St. John[2] wrote two useful volumes and the second Rajah-to-be (Brooke, 1866) published his *Ten Years in Sarawak.*

Boyle (1865) in the same period exploited that vogue for the exotic which was to become characteristic during the following century of so many Borneo books—both those concerning the British- and those about the Dutch-administered parts of the island. These included works such as those of Bock (1881), Furness (1902), Walker (1910), Mjöberg (1927), and, more recently, Ivanoff (1958). The exotic books have been at best exaggerated, at worst actively misleading—not least those of the 'noble savage' or 'glamorous primitive' school of photographers who have developed the market in recent years.[3] In the last category the notable exception is Hedda Morrison[4] whose pictures are as informative and true to life in Sarawak as they are beautiful.

Borneo did not only 'steal the hearts' (Cook, 1924) of the sensationalists, however; there were many who wrote out of a real feeling for and knowledge of the country and its people. Their experience and the length of time they lived in Sarawak varied; so do their accounts and viewpoints. Hose devoted a lifetime to the Rajah's service and produced several books,[5] although in the course

[1] 1846. Keppel, 1853, wrote again of his experiences in the 'Indian Archipelago' and included portions of the journal of James Brooke.

[2] 1863. St. John, 1879, also wrote a life of James Brooke.

[3] For example Wong, 1960 (entitled *Pagan Innocence*), and Bisch, 1961.

[4] 1957 and 1962; the latter, *Life in a Longhouse*, devoted exclusively to the Iban.

[5] 1912 (in collaboration with McDougall), 1926, and 1929 are especially important.

of them he repeats some of the same material. At the other end of the scale, Malcolm MacDonald (1956) only visited Sarawak briefly in a very senior capacity, but succeeds in communicating in his record a genuine sympathy for, and understanding of, Sarawak's people. In addition to the administrators and government officials who spent their working lives in Sarawak, there were also the missionaries: in particular, Perham,[1] Gomes,[2] and Howell[3] who was himself married to an Iban woman. Between them they produced the bulk of the major writing about Sarawak as it first became known to the world.

In more recent years the most prolific author, and probably the best known, has been Tom Harrisson. He first went to Borneo with an Oxford (and Cambridge) University expedition before the Second World War,[4] and returned during the Japanese occupation to live among the Kelabit people.[5] Subsequently, during his long post-war tenure of the curatorship of the Sarawak Museum and as government ethnologist, Harrisson wrote and edited many articles for the *Sarawak Museum Journal* and other publications.[6] He has also collaborated with Benedict Sandin,[7] himself an Iban and Harrisson's successor at the Sarawak Museum, in translating and preparing Iban texts and other material for publication.[8]

Although many of these works—especially the later writings of Harrisson and Sandin—contribute to our understanding of Sarawak

[1] Published in the *Journal of the Royal Asiatic Society* and included in Ling Roth's compilation, 1896.

[2] 1911 and 1917; he quotes extensively from Perham's material.

[3] Contributions to the *Sarawak Gazette*, some republished in the Borneo Literature Bureau compilation, 1963, but his principal contribution is undoubtedly the *Dictionary*: Howell (and Bailey), 1900; see also the supplement, Howell, 1961.

[4] In 1932, described in Harrisson, 1938. A second University expedition to Sarawak is recorded in Arnold, 1959.

[5] 1959a gives an account of this experience and the Kelabits.

[6] Among others 1959b, 1960, 1962, 1965a, 1965b.

[7] Sandin and Harrisson have worked closely together on a number of Iban studies, some of which are certainly Sandin's work, 1956, 1957, 1959, 1961, 1962a, 1964, and some of which are essentially Harrisson's, 1962, 1965a. Sandin and Harrisson appear as co-authors of their latest and most ambitious study, 1966, the lengthy paper on writing-boards.

[8] Sandin has also published several collections of Iban lore in Iban designed primarily as reading matter for the growing number of Iban literates (e.g. 1962b), but these also include interesting general and protohistorical material, such as that contained in Sandin's first book in English, 1967.

and the Iban in particular, even as a whole they cover only parts
of the anthropological material.[1]

South-East Asia has been called 'an anthropologist's paradise'[2]
and the variety of peoples and cultures is widely known. In Sarawak
alone the 1940 census classified a population of three-quarters of a
million into fifty-one 'races', three of which were subdivided into
eighty-one 'tribes'.[3] But in spite of the extensive literature a very
large section of this population has never been systematically described. This applies partly to the Iban who make up more than a
third of the total. After the response to early encounters with the
Iban, or Sea Dyaks as they were commonly called, and the excitement aroused by their reputation as head-hunters and off-shore
pirates had subsided, the attention of writers like Hose and Harrisson was diverted to the more 'interesting' Kayan-Kenyah-Kelabit
peoples. With the exception of a meticulous study by Haddon and
Start (1936), which is limited to Iban fabrics and weaving, little significant material appeared concerning the Iban between the time
of Howell's essays, published primarily in the *Sarawak Gazette*,
and the major study of J. D. Freeman.[4] Freeman lived among the
Iban of the Balleh in the Third Division of Sarawak from February
1949 until January 1951, and he visited Sarawak again from
December 1957 to March 1958 (1958b, 3). His main work deals
with Iban social organization and agriculture, although he has also
published papers on other aspects of Iban culture.[5]

[1] A number of anthropological studies have been undertaken in Sarawak
since the war. After an exploratory investigation by Leach, 1950, into the
possibilities for a social economic survey, the Colonial Social Science Research
Council sponsored the work of Morris among the Melanau, 1953, T'ien among
the Chinese, 1953, Geddes among the Land Dyaks, 1954, (see also a popular
account, 1961), and Freeman among the Iban, 1955a (and 1955b). Under
different auspices Needham worked among the Penan (see 1954a, 1954b, 1955,
etc.). Of these only Freeman's work has direct bearing on Iban studies; see
below.
[2] Hall, 1964, 5; Tarling, 1966, 9, calls it 'an ethnic museum'.
[3] Leach, 1950, 15, paras. 74 seq. discusses the classification of Sarawak
peoples.
[4] Freeman's work deals with Iban agriculture, 1955a, the subject of his
official report, published by H.M. Stationery Office, and social organization.
His study of Iban social organization has appeared in various forms, of which
the most important are the versions published for use in Sarawak, 1955b, that
included in Cambridge Papers in Social Anthropology, 1957a (ed. Goody 1958)
and 1958b, which make use of much the same material for slightly different
purposes.
[5] Iban augury, 1960a, for example; a note on the Gawai Kenyalang, 1960b,
and a paper on Iban pottery, 1957b.

It would be possible to justify a second study of Iban society on the grounds that circumstances in the Balleh might not apply to all Iban,[1] and comparative material from the Second Division, the oldest area of Iban settlement in Sarawak, would therefore be significant. It is also true that some of the conditions described by Freeman, in particular certain facets of shifting cultivation, no longer obtain in many areas. That, however, is not the purpose of this book. It does not set out to compare the Iban of the Second Division interior with the Balleh Iban, nor is it comparative in the wider sense.

Many of the peoples of Malaysia and Indonesia have long believed in spirits, the spirits of men both living and dead, spirits which inhabit living things, inanimate objects, and natural phenomena, not least the spirit of rice. In spite of Hinduism and the later influence of Islam, many of these traditional beliefs still exist among Muslim Malays and the peoples of Indonesia. The concept of the *samengat*, for example, is important to the peninsular Malays (see Skeat, 1900, 47 seq., *et al.*) and to the Indonesian Javanese (see, for example, Landon, 1949, 15 seq.). The same words, folklore, and taboos occur in different societies.[2] But although some ancient concepts have survived under old or new names, many have either disappeared or changed their character under the influence of other religions. Hinduism has touched the Iban, as the title for a deity (*petara*) and the names of some of the spirits imply.[3] But neither Hinduism nor Islam has radically influenced Iban religion which remains a cult based on a belief in the spirits of men, nature, and super-nature. Although many words belong to the regional vocabulary, the Iban have given them a meaning of their own as any reading of this text, should make clear.[4] It would be

[1] Leach, 1950, 27, para. 135, comments on Kayan influence among the Balleh Iban and suggests that to this extent they may not be entirely typical.

[2] To name only one example in each category: (*h*)*antu* is a widespread Malaysian name for (mischievous or evil) spirits; skirt-loss occurs as a theme in the myths and folklore of various Malay peoples; the taboo against the mockery of animals is general, and *plandok* mouse-deer stories are common throughout the region.

[3] For example, see below, pp. 100 seq.

[4] This applies to words of Hindu and Arabic as well as Malaysian origin like *petara*, *adat*, *samengat*, and *antu* (see below, Chapter VIII), which have key meanings in Iban religion. More general words, like those for the earth, *dunya*, sky, *langit*, and a district or area, *menoa*, which have also come into Malaysia from abroad, are part of daily Iban usage. Without being specifically religious,

fascinating to attempt to trace the sources of Iban religion—something which I hope at a later juncture to undertake—but this falls outside the bounds of the present study which is neither historical nor comparative. The literature on the Malaysian–Indonesian area and peoples is vast. It would expand the scope of this work beyond reasonable limits if a great quantity of comparative material (even parallels from the Ngaju) were to be included.

This book attempts to provide an ethnographical account of Iban behaviour, the religious beliefs which are the basis for their way of life, the framework within which these exist, and the ends to which they are directed. Freeman,[1] in passing, emphasized the 'cardinal importance' of the ritual acts and concepts expressed in the Iban rice cult, which is the centre of their religion, planning to 'deal fully with this most important and fascinating subject in a separate monograph'—a point which was taken up by Smythies (1956, 243) in his review of Freeman. Although this is a fact which has escaped the majority, as Freeman explicitly says, 'only when the inter-dependence of economics, social organization and ritual are understood can there be any genuine appreciation of Iban agricultural practice' (1955a, 32, para. 66).

In spite of the vast literature on Sarawak in general and the many references to the Iban in particular, no systematic study has been published on Iban religion and its significance for an understanding of their social organization and system of agriculture. Nor has Freeman yet produced the monograph he had in mind. The Iban themselves express the connection and interdependence of their social organization, agricultural practice, and religion most succinctly when they say: *adat kami bumai.* This means 'we farm (hill rice) and live according to the order revealed by the spirits.' The word *adat*, which is normally translated 'customary law', may mean much more than this. To the Iban it involves the basic values of life, their system of agriculture, as well as the code according to which their society is ordered. It also concerns the 'correct' manner of behaviour. *Adat* is applied not only to men but also to animals and to natural phenomena. This is a study not of Iban customary law, but of Iban *adat* in general, their way of life.

they have implications for the understanding of Iban beliefs. The Malay *nasip* (or *nasit*) also occurs occasionally among the Iban, but neither the word nor the Malay *nasip*-fortune concept is an authentic part of the Iban tradition.

[1] 1955a, 32, para. 66 (repeated in 1955b, ii. 13, para. 221).

The facts of Iban social organization and their rice-centred economy are followed by a summary of the principal myths, an account of their belief in spirits and ordered world-view, the pattern of the seasonal rice cycle, and a description of the major rituals which are the social culmination of one agricultural season and ritual inauguration of the next. Head-hunting is mentioned only in passing, and other aspects of Iban life might also have been discussed in greater detail. But this is an examination of Iban religion and the rice cult as it existed during the years just before and after independence in Sarawak—as it existed then, and not as it was more than a generation ago. Since its successful suppression in the 1920s, head-hunting has not played an active role in Iban behaviour. This book describes—in the ethnographic present tense—the situation, principally in the Second Division of Sarawak, as it was during the years 1959 to 1966.

Owing to recent legislation, and especially the government-sponsored rubber-planting scheme, improved communications, and educational amenities established under the Sarawak Development Plan of 1964 to 1968 and the First Malaysian Development Plan, the traditional Iban way of life is changing further. This way of life, the religious focus on the rice cult, an economy based almost exclusively on hill rice cultivation and social organization centred on the longhouse community of separate *bilek* families—this way of life which has survived for centuries, if not already close to extinction, is likely to disappear with the older generation of living Iban.

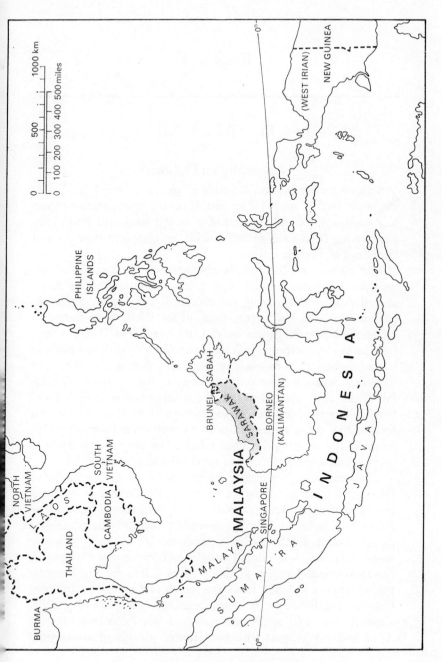

MAP 1. South-East Asia

PART 1

II. SARAWAK

Geography and Climate

SARAWAK lies between latitude 0° 50′ and 5° north and longitude 109° 30′ and 115° 40′ east. It covers approximately 48,300 square miles and consists of a coastal strip, 450 miles long and varying from 40 to 120 miles wide, on the north-west coast of the island of Borneo.

The climate of Sarawak is characterized by heavy rainfall, uniform temperature, and high relative humidity. The mean annual rainfall at Kuching, the capital, is 158 inches. For comparison, London has twenty-four inches, New York forty-two inches, and even Singapore only ninety-five inches. The distribution, however, is erratic: 'it is not unusual for rainfall at a place to exceed eight inches in one day, especially during the Northeast Monsoon, while a place forty miles away has no recorded rainfall' (Seal, 1958, 500). However, the weather is invariably hot and humid. The temperature ranges from 72 °F to 88 °F at mean sea level, with a mean temperature over twenty-four hours of 78 °F. At six in the morning the mean relative humidity over the year is 98 per cent, and 70 per cent at two in the afternoon.

The seasons are not clearly defined, but from the beginning of October to towards the end of February, the north-east monsoon brings particularly heavy rainfall. An exposed coastal belt such as Sarawak is influenced by the boundary layer of the north-east monsoon on its southern trends, giving rainfall of twenty inches or more. The heaviest rainfall usually occurs during November, December, and January. (Table 1 gives details for the five-year period 1951–5.) Apart from the north-east monsoon between October and February, it is not meaningful to speak of seasons, although the mild south-east monsoon usually occurs between April and July/August with two shorter periods of about eight

TABLE I

Records of monthly rainfall at Lubok Antu[1]

(in inches)

Year	Jan.	Feb.	Mar.	Apr.	May	June	July	Aug.	Sept.	Oct.	Nov.	Dec.	Total
1951	21·40	15·41	6·08	11·77	13·00	5·96	5·57	8·26	10·80	13·12	13·92	13·06	138·35
1952	12·33	8·62	12·02	10·94	13·30	2·81	8·71	5·22	10·30	9·67	18·90	9·65	122·47
1953	20·9	13·34	12·94	10·38	8·94	7·22	11·74	6·34	9·59	11·83	6·06	15·16	115·63
1954	13·18	11·18	9·31	14·86	5·04	6·39	8·52	11·20	8·16	12·04	12·63	12·48	124·99
1955	6·53	13·65	10·82	17·44	4·29	3·50	15·36	18·45	9·23	5·81	12·24	12·28	129·60
Mean	11·11	12·44	10·23	13·08	8·91	5·18	9·98	9·89	9·61	10·49	12·75	12·53	126·21

[1] From Seal, 1958, 519, Table 18.

weeks each separating the end of one 'season' from the beginning of the other.

Ecology

The island of Borneo, which is the third largest in the world, after Greenland and New Guinea, is covered in forest. It is estimated that 75 per cent of the entire island is under primary forest, and a further 10 to 15 per cent under secondary forest. Sarawak itself can be divided into three main zones: an alluvial and swampy coastal plain, an area of rolling country intersected by mountain ranges, and a mountainous region in the interior. The forests of the lowland area are dominated by 'the family *Diptero-carpaceae*'. 'In the montane zone the forest changes to oaks and chestnuts, with a sprinkling of conifers of the genera *Agathis*, *Podocarpus*, and *Dacrydium*. At an altitude depending on local climatic conditions, distance from the coast, and other factors, but usually around 4,000 feet, "moss forest" appears, characterized by rather stunted vegetation covered in dense wrappings of dripping moss' (Smythies, 1960, 15).

These botanical details fail to bring out the particular nature of the jungle. As an environment, tropical rain forest has certain characteristics which are significant to an understanding of the people who live there. Geddes (1961, 8) says that 'to try to understand the attitudes of the Land Dayaks, I believe that one must do more than study their economy, their politics, their mating and breeding habits. One should go into the jungle, quite often and sometimes alone.' This applies equally to the Iban, who for the most part inhabit the rolling forest-covered country of the montane zone.

This is a world of luxuriant vegetation, where wild fruit, vegetables, even bamboo and timber for construction abound, but perpetual humidity rots, insects undermine, and the jungle relentlessly encroaches on a clearing only briefly abandoned. It is not a harsh environment. It is easy to subsist, to obtain the basic necessities of life, but to approach permanence in the Borneo jungle is, in Iban circumstances, almost impossible. Signs of human activity disappear quickly; human achievement is at all times ephemeral. The outstanding characteristic, however, of life in the jungle is neither its comparative ease nor its difficulty; it lies in its unpredictability. Rain falls heavily out of season or sometimes fails to fall when most expected and most needed. Rice farms are liable to be devoured by swarms of pests against which the Iban are virtually powerless. Rivers which are both the source of water and the main means of communication rise overnight in sudden, destructive floods. Above all, disease and early death, poisonous insects, snakes, crocodiles, and other wild life strike one man and not another in an apparently irrational manner. It is the unpredictable, even capricious, character of life in the Sarawak jungle, to which the Iban has to adjust and for which he seeks an explanation.

Historical Background

From the fifteenth until the early part of the nineteenth century, Sarawak was in theory part of the Sultanate of Brunei. Provincial governors ruled on the Sultan's behalf and paid tribute to him. Around 1837, when Sarawak local groups were in revolt against the governor, Pangiran Makota, the Rajah Muda Hasim (from Brunei) 'moved there in order to bring the province back to its allegiance' (Runciman, 1960, 57). In return for assistance in restoring law and order, an Englishman, James Brooke, was promised the raj of Sarawak by Hasim. However, after Brooke's second visit to Sarawak in 1840 when the rebellion was successfully put down, this promise had yet to be fulfilled. Again in 1841 Brooke returned to Kuching to find the situation unchanged, but, after a sequence of dramatic events, he was successful in persuading Hasim to draw up and sign the document by which, on 24 November 1841, James Brooke was proclaimed Rajah and Governor of Sarawak.[1]

James Brooke, as the first Rajah of Sarawak, was granted additional lands by the Sultan of Brunei in 1861. His nephew and heir, Charles (Johnson) Brooke, the second Rajah, further increased the territory by cession, annexation, and purchase until, by 1905, it had been brought to its present size, more than twenty times that of the original raj granted to James Brooke. Sarawak had grown to cover the area drained by the Sarawak, Lupar, Rejang, Baram, and Limbang rivers, thus encompassing the entire north-eastern part of Borneo from Lundu in the west to Limbang in the east, and actually encircling the reduced Sultanate of Brunei.

In 1941 the third Rajah, Sir Charles Vyner Brooke, enacted a

[1] See Runciman, 1960, 56–67, whose description is based largely on the early accounts of Keppel, 1846, Mundy, 1848, and St. John, 1879.

new constitution to mark the centenary of Brooke rule. This was the first move towards democratic self-government. However, after the Japanese occupation from 1941 to 1945, the Rajah felt unable to restore Sarawak to its former relative prosperity with the resources available to him, and proposed cession to the British crown. In May 1946 a bill was duly passed by Council Negri, the State legislative assembly, and Sarawak became a Crown Colony. A new constitution in 1956 made provision for an elected majority in the legislature, and in 1963 the formation of the Federation of Malaysia brought independence to Sarawak as a member state of the new federation together with Sabah (previously known as North Borneo), Singapore, and the federated states of peninsular Malaya.

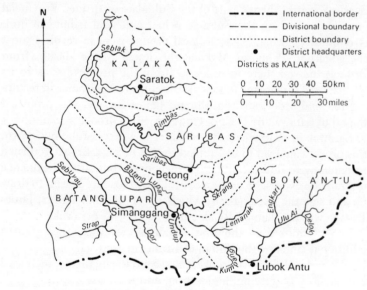

MAP 2. Sarawak: Second Division

Administration

For administrative purposes Sarawak is divided into five Divisions.[1] The senior administrative officer in each Division is the Resident. Each Division is divided into Districts (under District Officers) and sub-districts (with Sarawak Administrative Officers in charge).

[1] This describes the situation at the time of research.

Administration

TABLE 2

Divisions and Districts of Sarawak

Division	First	Second	Third	Fourth	Fifth
Administrative centre	Kuching	Simanggang	Sibu	Miri	Limbang
Districts	Lundu Bau Kuching Serian Sadong	Batang Lupar Lubok Antu Saribas Kalaka	Sarikei Binatang Sibu Kanowit Kapit Mukah	Bintulu Miri Baram	Limbang Lawas
Total area in square miles	3,464	4,129	22,465	15,094	3,190

TABLE 3

Second Division Districts: Area, Population, and Density[1]

District	Area (in sq. miles)	Total population[2]	Density (persons per sq. mile)
Batang Lupar	1,754	40,389	23
Lubok Antu	983	16,129	16
Saribas	741	28,292	38
Kalaka	651	24,612	38

[1] Jones, 1962, 29. (In the 1960 Census Report Batang Lupar is referred to as Simanggang, the name given to the Census District.) These figures for area and population density do not agree with those quoted by Leach, 1950, figure between pp. 46 and 47. The differences may be explained partly by the redefinition of District boundaries and partly by the fact that Leach did not have the final figures of even the 1947 census when preparing his report (as he states on p. 15).

[2] The 1960 Census Report (Jones, 1962, 29) also gives figures for 1939 and 1947 as an indication of population growth; these are as follows:

District	Total population			Percentage change
	1939	1947	1960	1947–60
Batang Lupar (called Simanggang)	29,146	31,537	40,389	+28·1
Lubok Antu	13,948	15,264	16,129	+ 5·7
Saribas	23,149	24,607	28,292	+15·0
Kalaka	19,682	21,262	24,612	+15·8

As shown in Table 2, both Divisions and Districts vary substantially in size. They also vary greatly in density of population. The greater part of the vast Third and Fourth Divisions is either very sparsely populated or uninhabited. Table 3 gives the area, total population, and population density of the Districts which make up the Second Division.[1] These are the original areas of Iban settlement and still comprise a very large part of Sarawak's total Iban population.

Population

According to the 1960 census all races in Sarawak numbered approximately three-quarters of a million. Just under one-third of the total in 1960 were Chinese living principally in bazaars and business centres, and approximately one-fifth Malays residing mainly in coastal regions. The largest single group in the heterogeneous population were the Iban (or Sea D(a)yaks) making up more than one-third, and these were found throughout the hill country (see Fig. 3). The remainder (as shown in Table 4) consisted of other indigenous groups: Land Dyaks, Melanaus, Kayans, Kenyahs, Kelabits, Punans, etc., of whom the Land Dyaks, then Melanaus, were the most numerous.[2]

TABLE 4

Population of Sarawak

Racial group	1960 Census	1965 estimate
Iban	237,741	246,000
Chinese	229,154	243,000
Malay	129,300	137,000
Land Dyaks	57,619	61,000
Melanau	44,661	46,000
Other indigenous	37,931	39,000
Others	8,123	8,000
Total	744,529	780,000

[1] Almost all surveys relevant to this study were undertaken in the Second Division, principally in the Undup, Lemanak, and Ulu Ai areas.

[2] For a discussion of the classification of Sarawak peoples, see Leach, 1950, 15 seq., and Jones, 1962, 47 seq., who refers to Noakes, 1950, Appendix entitled 'classifying the people'.

III. THE IBAN

The Name of the Iban

To the outside world the Iban were first known as Sea Dyaks. The word 'dyak' or 'dayak' has been widely used, in particular by the Dutch colonial administration in the East Indies, to signify any non-Malay (i.e., any non-Muslim) native. Chalmers thought that the word *dyak* meant simply 'man' in Land Dyak (Ling Roth, 1896, i. 42). Charles Brooke, however, states (1866, i. 46), in reference to the Land Dyaks, that 'the generic term Dyak (or properly called Dya by themselves) in many dialects means *inland*, although among many of the branch rivers the term is not known as being referable to themselves, further than its signification as a word in their language. Some of the interior populations . . . are called ka-daya-n.'[1] The Land Dyaks' word for inland is 'kadayo'. From this appears to have arisen the 'error of applying the name Dyak to all the inland tribes'.[2] Although Bampfylde[2] calls this the 'Dutch' error, it was common to both Dutch and English speakers. At the time of his compilation, Ling Roth wrote (1896, ii. 287, n. 5) that 'the name Dyak is here used in its generally but incorrectly accepted application to all natives of Borneo more or less wild'. This interpretation of the word has been queried, but whatever the derivation and meaning of 'dya' or 'daya' or 'dyak' itself, there is no doubt that as a description of indigenous Borneans it was early adopted by the Europeans.

James Brooke first encountered the Land Dyaks. In suppressing piracy he subsequently came across a distinct people who were superficially similar but different in language and culture: these he called Sea Dyaks, since 'these people frequent the ocean' (Ling Roth, 1896, i. 43). St. John (1863, i. 4) actually attributes 'Sea Dayak' as a term to the Malays. It is not unlikely that Brooke inquired of the Malays the name of the people and was given this description in answer.[3] Thus, through their association with the

[1] See also C. A. Bampfylde in 1882, quoted Ling Roth, 1896, i. 40.
[2] Ling Roth, 1896, i. 39, quoting C. A. Bampfylde.
[3] In a private communication A. J. N. Richards has suggested that 'Sea Dyak' might be a corruption of *sida iya*, a colloquial way of saying 'those

Malays engaged in off-shore piracy or on independent expeditions, the Iban became known to Europeans as the Sea Dyaks (Hose and McDougall, 1912, i. 188). Throughout a century of Brooke rule the Iban were known to the administration as Sea Dyaks: both the 1947 and 1960 Census Reports (Noakes, 1950; Jones, 1962) refer to 'Sea Dayaks'—the former including notes and an appendix on terminology (and classification)—but, as many writers, including the author of the second Census Report, have observed,[1] the name is inaccurate and misleading. The Iban are not a seafaring people in spite of occasional head-hunting forays off the coast; they are a hill people who live for the most part long distances from the sea and whose economy is agricultural.

While Sea Dayak survives as an alternative name, Iban has long been used throughout large parts of Sarawak. Iban is thought to be in origin a Kayan word. According to Hart-Everett (Ling Roth, 1896, i. 40): '. . . the Kayans habitually designate Sea-Dyaks as "Ivan" among themselves, whence the Dyaks have applied the name; but having no v-sound in their language, they say "Iban" . . . I have been informed, though I cannot vouch for the accuracy of the statement, that "Ivan" in Kayan is a term carrying with it a sense of opprobrium. . . . That on the Rejang the Sea Dyaks should have adopted the name given them by their enemies is very curious.' Needham (1955, 168) thinks it is most unlikely that 'Iban' would have been adopted had it been a term of derision. Another (tentative) explanation claims that 'Iban' or 'Ivan' means merely a 'wanderer'[2] but this has not been substantiated.[3] Whatever its derivation, Iban was adopted by the Sea Dyaks and quickly came into widespread use—especially in the Third Division, the Rejang and its tributaries. It was certainly in use some years before Haddon (according to Freeman)[4] 'introduced [it] to ethnographical literature' in 1901 (Haddon, 1901, 325); it occurs, for example, in a quotation from Hart-Everett (see above, Ling Roth, 1896, i. 40).

there', or, more idiomatically if less grammatically, 'them there'. This is entertaining, but, as he admits, not very likely.

[1] See, for example, Freeman, 1957a, 51, n. 1; 1958b, 43, n. 3; Jones, 1962, 51, which reads: 'Why the Sea Dayaks are *Sea* Dayaks is apparently obscure, all the more obscure for their being an inland people . . .', *et al.*

[2] Hose and McDougall, 1912, ii. 249–50; see also Hose, 1926, 7.

[3] Richards, 1959, 10, says 'Iban (or Ivan) was once said to be a Kayan word for wanderer, but it is only to be found meaning father, or mother-in-law . . .'.

[4] 1957a, 51, n. 1, and 1958b, 43, n. 3.

For a long time Sea Dyak continued to be the preferred name of the sophisticated who had received some Western education and, commonly, abandoned their traditional religious practices; and on occasion these would refer disdainfully to the others as 'Iban'. In recent years, more especially with improved communications, Iban has come into general use not just as the only name for information, broadcasting, and other official services in the Iban language, but for the people as a whole.

Among the Iban themselves the word can be used in three ways: first, in the ordinary sense to mean an Iban as opposed to a Land Dyak, Kayan, Malay, Chinese, etc; secondly, to mean an ordinary Iban as opposed to a healer or *shaman* (*manang*); and thirdly, to mean, quite simply, a person, as, for example, in the phrase 'is there anyone at home?' (*bisi Iban di rumah?*). The first sense is the most common. The name Iban is used principally to distinguish their own from other peoples, when necessary. For although the Iban recognize the common language, culture, and religion of their people, among themselves they continue to use the name of the river valley they inhabit as if it were the name of the people. They say, for example, '*nya orang Skrang*'—'that's an Iban (literally, 'a man') from the Skrang' or to mean merely 'that's someone from the Skrang', and '*sida Delok*'—'the people from the Delok'. They call themselves '*kami Undup*'—'we of the Undup' or '*kami Lemanak*'—'we of the Lemanak', or, quite simply, '*kami menoa*'—'we (people) of this district'.

Physical Characteristics

The Iban are a short-statured, brachycephalic people of proto-Malayan stock. 'Proto-Malay' is the term applied by Haddon (1901, 321) to the 'broad-headed' peoples of Sarawak as opposed to the 'narrow-headed' whom he calls Indonesian. In an appendix to 'The Pagan Tribes of Borneo' he says[1] of his Iban measurements that 'the cephalic index forms a gradual series, the median being eighty-three, and therefore shows brachycephaly.' The Iban have an average height of 5′ 2″ (see Haddon, 1901, 325) and have straight or wavy hair and pale brown or cinnamon-coloured skin.[2]

---

[1] Hose and McDougall, 1912, Appendix by A. C. Haddon, 339.
[2] Ibid. 340.

Hose and McDougall (1912, ii. 248) also call the Iban proto-Malays, but use the word in a different sense. 'We regard them as Proto-Malays, that is to say, of the stock from which the true Malays of Sumatra and the Peninsula were differentiated by the influence of Arab culture.[1] A large number of the ancestors of the present Iban were probably brought to Borneo from Sumatra less than 200 years ago.' Elsewhere, Hose (1926, 7) says that 'the Iban probably turned up in Borneo less than 300 years ago.' For neither assertion is there much real evidence.[2] To judge by his reference to Malay nobles in the same context, Hose may have drawn his conclusion from the system of indirect rule he encountered in parts of the Second Division of Sarawak. Although not improbable that the Iban at some stage came from Sumatra (some legends overtly suggest the possibility)[3] there is no historical evidence and no verifiable support for the theory that they were systematically introduced in significant numbers at that particular date.

Migration to Sarawak

According to their own traditions and remembered history, the Iban came to Sarawak by way of the Kumpang valley from the middle reaches of the Kapuas river (in what is now Kalimantan Barat, a province of the Republic of Indonesia). From Sarawak genealogies, it would appear that the Iban have lived in Sarawak for up to fifteen generations.[4] Thus the original movement into Sarawak ended rather than began around three centuries ago.

From the Kumpang valley, which remains one of the easiest access routes into Sarawak from Indonesian Borneo, some of the Iban moved further up-river towards Lubok Antu, some down-river to Engkilili. The main Lupar river, which they settled on first coming to Sarawak, is still known to the Iban as the *Batang Ai* —'the river'.

They invaded primary forest which was largely uninhabited but for isolated nomadic tribes who lived off wild jungle produce and game. Iban legends refer to these variously as Punan, Bukitan, and

[1] See also Hose and McDougall, 1912, ii. 250 and 252.

[2] Sandin, 1967, 28, estimates 'that the period of Iban pioneer settlement in the major rivers of what is now the Second Division of Sarawak *ended* somewhere around 275 years ago—roughly at the beginning of the eighteenth century' [my italics].   [3] Sandin, 1964, 513 seq. (see also Sandin, 1967, 2).

[4] Sandin, 1967, 28 thinks: 'The migrations . . . took place between eleven and sixteen generations ago.'

Seru. They were few in number, and, if they inhabited the upper reaches of the Lupar at all, retreated rather than oppose the more powerful newcomers.[1] Place and river names survive which the Iban associate with encounters with the earlier occupants of the area,[2] but it was not until they penetrated as far as the Saribas area (the Layar and Paku rivers) that the Iban faced other peoples in force and met real opposition.

After settling the middle Lupar, the Iban advanced into the upper tributaries, the Mepi, Engkari, Delok, and Jinggin. They also settled the Lemanak river, the Undup, and the Skrang. Undup Iban subsequently migrated first to Bukit Balau by Banting, thence to Sebuyau (under the leadership of a man named Gelungan), and from Sebuyau to the First Division, where, after defeating the local population, they settled finally in the Sadong and Samarahan valleys as well as at Lundu. The major migrations were in the other direction. Manggi is believed to be the name of the Iban who led the move into the Skrang (Sandin, 1956, 60–2). Legend says he died when trying subsequently to see the Seru Dyaks of the Rimbas.[3] Another Iban, Tindin, migrated from the Skrang and advanced up the Paku; others settled the Layar. Legend still preserves the names of the Bukitan chiefs who ruled in the upper Layar and the upper Paku, Entigar, and Entingi (also called Entigu). According to Iban genealogies, Demong, the son of Entingi, married Rinda, the daughter of Tindin, and from this union leading Saribas Iban trace their descent.[4] The Bukitan people were to a large extent absorbed by the Saribas Iban,[5] who, around the turn of the nineteenth century, went on to settle the Rimbas, Krian, and Seblak river valleys also, bringing them to the edge of the Rejang delta.

All subsequent migrations can be traced to one or other of the

[1] An Iban proverbial expression says 'Don't be like a Bukitan' (*anang baka Beketan*) signifying someone who rushes off in a hurry without showing proper respect.

[2] The rivers Sungai Para, Sungai Senoan; the ridges Tinting Adau, Tinting Indai Tupai; the mountain Bukit Sapindah, etc.

[3] Very little is known of the Seru. Two summary descriptions of the people and their language appeared in the *Sarawak Gazette* in 1901 (reprinted Bailey, 1963, and de R., 1963).

[4] See, for example, Sandin, 1956, 73, repeated in Sandin, 1967, 115.

[5] The extent of intermarriage (both with Bukitans and Malays) is illustrated by surviving genealogies; see Sandin, 1964 and 1967 (especially 107–9, 115). This is important for the discussion of certain peculiarities associated with Iban religion as practised in the Saribas; see below, pp. 56–9.

early river groups. In the initial decades of the nineteenth century the movement into the Third Division began. Before this, the Rejang valley and its tributaries had been only sparsely populated. The Tanjong, Kanowit, and Lugat peoples were already living in settled communities in the area now defined by Sibu and Kapit, but these were numerically few. Nomadic Bukitans and Ukits were living in the jungle, but were equally unable to offer effective opposition to the Iban invaders.

The nomadic Ukits consistently opposed the Iban invaders and endeavoured to check their advance for as long as they were able. The Bukitans, on the other hand, became allies of the Iban, as had happened in the Saribas. Eventually they adopted the Iban practices of rice culture and longhouse organization.

In their subsequent encounter with the Ulu Rejang peoples, the Kayans and Kajangs in particular, the Iban met firm resistance. The Kayans in the 1850s were strong enough to oppose the invaders. Enmity between the Iban and the Rejang peoples increased after a punitive expedition in which Iban forces were led by the Tuan Muda in 1859 to avenge the murder of the government officers, Steele and Fox, at the fort in Kanowit. An Iban longhouse was attacked and burned by the Kayan in the lower reaches of the Katibas in 1861, but in 1863 the Iban achieved their final revenge. The Tuan Muda led an expeditionary force numbering 12,000 men into the upper Rejang, where he defeated the inhabitants decisively. The Kayan were not again successful in checking the Iban invasion of their traditional sphere.

In spite of punitive expeditions and serious government attempts to control further Iban expansion and settlement, by the end of the nineteenth century even the tributaries above Kapit were populated by the Iban and the movement beyond the Rejang had begun. The Resident of the Third Division, in his report for the year 1900, mentions Iban migrations to the Oya, Mukah, Balingjan, Tatau, and Bintulu rivers (*Sarawak Gazette*, 1901, 59).

Unauthorized as well as authorized migrations continued well into the twentieth century and head-hunting expeditions were not infrequent until the Rajah's authority and law had become firmly established throughout the interior towards the end of the second decade. By then the Iban had migrated to all parts of the Third Division and much of the Fourth, where they settled principally in the area above Bintulu.

MAP 3. Distribution of the Iban in Sarawak

Distribution

Although the Iban now inhabit all five Divisions of Sarawak, as Map 3 clearly shows, the main concentrations are still in the Second and Third Divisions, the established areas of Iban dominance.

At the time of the 1960 census every district in Sarawak had a sizeable Iban population, but nine districts (out of twenty) had more than 10,000 resident Iban.

TABLE 5[a]

Sarawak Districts with over 10,000 Resident Iban

Second Division	Batang Lupar	27,870
	Lubok Antu	14,056
	Saribas	13,782
	Kalaka	14,926
Third Division	Sibu	15,009
	Kanowit	34,687
	Kapit	30,822
	Mukah	17,863
Fourth Division	Bintulu	15,756

[a] The figures are from the 1960 Census Report, Jones, 1962, 121.

Since independence, the Iban have been very active in the national and political life of Sarawak. Both the first two Chief Ministers (Dato Stephen Kalong Ningkan and Dato Tawi Sli) were Second Division Iban. The Federal Minister for Sarawak Affairs, Tan Sri Temonggong Jugah, is from the Rejang. But the pre-eminence of the Iban in Sarawak life has been hindered to some degree by factionalism.

IV. SOCIAL ORGANIZATION

Iban Administration: the *Penghulu*

ACCORDING to its geographical extent and size of its population (also, in some cases, the terrain), each river valley has one or more local 'chiefs'. These are called *Penghulu* which, in Iban, means literally 'one who leads'. In the traditional Iban context there was no area leader, and the title was used only of those who led head-hunting expeditions (*gayau*) or mass migrations (*pindah*). The modern office of *Penghulu* was introduced by the Brooke Rajahs and has since become part of Iban administration.

The duties of a *Penghulu* are largely magisterial. He functions as an arbitrator in customary law cases between longhouses and as a first court of appeal when the verdict of a village headman is in dispute. More serious offences are also brought before the *Penghulu*, since his powers are less limited than those of the headman; he is permitted by the government to impose fines up to $66.[1] Cases involving potential imprisonment or fines which exceed $66 are beyond the jurisdiction of a *Penghulu* and come before the District Court. The *Penghulu's* most important function remains as an arbitrator and adviser, and since litigation among the Iban is something of a national pastime, the *Penghulu* has a key role and makes a contribution of consequence. Independence and the advent of political parties combined with the greatly enhanced powers and influence of District Councillors have had a pronounced impact on the traditional status of *Penghulus*, although the office is still held in esteem.

The appointment to *Penghulu* is salaried. Before the Japanese occupation it was made by the government for life; *Penghulus* are now appointed for a limited period (of five years) on the basis of a local election. Although the office is not hereditary, it is not uncommon for the *Penghulu* to be succeeded by his son or other relative.[2] This is especially true when a *Penghulu* has been

---

[1] All figures are given in (Sarawak) Malaysian dollars: very approximately $8 = £1 sterling and $3 = U.S. $1 at the time of research.

[2] Freeman, 1955a, 10, para. 21, asserts that 'rank is not inheritable and

conspicuously successful in office. Since profound knowledge of customary law and precedent, respected judgement, and wide acquaintance with the area administered are prerequisites, the son, son-in-law, or other close relative of a retiring *Penghulu* is considered more likely to possess these than any other person. The tendency is, therefore, to look first for suitable candidates among the *Penghulu*'s immediate relatives, and only if these are found wanting, to seek elsewhere. Where a particular *Penghulu* has lost public respect, a rival leader for the area may evolve, and he naturally becomes a strong candidate for the succession.

An analysis of ten successions to the office of *Penghulu* in the Delok, Ulu Ai area, showed that in five cases the retiring *Penghulu* was succeeded by his son or son-in-law. Only once were the two not knowingly related at all and in this instance an existing *Penghulu*'s area had been divided into two. Nor is this a new phenomenon, as genealogies show.[1]

TABLE 6

Relationship of Penghulu *to Immediate Predecessor in Office*

Area	Relationship				
	Son	Son-in-law	Close relative	Distant relative	Not related
Ulu Ai/					
Delok	4	1	1	3	1
Lemanak	2			1	1
Total	6	1	1	4	2

The area in which one *Penghulu* has jurisdiction is known as his *pegai*. Both in terms of area and number of longhouses, the *pegai* vary extensively in size. The demarcation of a *pegai* is dictated partly by traditional groupings, partly by geography, and partly by the relative ease or difficulty of communication. The second smallest *pegai* in the Lubok Antu district in 1963–4 had only thirteen longhouses. (The smallest of eight was an exceptional *pegai*, created largely to ensure that a respected *Penghulu* was avail-

there is no institution of chieftainship. Iban society is classless and egalitarian . . .'. Although this is, theoretically speaking, true, it gives an incomplete impression of the *Penghulu*'s office in Iban society and the facts of succession, at least in the Second Division.

[1] See, for example, Sandin, 1967, 104–5.

able in the vicinity of the District Office at Lubok Antu.) Not only
was the *pegai* remote from District headquarters, but the longhouses themselves were for the most part distant from each other
and situated in broken and difficult terrain. But another *pegai*, in
the lower Skrang, for example, where the longhouses were sited
on a navigable river readily accessible to each other and the
District headquarters at Simanggang, had as many as thirty-four.

TABLE 7

Penghulu's *Areas in the Lubok Antu District*

Area	Number of longhouses
Lemanak (ili)	22
Lemanak (ulu)	16
Batang Ai (ili)	23
Batang Ai (ulu)	24
Lubok Antu (ili)	8
Lubok Antu (ulu)	15
Ulu Ai	13
Delok	17
Engkari	14
Total (9)	152
Average	16·9

The *Tuai Rumah*

Each longhouse has a headman (*tuai rumah*) chosen by a consensus
of the people in his village. Although he receives no salary, the
government officially recognizes the *tuai rumah* and considers him
the spokesman for his longhouse and representative of the community. The *tuai rumah*, however, is a *primus inter pares* with no
authority to issue orders. In spite of this, he is responsible for
arbitrating in disputes which occur within the longhouse community and may impose fines not exceeding $16. As a 'chairman'
he presides and maintains order over the court which is attended
by all parties directly involved in litigation as well as anyone who
happens to be interested. Although, when the *tuai rumah* is a
respected member of the community and a forceful speaker, his
influence is significant, he does not offer his own judgement having

heard both sides of the case. His function is to express the verdict of the court as a whole. When the court equivocates in deciding on the merits of the case, the case is usually heard again or appealed.

To the Iban, the *tuai rumah*'s traditional role[1] is to maintain the correct relations among longhouse members and between these and the spirit world: to ensure that the longhouse community does not become *angat*, literally 'hot', implying an unexpiated offence against the spirits (see below, pp. 113–5). Any offence against customary law, known or unknown, deliberate or unintentional, disturbs the relation. When the *tuai rumah* presides over the court of longhouse members which settles disputes and fines offenders, and he imposes the general verdict, he is restoring the community's state of spiritual harmony. The desired balance is re-established as soon as a fine has been paid by the offender and, in certain circumstances, a sacrifice offered (Richards, 1963, 2, makes the same point). If, in exceptional circumstances, the offender is not discovered and convicted, the *tuai rumah* may take the fine upon himself in order to restore harmony between the spirit world and men.

A new *tuai rumah* is chosen when the incumbent dies, becomes too old to continue in office, wishes to be relieved of his obligations of *tuai rumah*ship, or loses the respect of the community. The last happens in particular after a series of misfortunes (death, sickness, or poor harvests), which are thought to indicate that the community is *angat*, that is, not in a state of harmony with the spirits.

In these circumstances the community seeks a new *tuai rumah*. This is almost always a man, although not necessarily so. In 1962, for example, a woman (Chupi anak Buja) was the *tuai rumah* at Pruan, a longhouse of twenty-eight units near Simanggang, and she had been chosen in preference to her son-in-law. Like the office of *Penghulu*, the *tuai rumah*ship is not hereditary although it is usual for the son (or son-in-law) of the *tuai rumah*, sharing the same family room, to take over from his father if he appears to the community to have the appropriate qualities. But there is no rule of succession, and any adult member of the longhouse can, in theory, become *tuai rumah* when the office falls vacant. However, as in the case of a *Penghulu*, it is normal to look first for a suitable candidate among the retiring *tuai rumah*'s close relatives.

---

[1] In traditional Iban thought the *tuai rumah* has functions often coinciding with those of the *tuai burong*; see below, pp. 60 seq.

In spite of Freeman's contention (1955a, 10, para. 20) that there is no 'rigid dogma of succession: . . . any male cognate may succeed', it emerges from Table 8 that not only are the clear majority of *tuai rumah*s directly descended from their predecessors in office either by birth or marriage[1] (eight out of twelve in the Undup; seven out of ten in the Ulu Ai/Delok and ten out of eighteen in the Lemanak), but the cognate limitation does not apply. Succession via affines is frequent and the relationship, close and distant, may be affinal as well as cognatic (where not both).

TABLE 8

Succession to the Office of Tuai Rumah

Area	Relationship of *Tuai Rumah* to immediate predecessor in office					
	Son (incl. adopted sons)	Son-in-law	Other relative (cognate)	Other relative (affine)	Not related	Total
Undup	7	1	3		1	12
Ulu Ai/Delok	3	4	2	1		10
Lemanak	8	2	4	4		18
Total	18	7	9	5	1	40

The Longhouse

During his tenure of office, the headman gives his name to the longhouse community. The longhouse structure itself, which is characteristic of the Iban and a Borneo landmark, is usually found beside a river in the interior. The building is raised above the ground on tall posts, and may be several hundred feet long. Although superficially it appears to be a common community dwelling, the longhouse is, in fact, made up of a series of apartments each of which forms a cross-section of the whole. The individual apartment belongs to a single family unit which is responsible for constructing and maintaining it.

In cross-section each apartment consists first of a walled family room (*bilek*), where the hearth (*dapur*) is, and where the whole family eats. Parents, old women, and young unmarried women, as well as children, also sleep in the *bilek*. Next is a covered working and living area (*ruai*) which is without side walls and therefore

[1] This is borne out by recorded genealogies also.

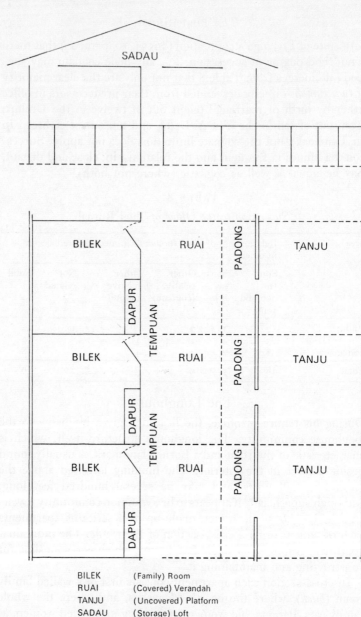

BILEK	(Family) Room
RUAI	(Covered) Verandah
TANJU	(Uncovered) Platform
SADAU	(Storage) Loft
DAPUR	Hearth
PADONG	(Raised) Sleeping area
TEMPUAN	Passage/work area

FIG. 1. Plan and Section of an Iban Longhouse

gives the impression of a common hall or gallery running the length of the longhouse. Finally, there is an uncovered open platform or drying area (*tanju*). Above the *bilek* and the *ruai* there is a loft (*sadau*), where rice, mats, baskets, and other household items are stored. The *bilek* invariably has a door leading to the *ruai*; not uncommonly, there is also an opening in the side wall(s) which gives directly on to the adjoining *bilek*.

The depth of the actual *bilek* is necessarily fairly constant in any one longhouse and is agreed before construction at a general meeting. Eighteen to twenty feet is average. The Iban indicate the 'size' of a *bilek* (and the entire family section of the longhouse) by referring to its width, and this may vary considerably even between *bileks* in the same longhouse. A common expression is *pemuka tiga depa*, meaning a width of three fathoms, that is, approximately eighteen feet. This is considered normal. Less than *tiga depa* is thought small; more than three is regarded as spacious and an indication of standing and comparative wealth in the community.

The number of *bileks* which make up a longhouse varies considerably. At the time when he was trying to check population movements and restrict Iban migration, the Rajah introduced a law forbidding longhouses of less than ten 'doors'. The list of regulations applicable to the Iban of the Third Division states explicitly[1] that 'No house of less than ten doors shall be permitted except with the written authority of the District Officer for some good and sufficient reason' and 'The person who erects the first post of a new house of less than ten doors without special permission shall be fined $25, all to Government, and the house shall be dismantled by the builders'. This law, however, is no longer enforced and many longhouses are of less than the official minimum without having the District Officer's specific authority.

The original tendency towards large communities, during the time that the Iban needed mutual protection, gave way to smaller houses, where the families found each other more readily compatible. Smaller communities also offered quicker access to farmlands. Recently there has been a return to larger groupings justifying the provision of schools and other amenities as well as improved communications with the outside world. But these consist normally, as at Batu Lintang in the Undup, of several distinct

[1] *Sea Dayak (Iban) Fines, Third Division*, 1940, Pt. V, ss. 10 seq.

longhouses in close proximity to each other, and not of one very long house.

The shortest longhouse in the Lubok Antu district (1963–4) had only two *bileks*; the longest forty-one. The arithmetical average

TABLE 9

Number of Bileks *per Longhouse*

(listed by *Penghulus'* areas)

Number of bileks	Penghulu						Total
	Inggol	Manchan (Lemanak)	Sigan	Jali (Batang Ai)	Manau (Lubok Antu)	Rangga (Undup)	
	Incidence						
2	2	1			1	2	6
3						1	1
4						2	2
5			1	1			2
6		1				3	4
7	2				1	1	4
8	1	5			1	2	9
9				3	1		4
10	3				1	2	6
11	2	2					4
12		1	6	2	1		10
13	1	3	1	2		1	8
14	2		1	2		3	8
15			1	3		3	7
16	3	2	1		1		7
17				2			2
18	2	1	1	4		1	9
19					1		1
20	1			2		1	4
21				3	1		4
22					1	1	2
23				1			1
24	1			1		1	3
25	1			1	1	1	4
26				2		1	3
28				1			1
29				1	1	2	4
30				1		1	2
31					1		1
33					1		1
34				1	1		2
41	1						1
Total number of longhouses	22	16	23	24	15	27	127

was 17·6. Table 9 gives the composition of all longhouses in the *pegai* of six *Penghulus*, two from the Lemanak, two from the Batang Ai, one from Lubok Antu (Lubok Antu district), and one from the Undup (Simanggang district). Out of a total of 127 longhouses, sixty-six, or fifty-two per cent, fall within the range of having from ten to twenty *bileks*.

The *Bilek* Family

The Iban term for a family sharing the same *bilek* and longhouse section is *sida sabilek*, literally 'they of the same *bilek*'. *Bilek* in Iban has come to mean not only the physical room but all the members of the family who share the same apartment as well as ritual restrictions and prerogatives, privileges, and responsibilities.

TABLE 10
Number of Persons per Bilek[a]

Number per bilek	Incidence						
	Lemanak longhouses			Delok longhouses		Undup longhouses	
	Melintang	Ancheh	Nyambar	Antas	Limbang	Chaong	Ganda
2	2	3		1		2	2
3	3	6		3	1	3	4
4	4	3	1	3	1	5	4
5	4	9	1	4	2	2	2
6	10	2	2		2	2	4
7	2	4	1		2		
8	3	4	2		1	1	2
9	1		4		1	1	
10	1	2	1				
11			1				
Total number of bileks	30	33	13	11	10	16	18
Total number of persons	166	173	101	43	60	72	82
Average number per bilek	5·5	5·2	7·8	3·9	6	4·5	4·5
Average for the area	6·2			5		4·5	
Over-all average: 5·2							

[a] *Temuai*—'visitor' and *kampar*—'lodger' are not included. While both are recognized categories of persons who may be associated with a *bilek*, they are rare and, by definition, temporary.

The *bilek* family is seldom numerically large and almost invariably genealogically simple. The usual number of *bilek* members lies between five and six. The arithmetical average for the entire Lubok Antu district was 5·4 persons per *bilek*. As Table 10 shows, the average for the three Lemanak, two Delok, and two Undup longhouses selected for intensive study was 5·2. The lowest number of persons occurred in the Undup where the figure was only 4·5, the highest in the Lemanak with 6·2.[1]

Composition of the *Bilek* Family

The *bilek* is the basic unit of Iban society, both ritually and economically. Ideally, it consists of a simple family: a man and wife, their children, together with one or two grandparents (either parents of the man or his wife, but not both). Although this occurs in fewer than half the cases analysed (41·5 per cent), the Iban consider this the ideal *bilek* family and each member has a distinct and significant role to perform at home in the longhouse and/or the rice farm. Out of 130 *bileks* in the Lemanak, Delok, and Undup, more than half (54 per cent) had only two generations sharing though these were not all simple families of parents and children; there was one case of grandparents sharing a *bilek* with their grandchildren. In just under 5 per cent there was only one generation: virtually all these were young couples who had recently established *bileks* of their own.

Table 11 illustrates the Iban preference for a family unit which comprises more than two generations and, at the same time, the rarity of married siblings, both with children, sharing the same *bilek*. There were only two instances in all the longhouses surveyed. The Iban sense of equality between siblings and between the sexes makes it difficult for married siblings with family responsibilities and conflicting spouse and sibling loyalties to share a *bilek* happily. But where this occurs, it is generally regarded as a good arrangement.

The normal practice is for one couple (with their children) to break away and set up their own *bilek* (called *bilek kadiri*) with a share of the original property. Partition is not uncommon; all but one of the 5 per cent one-generation families were instances of it. It is the solution not only to the conflicting loyalties of married siblings but to more general differences of opinion. When one part of the *bilek* feels it is doing more than its fair share of the work or

[1] Freeman's (1955b, 4, para. 14) figures for the Balleh District of the Third Division (Av. 5·75 and 5·78) fall in the same bracket. A word of caution must be introduced regarding the use of government statistics: official records almost invariably give a distorted view of *bilek* membership, since for census purposes the Iban normally include as *bilek* members all those 'temporarily' absent and a 'temporary' absence to the Iban may last many years and cover 'temporary' *bilek* membership elsewhere.

TABLE II
Composition of Bilek Families

Members	Lemanak			Delok		Undup		Total
	Melintang	Ancheh	Nyambar	Antas	Limbang	Jawan	Ganda	
Man and wife	1	2				2	1	6
Parent(s) and child(ren)	16	17	5	4	4	7	3	56
Parent(s) and child(ren) with spouse	2	2	1				3	8
Grandparent(s), child(ren), spouse(s) and grandchild(ren)	9	12	5	5	3	4	9	47
Great-grandparent(s), child(ren), spouse(s), grandchild(ren), spouse(s) and great-grandchild(ren)	1		1			1	2	5
Grandparent(s) and grandchild(ren)				1				1
Great-grandparent(s), child(ren), spouse(s), and great-grandchild(ren)						1		1
Parent(s), child(ren), and sibling(s) of parent				1	3			4
Grandparent(s), child(ren), spouse(s), grandchild(ren) and cousin of grandparent			1					1
Married siblings, spouses and children	1							1
Total	30	33	13	11	10	15	18	130

receiving less than its share of the rewards, partition provides a solution. Amalgamation of two *bileks* also happens, but this is rare.[1] It is usually due to the death of one or more key members of related *bileks*. There were two cases at Rh. Sa and Rh. Melintang during 1961 and 1962 which provide good examples. In one case a man (Putit) died childless, leaving a widow who had joined his *bilek*. His parents were already dead and she decided to amalgamate with her brother's *bilek*. In another case, a man (Brita) lost his wife in childbirth and died himself the following year: the *bilek* of his two surviving adolescent children was amalgamated with that of their father's brother. (Subsequently, however, they decided to have their own *bilek* again and partition took place.)

Recruitment to the *Bilek*

Recruitment to the *bilek* is by birth, adoption (which is common), incorporation (which is rare), or marriage. A survey of 450 persons (including children) in three Lemanak longhouses indicated that over 65 per cent were living as members of the *bilek* in which they were born and 28 per cent were members by marriage. Nearly 6·5 per cent were adoptive members, but as Table 12 shows, only two individuals (less than 0·5 per cent) had become members in some other way.

TABLE 12

Recruitment to Bilek *Membership*

	Manner				
	Birth	Adoption	Marriage	Other	Total
Number of persons	293	29	126	2	450
Percentage	65·1	6·4	28	0·4	100

An Iban child is born as a member of one *bilek* and acquires full membership, full hereditary rights and responsibilities within that *bilek*, irrespective of sex. In the event of divorce the child may be taken by either parent to another *bilek*, where it becomes a full member, but more usually it remains in the natal *bilek*. Adopted children have precisely the same status as natural children but, while they acquire rights in the *bilek* of their adoption, they lose them in the *bilek* where they were born.

---

[1] Freeman, 1955b, 23, para. 78, observes this too.

Incorporation is used to describe those cases where an individual becomes a *bilek* member without the ties of birth, adoption, or marriage. From time to time, outsiders work for and together with a particular family, and may after a period be incorporated as *bilek* members.[1] Occasionally, individuals are left without *bilek* relatives of their own and are incorporated into another *bilek*, though where they are the sole surviving *bilek* heirs this is tantamount to amalgamation.

Marriage

The commonest way in which an Iban becomes a member of a *bilek* other than the one in which he was born is by marriage. It is exceptional for an Iban man or woman to remain unmarried in his thirties. By the age of thirty-five, according to the census in 1960 (Jones, 1962, 197), only 3 per cent remained single. And it is fair to assume that some of these were Iban no longer living in traditional communities and that among the remainder a significant proportion were suffering from a physical or mental abnormality. Surveys in the Lemanak and Undup revealed only about 1 per cent of active and mentally normal individuals in their thirties who had never been married.

TABLE 13[a]

Marital Status of Men and Women Aged 35–9 Years

(rate per thousand)

Age group 35–9	Single persons	M.	F.	Married persons	M.	F.	Widowed persons	M.	F.	Divorced persons	M.	F.
Per mille	30	40	20	903	918	887	30	17	44	37	25	49

[a] Jones, 1962, 197.

On marriage the Iban joins either the husband's or the wife's *bilek*, where he or she acquires full membership while at the same time forfeiting membership and rights in the other. Freeman (1955a, 5–6, para. 8) calls the system 'utrolocal' which he defines as 'a system of marriage in which *either* uxorilocal *or* virilocal residence may be followed, and in which the rules of kinship and

[1] This was applied also to slaves before slavery was abolished in 1888.

inheritance result in neither form of domicile receiving any sort of special preference'.

Surveys show that among the Iban it is almost equally common for a man to join his wife's *bilek* (*nguang, ngugi,* or *nguai ka bini*) as for a woman to join her husband's (*nguang, ngugi,* or *nguai ka laki*). In the Balleh area of the Third Division, Freeman (1955b, 10, para. 36) found that out of a sample of 284 marriages, 145 (or 51 per cent approximately) were uxorilocal—that is to say, the husband had taken up residence in the wife's *bilek*—and 139 (or 49 per cent approximately) were virilocal, the wife living in the husband's *bilek*. His analysis of living married couples showed an even greater tendency towards uxorilocal domicile: 61 out of 109 (nearly 56 per cent). This slight bias was not borne out entirely by investigations in various parts of the Second Division where the surveys indicated that in practice one was as likely as the other. An examination of 307 marriages in the Lemanak, Delok, and Undup revealed that altogether approximately 54 per cent were virilocal and 46 per cent were uxorilocal; but the breakdown by river showed a varying emphasis.

TABLE 14

Domicile of Married Couples

Area	Type of Domicile		Total	Percentage	
	Virilocal	Uxorilocal		Virilocal	Uxorilocal
Undup	89	73	162	55	45
Delok	9	10	19	47	53
Lemanak	68	58	126	54	46
Total	166	141	307	54	46

Marriages are not arranged among the Iban. Young men and women are free to choose their own prospective partners, and the recognized procedure of night visiting (*ngayap*) enables them to learn to know each other. There are frequently difficulties in agreeing where the couple are to live: as members of either the husband's or the wife's *bilek*; this is mainly a practical problem, although emotional considerations enter, especially when the *bileks* are at a distance from each other. Much more serious is the objection to marrying the descendant of a slave (*ulun*) which, although forbidden public mention by law,[1] is still remembered, or one of

---

[1] Brooke anti-slavery law of 1888. According to Harrisson and Sandin (1966)

a family credited with the ability to curse (*tau tepang*)—rice, in particular.

Although marriages are in no sense prescribed, the young Iban are urged[1] to find a marriage partner among their own cousins provided they are not members of the same *bilek*. Consequently the majority of marriages occur within the longhouse community. An analysis (Table 15) of 126 marriages at three longhouses in the Lemanak showed that eighty-seven, or approximately 69 per cent, were between persons who were members of the same longhouse before marriage and only thirty-nine, or almost 31 per cent, were with outsiders—many of whom came from neighbouring communities and were in fact relatives.

TABLE 15

Residence of Partners before Marriage

	at Rh. Ancheh	Melintang	Nyambar	Total
Uxorilocal marriages:				
from the same longhouse	14	18	6	38
from different longhouses	8	9	3	20
Total (uxorilocal)	22	27	9	58
Virilocal marriages:				
from the same longhouse	23	21	5	49
from different longhouses	11	4	4	19
Total (virilocal)	34	25	9	68
(All) married couples:				
from the same longhouse	37	39	11	87
from different longhouses	19	13	7	39
Total	56	52	18	126

The extent of marriage to cognates and the complex relationships which, in consequence, tie a longhouse community together, emerge very clearly from a simple genealogical diagram of Rh. Limbang (Delok). Out of a total of sixty persons actually living as members of the longhouse, the names of 52 appear in Figure 2. And of the remainder, 7 are direct descendants of an affinal relative of Melaka.

100) the 'Shaman' Imban is regarded as 'low-class' because of his descent. In the Undup marriage by a 'respectable Iban' to a slave descendant (at Entebar) was definitely opposed, and everyone claimed to know who the slave descendants were.

[1] This is 'preferential' as the term is used by Needham, 1962, 8 seq.

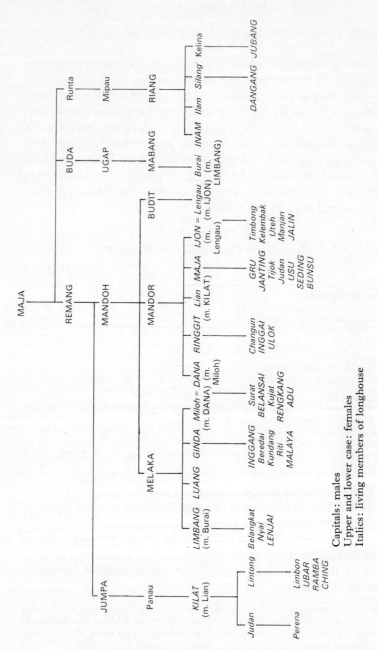

Fig. 2. Genealogical Diagram of Rh. Limbang

Capitals: males
Upper and lower case: females
Italics: living members of longhouse

The Concept of Incest

The Iban prefer marriage between relatives, except members of the same *bilek*, but they consider it essential that the relative should belong to an appropriate generation level. While the marriage of first cousins is encouraged,[1] *adat* rules prohibit (and threaten extreme consequences for transgression) the marriage of cousins who belong to adjacent generation levels. Beyond this degree, sanctions are less severe, but still apply to vertical as opposed to horizontal relatedness. The definition of incest is traced to the founder of the Iban pedigree, Seragunting, whose father was an ordinary man but whose mother was the daughter of the spirit Sengalang Burong. Seragunting himself committed incest, and the rules were subsequently taught him by his spirit grandfather (see below, pp. 89–90). The most stringent rules apply to members of the same *bilek*: brother/sister, parent/child, but uncle/niece, nephew/aunt relationships are also strictly prohibited. Figure 3 expresses the relative gravity of the offences.

Incest, however, is not merely a question of incestuous relations between members of the same *bilek* or their immediate relatives, but involves a complex system of relatedness and generation levels. Whereas incest between siblings and among immediate relatives of adjacent generations is the most serious offence and in no circumstances may the couple marry, marriage is permitted in other cases after certain fines have been paid and the spirits appeased. These semi-incestuous categories fall into two. The first covers second and third cousins as well as first and second (called *besapat*, literally 'having partition walls') and involves a heavy fine of from eight to fifteen dollars. The second includes third and fourth and fourth and fifth cousins (called *bekalih*, literally 'reversed' or 'inside out') and carries a lesser fine of from four to six dollars. After offering *plasi menoa* which absolves the offence against the spirit order, the couple are permitted to marry. *Plasi menoa* is the expression for the appeasement offering made when a serious offence against *adat*, such as murder or incest, has

---

[1] An astonishing observation of St. John (1863, i. 85) reads 'It is contrary to custom for a man to marry a first cousin, who is looked upon as a sister'. This is certainly not the case now, nor, to judge by genealogies, myths, and remembered marital histories, was it ever true. It is, however, significant that, among the Iban, *menyadi* is commonly used of a first cousin although, properly, this is the term for a brother or sister—to whom marriage is emphatically forbidden. But kinship terminology makes generation levels explicit at all times.

been committed and is considered liable to have undesirable consequences for the area as a whole. Incest unpropitiated is thought
likely to affect adversely not merely the guilty parties but other
members of the community and even the fertility of the land.[1]
Staking incestuous couples, the traditional punishment for unpropitiated 'high incest', was intended not primarily to punish
the guilty for their offence but to appease the spirits and restore
order.

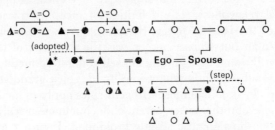

▲ ⬤ most serious offence: fine of 200 katis = dollars
     and payment of *plasi menoa.*
▲ ◑ next most serious offence: fine of 150 katis = dollars
     and payment of *plasi menoa.*
△ ◯ third most serious offence: fine of 100 katis = dollars
     and payment of *plasi menoa.*
 * half fine only for persons adopted as (young) adults

FIG. 3. Prohibited Degrees of Marriage

[1] Consequently when an unmarried woman becomes pregnant and refuses to
name the father (as ordained by customary law), it is assumed that she may be
guilty of incest, and she is required to make an appropriate offering. Ward
(1961, 98) says she incurs no penalty as such but is obliged to offer a pig;
Richards (1963, 29) says she is fined '40 Katis' (=dollars) and must offer *plasi
menoa.*

V. PROPERTY AND LABOUR

Property

NOT only is the *bilek* family the basic social unit of Iban society, it is also the basic unit economically. With one or two important exceptions, the members of a longhouse own no property in common and do not function economically as a community. Freeman (1955b, 46, para. 144) says that communal economic activity is limited to constructing the *tangga* (the notched log leading up to the house), which is common longhouse property. One should also mention the forge (*repun*) where iron tools are worked, since this too is usually a joint longhouse undertaking. In the years since the war, longhouse communities have even acquired common rubber mangles and rice mills. But with these exceptions the basic property-owning as well as social and economic working unit of Iban society is the *bilek*. *Bilek* property, which does not belong to any individual member but to the *bilek* family as a whole, falls into three categories: ritual property, prestige property, and productive property.

Ritual property, which may never be sold, consists of the rice seed (*padi pun*) set aside for the (sacred) central plot, charms (*pengaroh*), which are used in the rice cult, to prevent disease and for success generally, and also, where these exist, *antu pala*, the trophies of head-hunting raids. Prestige property in traditional thought was composed primarily of valuable jars (*tajau*), gongs (*tawak*), gold ornaments (*mas*), silver (*pirak*), other jewellery and woven cloth. Prestige property is sold only in the event of a serious emergency.

Ritual and prestige property may be acquired in different ways: by direct inheritance within the *bilek*, by partition of the *bilek*, by purchase from non-Iban traders and others, presentation, or acquisition otherwise. The last includes booty acquired in war as well as gifts revealed by the spirits, but applies in particular to trophies obtained on *bejalai*, the custom among men, especially the young, of going on expeditions for a period of time.

Productive Property

In economic terms the ritual and prestige possessions matter less than Iban productive property, the most important of which is undoubtedly land. Strictly speaking, land belongs to the spirit, Pulang Gana, who, according to Iban mythology, received a sod of earth for his inheritance and thus became spirit of the earth (see below, pp. 78–81). The Iban obtain permission to clear and farm through sacrificial offerings and ritual observance. In the same way they acquire general hunting and gathering rights to a particular area, but they do not 'own' the land.

In practice the right to use land is in most cases acquired by felling primary forest. Official publications[1] describe felling virgin jungle as 'creating customary rights' to land. Apart from acquisition by felling, land was occasionally obtained in the past by invasion (in the context of earlier mass migration and the defeat of local inhabitants who were either eliminated or absorbed). Rarely was the right acquired from other peoples in exchange for slaves, jars, gongs, or cannon (also in the context of migration and warfare).

Felling and farming for one season confer the right to use (in rice cultivation) a given piece of land on the *bilek* family and the *bilek* heirs in perpetuity so long as they remain in the area. Farming land, like other property, belongs to the *bilek* and not to the longhouse community. So-called customary rights in Sarawak have been called limited, obscure, confused, undefined, but they are not communal, as Richards emphasizes (1961a, 18).

In the traditional context of *pindah* migrations, 'the fact that virgin forest was in virtually unrestricted supply, resulted in little value being attached to secondary jungle' (Freeman, 1955a, 25, para. 55). Even in the Lemanak in 1960, where no virgin jungle remained except for limited timber and produce reserves, burial places (*pendam*) and specific taboo copses (*tanah mali*) mainly on hilltops, little or no value (in a monetary sense) was ascribed to the land itself. Although it was common to borrow land for a season, land was never bought or sold. Theoretically speaking, it was not the Iban's to sell or otherwise dispose of permanently, since it remained the property of Pulang Gana, although the Iban referred to it as their own and enjoyed exclusive rights to its use.[2]

---

[1] For example, *Sarawak Government Gazette*, pt. III, of 22 Mar. 1955.
[2] This is not peculiar to the Iban. See, for example, Spencer, 1966, 88,

In addition to land, most Iban *bileks* have small holdings of wild or semi-wild fruit trees, rubber, pigs, and poultry. These are also *bilek* property and inherited through the *bilek* heirs. In Iban eyes, however, the most important possession of the *bilek* is rice. The value of ritual property lies in promoting the growth of rice. Even prestige property is commonly associated with a plentiful harvest, or was acquired with the proceeds from the sale of surplus rice. Rice stocks are a measure not merely of wealth but of moral standing in the community. The good man is the man who observes the rituals, recognizes the restrictions, and honours the Iban *adat*; and the man who observes the appropriate rituals and respects the restrictions associated with rice-planting is also the responsible farmer, who is most likely to have a good harvest. *Bulih padi* ('to have a good yield, a good harvest') is the ultimate criterion. No man dares say it of himself; it is high praise of another. *Bulih* by itself connotes ample food resources, good health, the successful and honoured member of the community. Conversely, not to grow sufficient rice for the needs of your family is a shaming experience: it makes you *malu* (ashamed). Even when the wherewithal to purchase rice exists, the Iban are *malu* to buy and prefer, if at all possible, to borrow discreetly from their relatives what amounts to an advance on the next harvest.

Division of Labour

Since the *bilek* is the basic economic as well as social unit of Iban society, labour is divided among its members. Although there is no rigid division of labour, men and women, young and old, are expected to prefer certain occupations. Collecting firewood and drawing water are, by tradition, the paramount examples of man's work and woman's work. The newly married bridegroom, when he first visits his parents-in-law, invariably finds that the firewood reserves happen to be exhausted; he proves himself by collecting an ample supply. The young bride, when she first visits her husband's parents, is allowed to discover that there is no water, and she shows what a good wife she will make by going at once to the river.

where he says that 'Among shifting cultivators the principle of land tenure is the principle of usufruct'; also Conklin, 1957, 35, 'Land is a free good: tenure is by usufruct only.' See also, Richards, 1961a, 15.

Diary records of the activities of twenty persons at Rh. Ancheh, Sebliau, Lemanak, from January to December 1963 revealed the normal range and preferences. Seven individuals are chosen here to represent the main categories into which the Iban may best be grouped by age and sex:

1. Sawai (aged 19) is a typical young unmarried girl (*indu dara*).
2. Karin (aged 20), a young unmarried man (*bujang*), unfortunately injured himself while farming and therefore spent more days sick than would be considered normal, but he is in other respects a useful illustration of a young man without farm management commitments.
3. Burai (aged 22) is a woman recently married and without children.
4. Rentap (aged 49) is a typical *bilek* head, married, with children.
5. Mangai (aged 45) is Rentap's wife and a good example of an Iban wife and mother.
6. Ungkir (aged 64) is an old man, whose activities are almost entirely in and around the longhouse although he remains very fit for his years.
7. Banun (aged 63) is an old woman and frequently ill.

With the exception of illness (in this case Karin and the old woman Banun), there are few days in the year when the Iban remain idle. Even when keeping an eye on children or animals in the longhouse, the Iban commonly do something constructive also: men make nets or fish-traps, women weave baskets or cloth, or prepare rice. (Only the main activity is listed in Table 16.) Thus days spent in farm work do not exclude men stopping for firewood on their way home, or women looking for vegetables, as they commonly do.

Participation in religious festivals (*gawai*) is a serious undertaking, and is considered fundamental to successful rice cultivation as well as *bilek* and community health and prosperity, but it is also fun, a party with generous eating, drinking, and dancing. Major religious festivals generally occur in June or August (see below, pp. 195 seq.). Other rites, however, are spread throughout the year; in particular, the many minor occasions (often associated with an augury, dream, or other spirit encounter) when the Iban are prevented from farm work. Sacrificial acts apart, these

TABLE 16

Distribution of Occupations throughout One Year (Rh. Ancheh, 1963)
Main activities in man-days

	Sawai	Karin	Burai	Rentap	Mangai	Ungkir	Banun
Food production:							
Hill rice:							
cultivation	143½	127	153½	208	129½	10	4
preparation	61½		56½		62½	2	7½
total	(205)	(127)	(210)	(208)	(192)	(12)	(11½)
Other food crops:							
vegetable gathering	26½	1	29	2	52	1½	11½
fruit gathering	11½	14	4½	8	7½	1	1
other crops	1		7	3			
total	(39)	(15)	(40½)	(13)	(59½)	(2½)	(12½)
Hunting and fishing:							
hunting	7½	18	5	18½	6	1	
fishing	4	6	4	10	6½	41½	
total	(11½)	(24)	(9)	(28½)	(12½)	(42½)	(0)
Total (food production)	255½	166	259½	249½	264	57	24
Cash sources:							
Cash crops:							
rubber production	20	29	5	7			13
pepper cultivation				1	1		
total	(20)	(29)	(5)	(8)	(1)	(0)	(13)
Work for wages		8					
Total (cash sources)	20	37	5	8	1	0	13
Domestic activities:							
Housing and implements, etc.							
house maintenance		11	4	16	4	22	
tool-making		3		7		2	
mat-making	42½		18		35½	1	116
weaving	½		13		½		
fishnets and traps		3				80½	
boat-building		7				19	
collecting firewood		12½	4½	14½		1	4
total	(43)	(36½)	(39½)	(37½)	(40)	(125½)	(120)
Animal and child care:							
animal care	3½				2	4	15
infant care	½		1			150	
total	(4)	(0)	(1)	(0)	(2)	(154)	(15)
Total (domestic activities)	47	36½	40½	37½	42	279½	135
Non-productive days:							
Religious observances:							
rice cult	19	26	27	31	26½	14	16
other religious practices	9½	9½	8	9	10	7	6
total	(28½)	(35½)	(35)	(40)	(36½)	(21)	(22)
Sickness, rest, and amusement:							
sickness		36	4	2	10	4	82
resting/playing	9	33	6½	2	11½	2	66
visiting	5	16	14½	11		2	23
cock-fighting		3		11			
litigation		2		4			
total	(14)	(90)	(25)	(30)	(21½)	(8)	(171)
Total (non-productive days)	42½	125½	60	70	58	29	193

days provide an opportunity to go boar-hunting, fishing, or to undertake other necessary jobs about the house, according to age, sex, and responsibilities. The consequent variety provides the Iban with regular relaxation from his routine occupations in the rice fields; and hunting as well as fishing are frequently social occasions which are as enjoyable as they can be profitable.

As Table 16 also shows, rice cultivation occupies by far the largest part of the Iban year: it is spread throughout the twelve months from the *manggol* rites, which inaugurate the clearing of the farm land for a new season, until the harvest has been finally carried home, some eleven or more months later. Both men, women, old and young, participate, but, where possible, they prefer certain activities, though Freeman may exaggerate when he says (1955a, 79, para. 177) that, with the exception of farm managers, nothing will induce young men 'to participate in the essentially feminine duties of sowing, weeding, and reaping. To do so would be to excite the immediate ridicule of their fellows.' A comparative survey throughout different parts of the Second Division shows that, although particular occupations are definitely preferred by one sex or the other, most farming activities may be performed by either one if circumstances require.

TABLE 17

Farming Activities Performed by Males and Females

Activity	Lemanak		Undup		Kumpang	
Slashing (*nebas*)	M	F	M	F	M	F
Felling (*nebang*)	M		M		M	
Firing (*nunu*)	M	F	M	F	M	F
Planting:						
Dibbling (*nugal*)	M	(F)	M		M	(F)
Sowing (*menih*)	F	(M)	F		F	(M)
Weeding (*mantun*)	F	M	F	(M)	F	M
Reaping (*ngetau*)	F	M	F	(M)	F	M
Storing (*nyimpan*)	M	F	M	F	M	F

An analysis of farming activities (Table 18) in the Lemanak shows the breakdown of specific activities by age and sex. There are important differences between the old man who spent only twenty-nine days in rice cultivation and the cult, the young unmarried man who spent 156, and the young woman, married woman, and married man, who all spent a total of well over 200 days in activities associated with rice planting. As the figures show, both men and women participate in clearing, firing, planting, weeding, harvesting, and storing, although a young unmarried man weeds as rarely as possible.

TABLE 18

Man-Days Spent in Rice Cultivation and Cult (Rh. Ancheh, 1963)

	Sawai	Karin	Burai	Rentap	Mangai	Ungkir	Banun
Clearing and burning:							
slashing of undergrowth (*nebas*)	7	25½	29	34	2	0	0
felling (*nebang*)	0	14	0	11	0	0	0
firing (*nunu*)	1	0	2	3	0	0	0
Planting and weeding:							
planting catch crops (*betanam*)	1	1	2	1	2	0	0
dibbling (*nugal*)	0	16	0	20	0	0	0
sowing (*menih*)	20	0	16	0	19	0	1
weeding (*mantun*)	54	7	44	45	43	0	1
Harvesting and storing:							
reaping (*ngetau*)	44	35	42½	53½	54½	5	0
carrying in and storing (*berangkut/nyimpan*)	14½	15½	13	12½	6	5	2
Total	141½	114	148½	180	126½	10	4
Work at the farm: hut (*langkau*) construction, traps, guarding, etc.	2	13	5	28	3	0	0
Preparing the rice: drying in the sun (*nyembi*), pounding (*nutok*), milling (*ngisar*)	61½	0	56½	0	62½	2	7¼
Total	63½	13	61½	28	65½	2	7¼
Making metal tools: adze (*bliong*), bush-knife (*duku*), weeding-knife (*bikong* or *ilok*), harvesting tool (*ketap*), etc.	0	3	0	7	0	2	0
Making mats for drying rice (*prempan*), baskets for carrying rice (*lanji*), etc.	42½	0	18	0	35½	1	116
Sacrificial offerings and religious activities associated directly with the rice cult	19	26	27	31	26½	14	16
Total (activities associated with rice cultivation)	61½	29	45	38	62	17	132
TOTAL (rice cultivation, cult, and associated activities)	266½	156	255	246	254	29	143½

Felling, dibbling, and making metal tools are invariably men's work, although a woman would lend a hand dibbling if necessary. Constructing the farm hut (*langkau umai*) is also done by men, although women frequently assist. Sowing the rice seed and preparing the rice for consumption is women's work: this includes drying the grain in the sun, pounding, winnowing, and milling.

The only instance of a man participating in these activities was the isolated case of Ungkir who kept an eye on drying rice while at home in the longhouse (a question of keeping poultry and dogs away). Mat making is also done by women and most of the basket work; the rim, however, of many baskets is made of a length of stiff split cane which is bound into place by the men.

Carrying home the harvested rice and storing it in bark bins is done by both sexes. Young men take pride in carrying heavy loads; women carry much less. When storing, the women place the rice in baskets, the men do the actual storing in the bark containers. Similarly, the religious activities associated with rice planting are divided between the sexes. Women prepare the offerings (*piring*), but men perform the actual rites.

As a general rule, men prefer the physically demanding activities which give them an opportunity to display their strength. But there was a woman in the Kumpang (at Rh. Pidau) who used to take part in felling. As far as possible men avoid the monotonous and tedious tasks, like weeding, which are done singly or in small groups. They enjoy the festive activities of dibbling, even harvesting, and carrying home, which engage all the members of the *bilek* and others in the longhouse also.

Although the young and unmarried, self-conscious bachelors in particular, may resent an 'inappropriate' activity which they consider embarrassing or even shaming (*ngasoh malu*), men and women who are married and have children of their own are not unduly concerned with a precise division of labour. Rentap, as Table 18 shows, took a major part in clearing, planting, weeding, and harvesting. He would have helped in sowing, if necessary. Even the traditionally divided activities of fetching firewood and drawing water may be done by the 'other' sex when circumstances require. A woman without a husband or adult son frequently collects her own firewood and a man whose wife is sick or in childbirth may draw water for the *bilek*. Old men, like Ungkir, commonly fetch water when on 'watch' in the longhouse, and from time to time both Burai and Banun gathered firewood.

The *Bilek* Labour Force

The Iban division of labour is based on the ideal *bilek* composition, where three generations live together as a working family unit.

Owing to the numerical composition of the average *bilek*, the frequency of *bejalai* when young men go away on expeditions for months or even years at a time, as well as old age, sickness, and child-bearing, the number of active persons in the *bilek* labour team is often reduced. It is not uncommon for a *bilek* to be entirely without an active man or woman for a time. A survey at the height of planting in the Lemanak in 1963 showed that at two longhouses, Rh. Melintang and Rh. Ancheh, there were in actual fact fewer working adults than those who were either absent or too young or too old to make a direct contribution to economic activities.

TABLE 19

Number of Working Adults

	Rh. Melintang	Rh. Ancheh	Total
Number of active adult men	34	38	72
Number of active adult women	36	47	83
Total number of active adults	70	85	155

TABLE 20

Number of Children, Aged Persons, and Persons Temporarily Absent

	Rh. Melintang	Rh. Ancheh	Total
Number of children too young to make an economic contribution:			
Boys	36	33	69
Girls	33	28	61
Total (children)	69	61	130
Number of persons sick or aged:			
Men	7	8	15
Women	11	11	22
Total (sick and aged)	18	19	37
Number of persons absent:			
Men	9	8	17
Women	0	0	0
Total (persons absent)	9	8	17
TOTAL (persons sick, aged or absent, and children too young to work)	96	88	184

In these circumstances, the *bilek* family labour teams at Rh. Ancheh and Rh. Melintang were composed predominantly of two- and three-person groups.

TABLE 21

Bilek *Family Labour Teams*

Total number of active persons in labour team	0	1	2	3	4	5	6
Incidence at:							
Rh. Melintang	1	3	14	9	3	0	0
Rh. Ancheh	0	4	15	9	2	2	1

At Rh. Melintang there was one *bilek* where a senile woman lived together with her son, who was crippled, and two young grandchildren. The crippled son was able to perform the most necessary activities in rice planting, but relied heavily on reciprocal labour exchange arrangements (*bedurok*).[1] No fewer than seven *bileks* (approximately 11 per cent) had only one active adult worker. The majority, as Table 21 shows, had two, and a substantial number, three. Having in mind the preferred division of labour, the incidence of available active adult men and women in the *bilek* labour teams is significant.

TABLE 22

Number of Men in Bilek *Labour Teams*

Number of men in labour team		0	1	2	3
Incidence at:					
Rh. Melintang		3	20	7	0
Rh. Ancheh		2	25	5	1
Total	(63)	5	45	12	1
Percentage	(100)	8	71	19	2

[1] *Bedurok* is the name given by the Iban to a system of labour exchange by which a group, usually of relatives, works the farms of participants in turn during important stages of the rice cycle. A principle of strict reciprocity is followed, the work of a woman being considered equal to that of a man. (See also Freeman's account, 1955a, 82 seq., paras. 183–90.) Not only is *bedurok* thought to provide a more effective labour system, but most Iban prefer this to working alone—a common attitude in Borneo. Geddes (1954, 70) writes that "Land Dayaks do not like to work alone. They say that it makes the sun grow hot upon their backs, meaning that the work seems much harder when not done in company".

TABLE 23

Number of Women in Bilek *Labour Teams*

Number of women in labour team		0	1	2	3
Incidence at:					
Rh. Melintang		3	19	7	1
Rh. Ancheh		2	19	8	4
Total	(63)	5	38	15	5
Percentage	(100)	8	60	24	8

In all cases where the *bilek* is without the labour of an active adult man or woman, some modification of the traditional division of work is necessary. As the Tables 22 and 23 show, this occurs in about 8 per cent of all families.

Bejalai

The custom of *bejalai* continues to have a great appeal for young men. *Bejalai*, 'to go on a journey' or even 'to go for a walk', is used in the semi-technical sense of going on an expedition. Present-day *bejalai* is interpreted in many respects as the equivalent of head-hunting expeditions in the past. Other trophies have taken the place of heads: valuable jars and gongs, and even outboard engines.

These expeditions may be to the nearest town only, or as far afield as the Malayan mainland or Singapore. Of a total of sixty-two men who had been on *bejalai* from Rh. Melintang and Rh. Ancheh, forty-three (or 69 per cent) had been outside Sarawak.

TABLE 24

Bejalai *Destinations*

	Sarawak	Sabah (North Borneo)	Brunei	Singapore and Malaya	Total *Bejalai*
Rh. Melintang (out of 34 adult men)	10	8	8	4	30
Rh. Ancheh (out of 38 adult men)	9	7	12	4	32
Total (out of 72 adult men)	19	15	20	8	62

Not only the destination varies, but also the length of the expedition, which may be anything from a month or two to many years. One Lemanak Iban (Sumping) of Rh. Ancheh had been in Sandakan for over twelve years but was still considered a *bilek* member on *bejalai*. An analysis of twenty-seven cases of recent *bejalai* in the Lemanak (January 1963) showed that *bejalai* rarely lasts for less than one year and in more than 50 per cent of all instances takes between one and four years or longer.

TABLE 25

Length of Bejalai

	Total	Less than 1 year	1–4 years	More than 4 years
Incidence	27	3	14	10
Percentage	100	11	52	37

The majority of all able-bodied men undertake an expedition at some period in their youth. As Table 24 shows, out of seventy-two adult men at Rh. Melintang and Rh. Ancheh, sixty-two had been on *bejalai*, approximately 86 per cent. The remainder were either quite young or, in a few cases, physically unfit. *Bejalai* is commonest among those who are still unmarried, and again those in their twenties or early thirties who are in most cases married but have not yet assumed responsibility for a *bilek* family. Of those on *bejalai* from Rh. Melintang and Rh. Ancheh during the 1962–3 season, percentages in various age groups were:

TABLE 26

Ages of Those on Bejalai

Age	17–20 years	21–5	26–30	31–5	36 or over
Percentage	39	21	25	15	0

The appeal of *bejalai* overrides the domestic requirements of rice cultivation, and the Iban accept that even at crucial times in the rice cycle a significant number of young men will be away. At the height of planting in 1963, when men are expected to dibble, over 20 per cent of the potential male labour force at Rh. Melintang, for example, was absent on *bejalai*.

TABLE 27

Numbers on Bejalai *during Planting, 1963*

	Rh. Melintang	Rh. Ancheh
Number of total potential male labour force	43	46
Number of men on *bejalai*	9	8
Percentage of potential force	21	17

Farm Management

It is not until the Iban becomes the senior *bilek* member (*tuai bilek*) and assumes the practical leadership of *bilek* affairs and responsibility for farm management that he is obliged to remain at home. The *tuai bilek* need not be the same as the senior hereditary (natal) member of the *bilek* (*pun bilek*), who, as emerges from the Table of domicile of married couples (Table 14), is as likely to be a woman as a man. The *tuai bilek* is normally a man although there were altogether three women *tuai bileks* at Rh. Melintang and Rh. Ancheh at the time of the survey. Of these, two were widows without adult sons or sons-in-law to share the *bilek*; the third was a young woman, unmarried, sharing, for special reasons, a separate *bilek* with her younger brother who was only just adolescent.

TABLE 28

Ages of Tuai Bileks/*Farm Managers*

Age in years	Incidence at: Rh. Melintang	Rh. Ancheh	Total
15	1	0	1
16–20	2	0	2
21–5	2	2	4
26–30	6	5	11
31–5	4	2	6
36–40	3	6	9
41–5	6	3	9
46–50	5	10	15
51–5	1	4	5
56–60	0	1	1
61 and over	0	0	0

As Table 28 shows, the age of the *tuai bilek* and farm manager varies considerably. Ideally the Iban is approaching thirty before assuming responsibility for a *bilek* and farm management. In practice, the great majority of *tuai bileks* (79 per cent approximately) fall into an age group beginning somewhat under thirty and continuing to the age of fifty. A breakdown of the sixty-three *bileks* of Rh. Melintang and Rh. Ancheh shows the percentage per age group.

TABLE 29

Percentage of Tuai Bileks *in Age Groups*

Age group	Incidence	Percentage
25 years and under	7	11
26–30 years	11	17
31–50 years	39	62
51 years and over	6	10

By the time he becomes *tuai bilek*, the Iban is expected to have had the opportunity to slake his wanderlust, to marry, establish a family, and reach the stage where he feels the urge to settle down and assume social and ritual responsibility for his *bilek*. At the same time, his parents or parents-in-law, if he has taken up domicile as a member of his wife's *bilek*, have reached the age where they no longer can be, or wish to be, primarily accountable for farming activities. As *tuai bilek* he is accepted as a mature and responsible member of the community and has a number of ritual and social obligations to fulfil.

1a. View of an Iban longhouse

1b. Interior of a longhouse

2. Hill rice farms in the Second Division

PART 2

VI. RELIGIOUS SOURCES

Uniformity of Iban Religion

THE early travellers were not impressed by Iban religion and understood neither its nature nor importance. Boyle (1865, 213) says categorically that 'in regard to their religion much cannot be said, for none exists.' Low (1848, 174) is only slightly less sweeping; he writes that 'the religious observances of these people are very little known, but in their state of civilization it cannot be supposed to extend beyond a few superstitions and belief in spirits of woods and mountains.'

It is surprising that the early writers did not discover the extent to which religion pervades all aspects of Iban life. Perhaps their own definitions of religious activity and thought were such that they failed to appreciate the nature and function of Iban religion. One of the most remarkable aspects of Iban existence is the way in which religion is almost synonymous with an ordered life and ritual enters into most activities. As Freeman (1955a, 28, para. 59) says, the Iban are 'an extremely religious people'. However, Iban religion is neither solemn nor set apart from the routine activities of daily life and it finds its principal expression in agricultural practice and the social order.[1]

The Iban have lived for generations in widely separated river valleys, and during their migrations they have come into close contact with other peoples. It is, therefore, to be expected that Iban religion—their agricultural rituals and ordering of society— might vary from district to district. Some differences certainly exist, but those who know the Iban well are constantly impressed by the homogeneous quality of their culture. Knowing that the social order and customary law are rooted in Iban religion,

[1] For an interesting account of a similar relationship which exists between religion, daily life and, in particular, agriculture among the Land Dayaks, see Howes, 1960.

A. J. N. Richards, at that time Resident of the Second Division, decided in 1961 to convene in Simanggang a meeting of traditional and religious leaders to discuss the standardization of Second Division (Iban) law, the formal core of the Iban way of life. The meeting,[1] at which I was present, was attended by thirty-five Iban gathered from all over the Division: apart from a few *manang* (*shaman*/healers) (see below, pp. 59–64; also 142 seq.), these were all either recognized community leaders (*penghulu* and *tuai rumah*) —hence also *tuai burong* in many cases, religious incantation experts (*lemambang*), or, as is not unusual, persons combining more than one office.

Never before had Iban from such a wide area been assembled to discuss their religion and customary law, and they were at first guarded and suspicious of each other. It is, however, hardly true that the delegates were intimidated by two 'non-Iban' chairmen, as one account implies.[2] One of the two chairmen who, in fact, conducted most of the proceedings was Hermanus Assan, himself an Iban,[3] son of a famous *penghulu* and, in his youth, a novice *lemambang*. After some initial hesitation, the meeting was remarkable not only for the light thrown on Iban religion but for the constructive, relaxed atmosphere which prevailed, and the direction which enabled the speakers to make their individual contributions.

It was not intended to produce a canon of Iban belief, but in discussing the religious assumptions which underlie customary law, the delegates spoke at some length on most aspects of their religion and one particularly interesting conclusion was the degree of uniformity which this discussion revealed. Of course there were local variations, differing details of expression and emphasis, but, considering the distances involved and the difficulty in communication, the tradition remained remarkably uniform. With one partial exception, it can be said that Iban religion does not vary in fundamentals from one river group to another.

The partial exception is the Saribas-Krian bloc, which differs

---

[1] A full account was published in the *Sarawak Gazette*, Richards, 1961b.

[2] Harrisson and Sandin (1966, 98). Harrisson did not attend, nor did Mujah, the principal authority for this account. As Richards stresses (1967, 489: 'Mujah is not known outside his own district . . .'), Mujah is certainly not the only *lemambang*, nor even the most famous *lemambang*, in the Second Division. In view of his Krian origins, he may even represent a variant point of view. See also Richards, 1968, 132.

[3] This point is made also by Richards (1967, 489), in his review of Harrisson and Sandin, 1966.

from the remainder not only in characteristics of language but in parts of their religious practice. In 1900 Howell and Bailey (1900, p. vi), in the preface to their dictionary, had described Iban as the language of a number of tribes which could be conveniently divided into five groups. They mentioned the Balau and Undup, Saribas and Skrang, Batang Ai and Lemanak, Sebuyau and Bugau, Ulu Ai and Engkari. These classifications were based largely on the extent of Malay linguistic influence. In the words of the preface (ibid.), 'the Ulu Batang Ai or Ulu Ai Dyaks, who live further up the Batang Lupar river than any other people, probably speak the purest dialect of the Sea Dyak language, but their accent is harsh and their speech rough-sounding and unpleasant compared with that of those who live nearer the sea.' Although the Iban use the names of the river valleys they inhabit to denote themselves, they cannot realistically be divided into five distinct groups. In head-hunting days, there were alliances between certain groups, the Undup and Balau, for example, and these consequently intermarried. In settled areas, the pattern tended to be a (somewhat unstable) alliance with the neighbouring river and enmity with the one beyond or adjacent to that. The Undup Iban, for example, were enemies of the Lemanak, and the Lemanak of the Engkari. Although among traditional enemies intercourse (and intermarriage) was slight or non-existent, this alone does not account for differences in language, and the distinctions of Howell and Bailey are to some extent artificial. There is no important difference between the Ulu Ai and the Lemanak in either language or practice and, although the Undup language shows slight traces of Malay influence, the original Iban remains relatively pure. But among the Saribas (and lower Skrang, which is very close) the intonation is perceptibly different and even the vocabulary has a number of peculiar forms. While the interior peoples have remained largely isolated, those 'who live nearer the sea', in particular the Saribas people, have been exposed to other influences—not only Malay.[1]

[1] Sandin, 1964, with respect to Malay influence demonstrates the 'impurity' of the Saribas Iban by his genealogies which show both the extent of Iban exposure to the Malays and Malay exposure to the Iban. He says, 514, that '. . . when they refer to Malays these are not . . . necessarily Malay in the "Malayan" sense. Usually they are animist "Dayaks" . . . who, on coming down nearer the coastal contacts have been converted to Islam. They then "masok Melayu", become Malay.' For Bukitan influence see genealogies in Sandin, 1956, 73 seq., repeated 1967, 115 seq.

Although the interior of the Second Division may have been sparsely inhabited by nomad hunters at the time of the Iban advance, these retreated rather than oppose the superior Iban forces, and according to tradition, the Iban encountered no significant opposition until they reached the Saribas area (see above, p. 19). Saribas legends and genealogies contain not only the important example of a dynastic marriage between the child of an Iban and a Bukitan chief (see above, ibid.), but assume extensive intermarriage. Throughout their history it has been Iban practice to adopt ideas from the conquered when this suited them (the *ajat* dance, tattoo patterns, and possibly even the use of a hornbill effigy, have all been traced to Kayan–Kenyah origins,[1] also the use of the *palang* penis-pin). Consequently when it appears that the Saribas-Krian bloc differs from the remainder not merely in intonation but in one important religious concept, the inference is that this was adopted from another source and is not a part of traditional Iban religion which was arbitrarily discarded elsewhere.[2]

What differentiates the Saribas-Krian Iban is the importance they attach to the *gawai antu* (feast of the dead) which culminates in the *timang jalong* chant. It has been implied (Harrisson, 1962, see especially 13–14) that this is a pale relic of an original secondary burial cult which has not survived elsewhere. A minor *gawai antu* occurs in the Undup but in the Ulu Ai burial rites are straightforward and the postponed *gawai antu* largely unknown. Two explanations are possible: either the elaborate *gawai antu* and its wider implications were originally part of Iban religion and have for some reason been 'forgotten' or rejected by the Batang Ai, and their spiritual heirs, or, alternatively, elaborate (postponed) burial rites were not part of Iban belief as imported to Sarawak, and have been grafted into the system by the Saribas-Krian Iban in the

[1] The Iban are themselves aware of this. They say, for example, that to dance the *ajat* especially well is to 'dance like a Kayan' (*ngajat baka Kayan*). They also trace many of their tattoo designs to the same source; to an outside observer Iban tattoos often look like coarse or modified copies of Kayan designs. Unlike the Kayan and Kenyah, the Iban are not especially adept at wood carving (except knife handles), but they carve impressive hornbill effigies although the hornbill is not an augural or special bird to the Iban, whereas Harrisson, 1960, 37, quotes an authority saying that it was an omen among the Kayan.

[2] Richards, 1967, 488, agrees with this conclusion. 'The people of this group [viz. the Saribas-Krian] are mixed in race and culture, not only with the previous inhabitants . . . but also with Malays and Chinese to a greater extent than other Dayaks. They are not typical . . .'. See also Richards, 1968, 132, in reply to Harrisson and Sandin, 1968, 131.

process of assimilating the Bornean tribes who lived in the territory before them.

With this exception occurring in the Saribas-Krian[1] the general uniformity of Iban religion is remarkable, as was made clear at the proceedings of the Simanggang conference. The religious beliefs and practice which survive in the Ulu Ai and neighbouring areas are common in all essentials to other Iban of the Second Division river valleys and their descendants who have migrated beyond. And, like their language, which is 'rough-sounding and unpleasant', but the 'purest' form of Iban (Howell and Bailey, 1900, p. vi quoted above), Ulu Ai practice is very probably that which has been least influenced by non-Iban peoples. And the Lemanak Iban remain close in most significant respects to the Ulu Ai.

That the Iban already practised shifting hill rice cultivation when they entered Sarawak is supported not only by the fact that the Iban considered this characteristic as a distinguishing factor at the time, but also by the migration itself. The unending search for fresh jungle prompted the Iban to move first into Sarawak's Second Division and subsequently into the Third and other Divisions. The rice cult is closely bound up with the myths concerning Pulang Gana which are known to the Iban everywhere; so also are those concerning Sengalang Burong, which define the system of augury (considered vital to successful rice cultivation), ritual celebrations and the ordering of society. These constitute the core of Iban belief.

Religious Personnel

The personnel of Iban religion, the experts, are those individuals who have specific roles in relation to rice cultivation, augury, ritual celebrations and the ordering of society. They act as a channel between the world of immediate experience and its spirit antecedents and influences. The leading exponents of these roles in Iban society are four, although one or more functions may be vested in the same person. They are the *tuai burong* or augur, the *tuai rumah* or village headman, the *lemambang* or ritual incantation specialist, and, lastly, the *manang—shaman* or 'healer'.

[1] Richards, 1968, 132, also draws attention to the significance of Burong Malam in the Saribas, but this is less important.

(a) The *Tuai Burong*

The most important person in everyday life is the *tuai burong* (see below, pp. 135, 159–63). He is a man of considerable standing in his own village and in certain cases his reputation may extend much farther afield. Dadup, for example, a *tuai burong* of the extreme Ulu Ai had in his younger days been a pupil of Busang, from Kesit in the middle Lemanak, and Iban used to come from far to meet Ulak, a well-known *tuai burong* of the Kumpang valley.

The *tuai burong* is the augur, but he is not merely an augury expert. He is, above all, favoured with the spirit attention which expresses itself regularly in omens and dreams. As omens and dreams are open to interpretation, the *tuai burong* has not only to receive regular spirit guidance in this manner but to be capable of interpreting it. The proof of his correct interpretation is assumed to lie in the success of his own undertakings in particular and in the well-being of his longhouse community generally. The *tuai burong*, through his dreams, his augury, and in his ritual activities, leads the community, and because he is responsible for the omen sticks (*megai kayu burong*) he is known as the foundation or base of the longhouse (*pun rumah*). If all goes well with the community and it continues to have satisfactory harvests, the *tuai burong* remains in office. If, however, there are two or three bad years, it is assumed that the *tuai burong* either lacks the fortune to attract the advice of the spirits, or the ability to interpret their guidance correctly, and he is replaced.

The office of *tuai burong* is not inherited, although there is no reason why a son should not inherit from his father the same propensity, skill, and good fortune which would enable him to qualify. The essential qualification is success, success in rice farming. Consequently, when the community seeks a new *tuai burong* to lead the community, it is customary to seek among those who are regularly successful (*ni orang ti sebak bulih dia nanya*). When a *tuai burong* has been provisionally selected by the community as a whole, it is expected that his appointment will be confirmed to him in a dream. Should the spirits fail to give their approval in this way, the provisional *tuai burong* does not qualify to take office and it becomes necessary to consider an alternative candidate.

The *tuai burong* leads the longhouse community in most daily religious matters and especially those concerning rice cultivation.

The rice cycle and farming activities are so closely bound up with both admonitory auguries and religious prohibitions that the *tuai burong* is in constant demand. And just as the standing of an individual *tuai burong* is related to his personal success, so successful farming is the measure of a community's healthy relations with the spirit world. The code of social behaviour and religion which the *tuai burong* is called upon to interpret are designed to maintain the right relations between men and the spirits.

(*b*) The *Tuai Rumah*

Administration of customary law and the social code as such, the *adat* in its restricted and technical sense, falls to the *tuai rumah* (see above, pp. 25 seq.). Unlike the office of *tuai burong*, the *tuai rumah* is officially recognized by the government, although the position carries no emoluments. The functions of *tuai rumah* and *tuai burong* are distinct, but in practice it is often the same man who performs both. This was the case in approximately two-thirds of the longhouses studied in the Lemanak and Delok. In the past, while the Iban remained comparatively isolated and *pindah* migration was a recurrent event thought to depend for its success on spirit favour and the correct response to spirit guidance, the *tuai burong* was almost invariably also *tuai rumah*. In recent years, a more settled way of life and the expectation that the *tuai rumah* will act as host to visiting officials and as spokesman or longhouse representative before the authorities, have come to demand qualities which the traditional *tuai burong* did not need nor always possess.

(*c*) The *Lemambang*

Members of the third category, the *lemambang*, have been called (Richards, 1961b, 138) 'priests . . . and sometimes judges, as in the old Celtic sense'. Harrisson and Sandin[1] refer to the *lemambang* as 'fully initiated shamans', and regard them as the arbiters of Iban religion. Howell, who in most respects has been considered the greatest authority on the Iban and their language, and was himself married to an Iban, defines *lemambang* as a 'patron saint' (Howell and Bailey, 1900, 92). This is a surprising entry, particularly since elsewhere he describes the principal functions of the *lemambang*

---

[1] 1966, 70, and 1966 *passim*: definition of *Lemambang-shaman* on p. 37, but note especially pp. 42 seq.

correctly. Under the *gawai* entry in his dictionary (ibid., 48) he speaks, without once using their name, of 'certain men who have given attention to that branch of Dyak lore and are able to chant the invocations (*pengap*) [see below, pp. 64 seq.] walk up and down round these offerings singing their monotonous song. . . . This chanting lasts for several hours and is indeed the important religious ceremony connected with these four Feasts.'

The *lemambang* may perhaps be called a priest but he is not the ultimate authority on Iban religion. His concern is with intoning the ritual incantations, called *pengap*, which form a central part of major ceremonies (*gawai*). These occur intermittently. Although extremely important, they are not as significant in the context of day-to-day religion as are omens, dreams, and social ordinances. They are, however, extraordinarily interesting since they comprise long versified accounts of personalities and life in the spirit world. They provide the dramatic, personified background to the code governing agriculture and social conduct.

The *lemambang* may be either a man or a woman. Harrisson and Sandin (1966, 37) say 'hermaphrodite (ideally)', but this view is not normally articulated by the Iban. There may be some confusion arising from the long, apparently feminine, dress used by *lemambang* on ritual occasions, which is intended not to represent female clothing but to afford symbolic protection on the journey through the spirit world. Unlike many references to *manang* of dubious masculinity, there is no evidence to support transvestite or hermaphrodite *lemambang* and no instances were encountered. The majority of *lemambang* are men, but a good number are women. From 1960 on, one out of four reputable *lemambang* in the Ulu Undup was a woman, and in 1964 both the *lemambang* novices at Nanga Delok were girls.

To become a fully recognized *lemambang* presupposes in the first place a vocation, a call experienced and confirmed in a dream. It also takes a lengthy period of training. This is not so much a question of 'initiation', but a process of apprenticeship and practice which culminates in general acceptance as a qualified *lemambang*. During the first stage one or two interested young men (or women) spend a series of long evenings with an experienced *lemambang*. They endeavour to memorize choruses and repeated passages. At the next *gawai* festival, the novices follow the *lemambang* as a chorus (*ngelambong*), repeating appropriate sections after him. In time, if they persevere, and have the facility for remembering by heart many hours' worth of verse, they graduate to officiating as *lemambang* themselves. Although a few *lemambang* are acquainted with incantations used in different contexts and on different occasions, it is normal to specialize in one or possibly two. The incantations include the full names, honorifics, and nicknames of the spirits. These are unfamiliar in detail to Iban other than the *lemambang*; even the *tuai burong* rarely knows them fully. The *lemambang*, however, does not necessarily understand the precise role of the named spirits in augury or other rites, and does not, qua *lemambang*, participate in these. Less than being a priest, since he does not perform ritual acts, it is probably truer to say, as Scott (1956, 103) does in his dictionary, that the *lemambang* is the 'bard' of Iban society, albeit the liturgical bard or cantor.

(d) The *Manang*

The fourth category consists of the *manang*.[1] Also these have been called 'priests'[2] but, in fact, their functions are not priestly. They are healers, possibly *shamans*, whose role is related exclusively to treating the sick—understood to include the sick in both spirit and body.

Whereas the *lemambang* was not recognized or understood, the *manang* has been familiar since the earliest writers on the Iban, and has attracted continuing attention. Two characteristics may account for this. The first is the blindness or poor sight commonly found among *manang*. The second, and more exotic, is the phenomenon of sex change.

Blindness, or part blindness, which in ordinary Iban life is a handicap so severe as to make a man almost totally dependent on his *bilek* family, could be interpreted as an asset in dealings with the spirit world. The spirits move mainly at night and they see in the dark, when the Iban cannot normally see; conversely blindness may be taken to imply spirit sight. Sex change also sets the *manang* apart. He is neither a true Iban man nor woman with their customary characteristics and undertaking their usual tasks. He belongs to a different order and this is his source of power, since he is commonly a person who in the ordinary Iban context counts for little.

---

[1] For a full account, see below, p. 142 seq.
[2] As early as, for example, St. John, 1863, i. 73, and as recently as Wulff 1960, 130.

Like both *tuai burong* and *lemambang*, the *manang* is called in a dream and no man becomes a *manang* without this stamp of spirit approval. The vocation may be accompanied by instruction from an older established *manang*, who also provides the core of the novice's equipment. The instruments consist primarily of stones, bones, and similar objects believed to have spirit properties. These are used in diagnosing the condition of his patient and during treatment. Treatment is directed at individuals and the *manang*'s role is as a healer of individuals. Although individual illness may spring from wider *bilek* causes and have implications for the community, since Iban religion is in most respects essentially a *bilek* or community affair, the *manang*'s main contribution to an understanding of Iban conduct and belief lies in explaining the nature and behaviour of the spirit/soul and in interpreting sickness in man's relations with the spirit world.

The Oral Tradition

Knowledge of Iban mythology and their conception of the spirit world is contained in a rich oral tradition. There are a number of recognized (literary) forms: *pengap, sampi, pelian, tusut, kana, renong, pantun, jerita tuai, ensera.*

The extensive oral tradition can be divided into two. One part, which is the more important, concerns specifically the origins of Iban custom, the rice cult, augury, and social organization. The other is comprised largely of legends from the heroic past, which serve partly as entertainment, as well as songs and stories. *Pengap, sampi, tusut* and the others differ both in form and purpose. Each has a distinct function and none by itself presents a complete picture of Iban mythology. *Pengap*, for instance, assume a knowledge of *jerita tuai*, *sampi* of *pengap*, and so forth. Of the sources, part belong to a poetical tradition, which in Perham's view (Ling Roth, 1896, i. 170) 'like all Dyak lore . . . is prolix in the extreme, and deluged with meaningless verbosity'. Others are expressed in the language of everyday prose.

(a) Pengap

Pengap provide the richest 'poetical' source. *Pengap*, which are also known loosely as *timang* (the verb *nimang* means 'to sing praise') are long incantations used at festivals (*gawai*) (see below, pp. 200 seq.). They commonly last from sunset to near sunrise the following morning, although on very special occasions, they may be carried over for several nights. In essence the *pengap* describes a journey to spirit territory in order to fetch the principal spirit(s), in whose honour the festival is celebrated and whose presence and favour are particularly desired. The incantations include elaborate allusions to spirits met on the way, their names and honorifics, their relationships, where they live, and what they do.

The *pengap* are poetry and extensive use is made of repetition, alliteration, onomatopoeic expressions, and even largely meaningless words with decorative intent (*bungai jako*). Repeated onomatopoeic words are especially common in introductory verses. For example:

> *Taing taing isau unding* . . .
> The (*taing*) clink of the knife blade . . .
>
> *Taung taung belumbong nibong* . . .
> The (*taung*) thud of chopping palm . . .
>
> *Trai trai betenchang ratai* . . .
> The (*trai*) sound of beating dry bamboo . . .

As an instance of Iban poetic usage, the Bemban/Bembu river is described:

> *Sungai Bembu, sungai Bemban,*
> *Spiak mabu, spiak dalam.*
>
> River Bembu, river Bemban,
> One side shallow, one side deep.[1]

The form of *pengap* follows a definite pattern and this changes little, but the embellishments vary from place to place and person to person. Even in the nineteenth century, it was apparent to Perham (Ling Roth, 1896, i. 168) 'that, in different tribes or clans, different renderings of the *pengap* . . . may be found'. The *pengap* are less esoteric chants, the prerogative of an initiate circle as has been implied (Harrisson and Sandin, 1966, 40 seq.), than elaborate incantations which, due to their length and intricacy, are familiar only to those—the *lemambang*—who have been specifically and painstakingly instructed.

Since the *pengap* are often exceedingly long, the process of

[1] Similar examples occur in many of the texts quoted by Harrisson and Sandin, 1966.

committing their contents to memory is not easy. In learning to memorize *pengap* and to provide cues which will serve as subsequent reminders, the *lemambang* novices use inscribed or incised boards. These boards, which are called *papan turai*, have recently been the subject of study and two substantial articles subsequent to the earlier passing references.[1] Because of their intrinsic interest and the fact that they were, apparently, unknown to earlier writers like Howell, there may be a tendency to attribute undue significance to their 'discovery'. It is difficult to accept the assertion that *papan turai* are an Iban 'Book of the Word' or something like the 'Acts of the Apostles'—a recorded, unchanging 'New Testament'[2] by which to measure current religious belief and practice.

Papan turai, however, provide clues to the interpretation of Iban 'texts', although their use is limited to *pengap*, *sabak* (a mourning chant similar to *pengap* which occurs most widely in the Saribas) and possibly *tusut* tables. *Papan turai* are not used for prayers (*sampi*), augury (*beburong*), customary law (*adat*), and so forth.[3] They are, therefore, only familiar to *lemambang*, who are trained in the ritual incantations. In recent years, perhaps because of a growing awareness of Malay *Jawi*, Chinese script, and Western writing, the Iban have been reluctant to display *papan turai*, possibly for fear that these should seem inferior, or conceivably because the Iban no longer considered them important. In remoter

[1] Morrison (1962, 80–1), shows photographs of *papan turai* (in the brief explanatory caption translated as 'memory tablets'); Jensen (1964, 544), has a passing reference to the nature and purpose of the boards; Harrisson (1965), devotes an article to a detailed study of a *sabak* chant (similar to the *pengap*) based on a *papan turai*; and Harrisson and Sandin (1966) contribute a long paper to the special monograph of the *Sarawak Museum Journal* which deals specifically with *pengap* and *papan turai*. (See also Jensen (1966, 29–30), in the same volume).

[2] Harrisson and Sandin, 1966, 66–7. 'The festival chants based on the *papan turai* are a Book of the Word for the newer Iban bird augury and all that went with it. . . . They are something like the Acts of the Apostles . . .' (66). 'Thus the Sengalang Burong "texts" acting as the New Testament (or part thereof) still carry on from and tie in with all kinds of other material, the rest of the Iban metaphysical Bible, new and old, Almighty God, petrified charms, whispering cricket, earlier creation myths, diving contest . . .'. Harrisson and Sandin's argument is weakened by their examples of *papan turai* which are all derived from the same cultural sub-group, the Saribas-Krian, (see especially 98–100) which more than any differs in important respects from other Iban groups (see above, pp. 56 seq.).

[3] This point and the following description occur also in Jensen, 1966, 29–30.

parts of the Second Division, where the boards still exist, there is no indication that the *papan turai* are or were ever considered secret; they are not revered in the manner that *Kenyalang* hornbill effigies for example, continue to be. *Papan turai* are in fact occasionally discarded together with other longhouse bric-a-brac.

The boards are marked with symbols representing stages, in particular persons and places, encountered or passed in the course of the *pengap* spirit journey. The *papan turai* 'characters' are personal to the extent that the individual selects an ideograph which will remind him or her of a particular 'verse' or stage in the journey through the spirit world. 'The way people write is not the same; each one does it his own way' (*tulis orang enda sabaka; siko ngaga ka diri*). The signs may or may not be understood by another *lemambang*: for example, a Melugu, Dor, *lemambang* was able to 'read' nearly half the signs on a Lemanak board, but his understanding of the characters was partly derived from his knowledge of the stages of the journey. It is not certain whether the use of 'standard' characters should be attributed primarily to common patterns of Iban thought and analogy or the direct influence of the *lemambang* who instructs the novices (thus channelling traditional ideographs) or a combination of the two. But it is certain that similar symbols are found on boards in widely separated areas and are immediately intelligible.

The quality of the actual 'writing' varies greatly. It depends partly on the artistic ability of the writer (*niteh ka pemandai orang ngukir*), partly on the care he chooses to devote to the board in question. On the one hand, roughly marked characters occur, done quickly with a stub of wood and paint on an indifferent piece of wood, and, on the other, exquisitely carved *papan turai* are found with elaborate decorations on polished wood. The medium is not itself important. Traditionally it was charcoal, the only appropriate writing material available, but *papan turai* were sometimes incised; more recently paint is often used or the signs even written on paper in pencil or ink.

(b) *Sampi*

Sampi are invocationary prayers used on virtually all ritual occasions. They begin with the cry 'Oha' repeated three times,[1] as

---

[1] Similar to the widespread introductory shout which occurs for example in the Greek, Anglo-Saxon, Norse, Celtic, and Old French oral traditions.

a summons to the spirits, and almost invariably continue by describing the favour or assistance which the relevant spirit(s) is asked to give. Like *pengap*, *sampi* are poetical in form: they employ repetition, alliteration, and decorative words with no real meaning. They vary greatly in length, according to the occasion and the officiant, from short prayers of less than twenty lines on the arrival of a guest, to lengthy invocations, as at planting (*sampi nugal*), which may last for an hour or more.

Other than the ability to memorize and repeat a prayer, no particular qualifications are required of the officiant. At Rh. Ancheh twenty-seven *tuai bileks* out of thirty-three (almost 82 per cent) were capable of reciting the usual *sampi*, but only twelve (about 36 per cent) remembered the elaborate longer invocations, and on occasions when these were essential, made their services available to related *bileks*.

Sampi are commonly associated with the *biau* ceremony in which a live fowl is waved over a food offering (*piring*) or honoured guest, and subsequently killed in expiation (*ginselan*) (see below, p. 77). *Sampi* provide the clearest picture of the spirits associated with specific rites and undertakings and their functions.

(c) *Pelian* and *Pantun*

Prayers for the sick (*pelian*) fall into a distinct category. They are also poetical in form but are intoned exclusively by the *manang* in association with healing rites (see below, pp. 148–9). They normally last for several hours and occur at night. *Pelian* concern the experiences of the sick or dying person's spirit or soul in its encounter with the spirit world.

Pantun, which in the Saribas are known as *renong*,[1] are songs, often drinking songs, which are sung at festivals and parties in honour of guests or other individuals. Although they commonly contain allusions to the myths and oral tradition, these references are incidental. *Kana* is the name given to legendary accounts when these are expressed in rhythmical or semi-poetical forms; Maceda (1962, 494) in a recent survey of Iban music was unable to find a 'singer of legends (*kana*)'.

---

[1] Maceda, 1962, 495, says *renong* is the name for a 'similar-type' of song.

(d) *Tusut*

Tusut are ancestral tables or genealogies, and are considered extremely important by the Iban as much to establish their spirit pedigree (since the *tusut* of prominent and remembered Iban are traced back to the spirits from whom they claim descent) as to determine their own more immediate relationships.

There are also non-human *tusut* which trace the origins of animals, fish, and important fruit trees. These, in particular, are semi-poetical, especially in the remoter, mythological parts, and are remembered in blocks. *Tusut* are normally familiar only to those Iban who take pride in their ancestry. In five Delok longhouses, only six individuals were able to recite their *tusut* accurately although many remembered sections and were able to suggest emendations when others attempted to recall them.

Neither *pengap* nor *sampi* (let alone *pelian, pantun,* or *tusut*) retell the myths. They assume knowledge of them and refer, incidentally, to relationships, places, experiences, etc., which they dramatize and amplify. The *pengap* project into dramatic form the assumptions of Iban religion which finds practical expression in the rites associated with the rice cult, augury, and the code of social behaviour.

'Prose' Myths

Apart from the poetic tradition, there is a large body of 'prose' in the oral tradition. Whereas the poetic tradition depends largely on its form and is frequently recited by rote without grasp of the meaning (including, as it does, expressions which are in themselves incomprehensible to the majority of the Iban, apart from words which are actually meaningless), the prosaic tradition is related to the recollection of (legendary) events and ritual procedure.

Jerita tuai are the traditional accounts of the 'heroic' age;[1] these are the 'prose' equivalent of poetical *kana*. They are often introduced by '*dulu kalia*' which means 'in ancient times', 'in the remote past', or 'once upon a time'. Although they may be told as much for entertainment as for instruction, they record in detail Iban myths and protohistory. *Jerita tuai* include the stories relating to the principal spirits: Pulang Gana, Sengalang Burong,

---

[1] *Jeluta* may be used with the same meaning.

Samerugah, Seragunting and others, but also the escapades—
affairs, intrigues, rivalries—of the lesser spirits or heroes of Iban
lore: Kling, Laja, Kumang, Lulong, Tutong, the inhabitants of
Panggau Libau.[1]

There is no rigid distinction between *jerita* and *ensera*,[2] folk
tales told almost exclusively for entertainment, although *ensera*
are in no sense believed to be literally true. *Ensera* describe, among
other happenings, the doings of Apai Saloi, the endearing simple-
ton of Iban folk lore, and plandok the mouse-deer (see below,
p. 109, n. 1) who, in spite of his physical vulnerability, outwits and
overcomes much larger and more powerful animals—an ability
much admired by the Iban. There are also fanciful 'just so' stories
to explain, for example, why the sun is brighter than the moon,
and so forth.

Certain individuals have a particular gift for story-telling and
may acquire a reputation even beyond their own longhouse, but
almost all the older generation (it is expected of grandparents)
know some *ensera*. They have no religious or ritual significance.

[1] See, for example, Ling Roth, 1896, i. 311; also Harrisson, 1965a, 25,
n. 22. 1.

[2] Harrisson and Sandin (1966, 69), say of *ensera* that 'their position, from the
present angle, might once more be compared, in western terms, to the relationship between the stories of Hans Christian Andersen and the Book of Job, or
with a devout Anglican's "Alice in Wonderland" and the sermons of Cardinal
Newman ultimately R.C.'.

VII. MYTHS AND LEGENDS

Mythology

THE substance of most myths is expressed in the prose form of *jerita tuai*, but the poetic embellishments occur more fully in *pengap*; variant descriptions and names, in particular. Although they also serve to entertain, the myths are told with the primary purpose of explaining Iban behaviour and the potential consequences of wrong behaviour. The major myths all culminate in a description of one (or more) aspects of Iban social, religious, or cult practice. To this extent they establish precedent (cf. Malinowski, 1963, 291).

Iban mythology links the 'palpable untruth' of the myths proper, the possible factual basis of certain legends, and the empirical truth of recent history. For example, the spirit Sengalang Burong is the focus of important myths; legends connect him with Kling, the legendary Iban hero, who combines spirit properties with very human qualities and encounters; and present-day Iban trace their descent to Sengalang Burong through his daughter's marriage to a mortal.

The main myths all concern the spirit ancestry of the Iban and the origins of their religious beliefs, ritual, and social code. Although these are remarkably consistent, some variants and even contradictions occur. The names of the principal spirits do not vary: Sengalang Burong, Pulang Gana, and so forth. Sengalang Burong's part-mortal grandson is known by some as Surong Gunting and by others as Seragunting, but this represents only a 'textual' difference, almost of pronunciation. Surong Gunting's father, however, is sometimes called Menggin, sometimes Siu, and the moment the myths describe subsidiary relationships and events in detail, the inconsistencies become numerous. Sengalang Burong and Pulang Gana are brothers in some accounts, but many of the myths concerning one make no reference whatsoever to the other and they take place in entirely different parts of the universe. A sister of Sengalang Burong, Ini Inee Rabong Hari, is on occasion credited with restoring to life the sister of a man called Lemambang, but genealogical tables imply that the woman was not yet born.

F

Closer examination also reveals examples of incestuous marriage across generation levels in the spirit world.

The Iban see no need to resolve the inconsistencies (cf. Leach, 1954, 265, *et al.*). Nor do they appeal to the authority of *papan turai* or any one person'[1] It is correct that certain individuals have a reputation for knowing the mythology and these are frequently asked to recount the myths in whole or in part, but no single individual has broad authority. And the *papan turai* do not function as a scriptural check, since these really concern *pengap*. Insistence on empirical truth or a precise definition of time (hence also relation levels) is alien to the nature of Iban mythology. The Iban say that the myths do not lie (*nadai bula*); they call them 'true', *amai* or *amat*, but these same words are used to convey emphasis also, with the meaning 'indeed' or 'very'. As an Iban explained, the myths were not empirically true in the way that the bowl of rice before us was true, because, he said, 'I have never seen these things with my own eyes' (*mata aku empu nadai meda*), but, he added, the myths were true (*amat*) nevertheless.

The truth of the myths lies in their capacity to explain to the Iban's satisfaction the functioning of his religion. The consequent state of affairs provides the test of their truth. Where Iban communities prosper, this is credited to their ritual acts and religious behaviour, as set out in the main myths. On the other hand, poor harvests, sickness, or suffering do not cast doubt on the validity of the myths, rather on the Iban interpretation of appropriate behaviour, since it is 'known' that the universal order as explained in the myths was responsible for prosperity in 'the past'.

This does not mean that Iban time can be sharply divided into the 'sacred' and the 'profane'.[2] The mythology implies a gradual transition to the reality of present-day experience from the remote mythical epoch when spirits and the ancestors of the Iban shared the same world (*aki ini kami agi begulai enggau sida Sengalang Burong*). The principal spirits of the main myths are still 'alive' and active and have as much relevance to living Iban as they did in the mythical past. To this extent they belong to a different category of time. Between them and the ordinary Iban come the

---

[1] As suggested in respect of Mujah, Harrisson and Sandin, 1966, 42. Richards (1967 and 1968) agrees that there is no justification for the 'canonical' authority claimed.

[2] See, for example, Eliade, 1958, 388 seq. for a discussion of these categories.

legendary heroes, part spirit, part human and Iban. The period of their dealings with men and spirits is more precisely placed: they flourished after the time of the principal myths, but before the events of more recent remembered history.

Creation Myths

Accounts of the original creation, the origin of the world and mankind are confused, but these are not considered particularly significant. Various versions have been recorded over the years of contact with the Iban. Horsburgh (Ling Roth, 1896, i. 299) in the last century mentions 'Rajah Gantallah' who sounds very like 'Raja Entala' of a version heard in the Undup in 1964. Horsburgh's account is said to be from the Skrang (called 'Sakarran').

In the beginning, existed in solitude Rajah Gantallah, possessed of a soul with organs for hearing, speaking, and seeing; but destitute of any other limbs or members. . . . By an act of his will, Rajah Gantallah originated two birds, a male and a female, after which he did not directly produce any creature, his will taking effect through the instrumentality of these birds. . . . They created first the sky, then the earth, and then Batang Lupar . . . which was the first of waters and the mother of rivers [see above, p. 18]. Finding that the size of the earth considerably exceeded that of the sky, they collected the earth together with their feet, and heaped it into mountains. Having completed this work they attempted to create mankind. For this end they made the trees and tried to turn them into men; but without success. They then made the rocks for the same purpose. These they shaped like a man in all respects; but the figure was destitute of the power of speech. They then took earth, and, by the aid of water moulded it into the form of a man, infusing into his veins the gum of the Kumpang-tree which is of a red colour. They called to him—he answered; they cut at him— blood flowed from his wounds; as the day waxed hot, sweat oozed through his skin. They gave him the name of Tannah [*sic*] Kumpok, or Moulded Earth.

Dunn[1] records a similar account of the creation. Two spirits, Ara and Irik, were floating in the shape of birds over a vast expanse of water. Swooping down, they gathered from the water two solid substances like eggs. From one of these Ara formed the heavens, from the other Irik formed the earth. The earth, however, exceeded the expanse of the heavens, so the two gods compressed the earth

[1] 1963, pp. 21–3, originally a paper read before the Manchester Geographical Society in 1887.

within the limits of the sky. In consequence, vast upheavals occurred on the face of the earth producing rivers and streams to water the valleys and the plains. As soon as these had been created, plants and trees appeared spontaneously. Finally the two spirits, seeing that there was no one to inhabit the earth, decided to create mankind. They thought of trying to form a man from a tree, but the first trees they struck only produced a white sap. Even when at last blood-coloured sap trickled from a tree and they shouted to give it life, it failed to respond. Eventually they turned to the earth and moulded two human beings, one male and one female. Again Ara and Irik shouted to animate the earth men, who came to life and shouted in return. These were called Tanah Kumpok.

Howell[1] divides the story into three separate accounts: in one, mankind is created from the Kumpang tree, which has red sap; in another, earth is used; and in a third, two birds, Iri[2] and Ara, are the creators.

The most recent published version (Sandin, 1962b, 5–6)—in Iban—names Kree Raja Petara (king of the spirits) or Raja Entala as the original creator. This is similar to a version personally recorded in the Undup. Raja Entala and his wife discussed the fact that neither heavens nor earth, nor river nor any other living thing existed. They decided to scrape together the dirt from their bodies, and with this they created the earth. Again they gathered dirt and created the heavens, but the sky was not expansive enough to cover the earth. Raja Entala, therefore, compressed the earth, thus producing hills and mountains, rivers, valleys, and plains. Bracken and ferns grew first, then grasses and trees appeared (which is the natural order of regeneration in Sarawak). Pisang Rura, a banana variety, was one of the plants. Pisang Rura seduced Burong Iri, the bird Iri, and from their union fish are descended. Raja Entala and his wife were still not satisfied, since there was not yet anyone to possess the world and enjoy it. So they cut down a *bangkit* banana and from the stem Raja Entala fashioned the likeness of himself and his wife, with eyes, nose, arms, and legs. For blood he used the red sap of the Kumpang tree. His wife then covered the image with a *pua* (hand-woven and dyed Iban textile used on

---

[1] 1963, 20. This account was originally published in the *Sarawak Gazette* in 1909.

[2] Without a final 'k'. In Iban the final 'k' commonly serves to indicate a glottal stop—a characteristic of the language.

all ritual occasions) and, after Raja Entala had shouted at it for
the third time, it stirred and came to life. The two first men in
this account were called Telichu and Telichai. Telichai is sometimes considered the ancestor of Menggin, husband of the spirit
Sengalang Burong's daughter and father of Seragunting, who
stands at the head of the Iban pedigree. Telichu is said to be the
ancestor of demons and evil spirits: Antu Grasi.

A different story from the upper Lemanak says the first man
dwelt alone among the shoots of *aur* bamboo. After a time he
noticed a curious swelling in the calf of his leg, and when he cut
it open, a human being appeared. God, vaguely called Petara, gave
her a name (Seti Awa) and said she was to be his wife. The man
killed the couple's first offspring and planted them about his farm,
where they were transformed into cucumbers, spinach, rice,
pumpkins, and gourds.[1] Wherever he happened to touch the
undergrowth with their blood, it was turned into ferns and bamboo
and all the other edible leaves and plants which are so important
to the Iban. But it is forbidden to eat the shoots of the *aur* bamboo
lest there be death as among the children of the first man.[2]

Common to most versions of the creation is a vague belief that
a deity at some time crumpled up the earth to fit under the sky,
which explains their relative appearance and accounts for the
landscape. Iri(k) occurs in several creation accounts but is not
otherwise important, or even mentioned in any other context. The
Kumpang tree, with its distinctive red sap, is a natural object of
interest. It is used to make human effigies (*pentik*) for magical
purposes. Similarly, in certain *manang* ceremonies, the *bangkit*
banana is employed as an embodiment for the human soul.

There is little sense of a specific 'in the beginning' in Iban
thinking and less concern with ultimate origins.[3] In their equatorial

---

[1] In a somewhat different myth, the sister of Pulang Gana, Siti Permani, is
cut up into pieces which are transformed into pumpkins, rice, etc. This is one
of many cases where details and incidents are transposed from one myth to
another.
[2] There are many restrictions concerning *aur* bamboo. It was traditionally
used as the stake when incestuous couples were sacrificed (see above, p. 40),
and clumps of *aur* are believed to commemorate such events.
[3] Monberg, 1966, 31, notes on the island of Bellona in the Solomon Islands
a situation similar to the Iban. Not only were the origins of the universe of no
special interest to the islanders, but, he continues: 'It is . . . characteristic that
none of those gods who were of ritual significance took part in the creation of
the world, and this act was never referred to in the rituals.'

jungle the Iban are perpetually made aware of the cycle of birth and death, growth and decay, in a context which seems always to remain the same. This may be one reason why they show comparatively little interest in the first beginnings of life and see its end as a returning cycle.

Simpang-Impang and the Beginnings of Rice Cultivation

With the myth of Simpang-Impang begins the description of the origins of Iban belief.[1] According to the story, a man in the remote past discovered that someone or something had been at his rice. When subsequently he observed a snake descend from above and lick up his rice, he killed it. A huge body then came down from the sky and filled the valley. The man cut up the body and cooked it in bamboo sections, but while it was cooking the womenfolk laughed at sounds emerging from the bamboo.[2] Consequently the sky turned black and it rained for forty days and nights. The great flood which ensued submerged the entire country and just one peak remained uncovered.[3] Only one person survived the flood. She was called Dayang Racha. When she was making fire by rubbing sticks together, a small piece flew up and touched her vagina. In this way, Dayang Racha became pregnant, and in time she produced a child named Simpang-Impang, so called because he had only half his parts.

When he grew up, Simpang-Impang contemplated suicide by allowing himself to drift out to sea, but he was persuaded by a strange creature, whom he encountered, to stay and allow himself to be adopted by her. She revealed that her name was Indai Jebua.

[1] In one form or another the myth occurs widely. It was already recorded by Perham in his *Sea Dyak Gods* (Ling Roth, 1896, i. 301). Sandin, 1957, also gives a version. See also Dunn, 1963, 22.

[2] The reference to laughing at the sounds emerging from the bamboo is relevant. It is a serious offence among many Malaysian peoples to mock 'natural' behaviour—the antics of an animal, for example. The consequence is invariably a calamity which takes a 'natural' form like violent wind, rain, storm, or barren soil, and is generally associated with petrification of the offender to serve as a reminder. A well-known story among the Iban tells of a young girl who, when basket-fishing in the river, laughed at a fish which leapt up and touched her breast, saying that even her lover dared not touch her so. There was a terrible storm and she was turned to stone.

[3] References to a great flood occur in other stories also; see, for example, Dunn, 1963, 22–3.

Simpang-Impang noticed that at times she became hairy and seemed to behave like vermin, regularly bringing home grains of rice. It fell to Simpang-Impang to look after her children and while Indai Jebua was absent these turned into vermin and were particularly naughty. On one such occasion Simpang-Impang threw boiling water over them, which scalded them. When their mother came home, he told her they had knocked over the pot but she preferred to believe the children and ordered Simpang-Impang away. She then disclosed that she was in fact no other than the Vermin Spirit, but having adopted Simpang-Impang she gave him three enormous rice seeds for his inheritance.

After wandering about for three days, he decided to dry the seeds in the sun. While they were drying, a gust of wind blew them and they broke into many pieces, about the size of seeds as they are known today. When the Wind Spirit refused to pay damages, Simpang-Impang led a body of supporters against him. As they were about to assault his house, the Wind Spirit called out to Simpang-Impang and said to him, 'Don't you know me? I am the greatest friend of your father, Kusok', and he explained to Simpang-Impang who his father had been. The father of Simpang-Impang was no other than Kusok, the Fire Spirit, and he always works together with the Spirit of the Wind. Finally, the Wind Spirit agreed to compensate Simpang-Impang and offered him, in payment, a gong which was only to be beaten in extreme circumstances to stop the wind blowing.[1]

On his way home, it fell to Simpang-Impang to give names to all living creatures, to the snakes, to the trees, and to the other forms of life which he had encountered on his journey. During the meeting when the names were given—which was attended by the spirits—a cock flew over the heads of those present and excreted. Pulang Gana, who was there, decided that on this occasion the cock should not be punished by death for its impertinence, but agreed that henceforth, when addressing spirits, an offering should first be sprinkled with the blood of a cock. This is given as the mythological explanation of the *biau* ceremony, which initiates invocations, and the *ginselan* expiation rite. A cock is waved, then killed, before its blood is used to touch the sacrifice and the officiants—sometimes directly from the neck, sometimes with the tip of a feather dipped in the blood.

[1] This remains Iban practice during particularly violent storms.

The myth is rarely repeated as a whole; different versions exist and discrepancies are common. While in almost every case the person of Simpang-Impang encounters the Spirit of the Wind, Antu Ribut, in some accounts the spirit from whom he acquires the rice seed is the Spirit of Sparrows, Pipit, and not the Spirit of Vermin. One detail, found in many accounts and very popular with the Iban, insists that the seed of rice was not given but stolen. According to a Delok version, Simpang-Impang and his brother(?) Empang Raga tried on three occasions to steal rice seed, which they particularly liked, from the Sparrow Spirit. On the first attempt they put it in the blow-pipe dart-case which they had with them, but she found it. On the second occasion also she discovered it on their person, but the third time they had the bright idea of secreting a seed beneath the foreskin.[1] Thus they were successful and acquired rice for themselves.

The flood is common to most versions; also common is the implication that there was once an epoch of comparative ease and plenty (when rice seeds were significantly larger) and, thirdly, that the Iban or their mythical ancestors surreptitiously found their way to the knowledge and possession of the desired rice, which is derived from the spirits. In connection with these stories are the myths describing the naming of animals and the allocation of relationships within the natural order.

Pulang Gana and the Origin of the Rice Cult

Of paramount importance are the myths concerning Pulang Gana.[2] Incidents and details vary slightly, but in every instance Pulang Gana is the spirit who has the earth as his domain and gives growth to the rice. The stories explain in different ways how he came to inherit or acquire the earth, but they are all agreed that it is his. In all versions, Pulang Gana frustrated the efforts of the first rice

---

[1] The myth obviously belongs to a time before circumcision became general among the Iban, as it is now. For a fuller account of this version, see Jensen, 1966, 19–20.

[2] In invocations, Pulang Gana often stands in apposition to 'Raja Sua' as a second name or title. The Land Dayaks also recognize a god of the 'countryside' called Pula Gana, Rajah Suwa (Geddes, 1954, 78). Both Sua and Suwa show obvious signs of Hindu connections and, like Siva, are spirits of fertility.

farmers until they learned to show the necessary regard for the earth by making sacrificial offerings. This remains the basis for the rituals associated with rice planting.

Pulang Gana is said to be variously one of three, five, or seven siblings. In an Undup version of the story,[1] which is probably confused, Pulang Gana was born to Simpang-Impang (in this case apparently female), who produced only blood at her first delivery.[2] The blood was thrown away into a hole and became Pulang Gana who lives in the earth, which is his. The central part of this account, however, conforms to the usual form of the myth. When the 'brothers' of Pulang Gana began clearing jungle for a farm without Pulang Gana's permission, he restored the trees and undergrowth to life nightly after they had returned home. When the brothers found for the third time regenerated jungle where their clearing had been, they decided to keep watch. That night they discovered Pulang Gana spiriting the branches, the bark, the chippings, and the trees back to life. They tried to catch him, but he revealed to them his identity and explained that the earth was his. The brothers asked him what the correct procedure was in requesting the use of it, and Pulang Gana instructed them. Before clearing jungle for a farm, the Iban were required to offer jars, bracelets, shells, ornamental shells, glass beads, etc. These are all symbolized in the *piring* food-offering or sacrifice.

A normal Iban *piring* offered to a spirit includes all that is usually given to a guest and is prepared in the same order: first items for chewing and smoking, then 'real food' as the Iban understand it—which means rice, and finally the optional extras. The actual *piring* consists of boiled rice (*asi*), puffed rice (*rendai*), sweet (glutinous) rice (*pulut*), salt (*garam*), sago or rice cakes (*tumpih*), betel nut (*pinang*), sireh leaf (*sireh*), and other chewing ingredients, gambier leaf and lime, tobacco and leaf for smoking, topped by a hen's egg and a cup of rice 'beer' (*tuak*). The *piring* may be in one or more portions and each simple *piring* must include all items (except, sometimes, the egg). Normally the *piring* is threefold, fivefold, sevenfold, or even ninefold, in which case each ingredient is split or divided into that number of pieces or portions—except, again, for the egg.

[1] Recorded near Batu Lintang in 1960.
[2] Howell's version, 1963, 19, says Pulang Gana was born 'without his members'.

Apart from explaining the origins of the *piring*, which is a focal point in Iban ritual, the myth stresses the nature of land tenure. The Iban farmer does not 'own' land: it continues to belong to the spirit, that is, Pulang Gana (see above, p. 42). Through the correct ritual procedure the Iban leases the use of it and acquires rights to the harvest. The appearance of Pulang Gana to his brothers after their attempted clearing, his revelation of himself as the spirit of the earth and his explanation of the appropriate ritual are common to all accounts.

Another version (Howell, 1963, 19) calls Petara (the general title for a spirit) the father of limbless Pulang Gana, and when the second child born to 'Petara' proved to be a girl with no nose, she was set adrift on a river and became Rajah Jewata, Spirit of Fishes. The third child was without any human form and was placed on a bough of a tree where it became an orchid. The fourth child was a girl named Siti Permani, and she was cut to pieces, the bits becoming rice, pumpkins, and other plants. The fifth child was a boy called Blang Pinggang because he had a white stripe around his waist; he later became Ini Anda and lives in the heavens. The sixth child was transformed into animals and birds, while the seventh was a girl called Dayang Petri.

In yet another (and perhaps the most widely accepted) version, Pulang Gana is tricked by his six brothers and one sister,[1] who are all relatively human spirits. After finding a pest in his vegetable plot, Pulang Gana tracks down a porcupine which escapes from him into a hole in the mountain-side. He goes after it in pursuit. After a long time, he emerges as from a tunnel into another land. This is the territory of Samerugah. By chance Pulang Gana succeeds where all others have failed in curing the slave of Samerugah, who has been seriously ill. He is rewarded by being given the choice of Rajah Samerugah's seven daughters for his wife. He selects the youngest, whose name is Serintun Tanah Tumboh Yak Serindak Tanggi Buloh. But when he returns home once more, Pulang Gana discovers that his family has given him up for dead and divided up the property without assigning him a proper share. According to one account he was given earth as his lot during the 'burial'; in another, when he complains to the eldest brother on his return that he has received no portion of the property, the brother merely replies 'It's too bad', picks up a lump of earth,

---

[1] Sengalang Burong is commonly said to be one of the siblings.

and says, 'Take this.' Thus the earth becomes Pulang Gana's property as he subsequently reminds his brothers when they begin to farm.[1]

Pulang Gana is thought to live underground at the mountain range called Giling Chiping. Messengers are sent there to summon him during the whetstone festival (*gawai batu*) when sacrifices are made in his honour and his blessing is invoked at the inauguration of a new farming season (see below, pp. 198 seq.). Pulang Gana attends the festival accompanied not only by his wife, but also by his daughter, Benih Lela Punggang Tengian Dara Bintang Tiga Datai Ka Jelan,[2] his son-in-law, Aji Ti Brani Ngilah Bulan Suka Raja Rengayan, and two slaves, Bengkang Bujang Penyadong (the Slow Lemur) and Ingkat Apai Renggat Pangkong Tutong (the Tarsier)—both subfusc or subterranean animals.

Pulang Gana is not only invoked during all the rites concerned with rice cultivation and fertility, but also at the construction of a new longhouse. When the first and central post is erected in the ground, a pig is sacrificed as a propitiation to Pulang Gana. He is also invoked when the entrance ladder (*tangga*) is placed in position after construction, and at the house inauguration ceremony of *mangkong tiang*[3] a sacrifice in his honour is placed above the hearth, which is made of earth. Both the actual longhouse and agriculture are rooted in the earth and, therefore, in the realm of Pulang Gana. Finally, before burial, rice is sometimes scattered on the ground in compensation for use of the land, but this practice is not universal.

Although the Iban had been taught by Pulang Gana the necessary procedure for inaugurating a rice farm, they were not conspicuously successful (see also below, pp. 88 seq.). An important myth which relates to Samerugah offers an explanation. All versions of it incorporate Samerugah by name, although his actual role varies; some mention Pulang Gana, others merely 'Petara'—without further definition. But it is ultimately revealed through Samerugah that the farmers have poor harvests because they use

[1] According to Harrisson, 1965a, 37, when Pulang Gana returns to find that his brothers have divided up the family property leaving no share for him, Samerugah, his father-in-law, '. . . porcupine wise, helped him remould the earth out of the hearth-earth remains'. (See also ibid., p. 47, n. 57. 4.)

[2] Whose name contains both the words for seed (*benih*) and the constellation Orion (Bintang Tiga). See below, pp. 155–6.

[3] See Howell, 1900, 116, entry under *pangkong* and n. 1 above.

the personal names of their parents-in-law—which is forbidden. This remains the most rigorously observed of all Iban prohibitions, even among educated Christian converts in government employment.

During the first season, one sowing basket of seed gave only one basket in yield, and the next, one whole carrying basket of seed produced only one carrying basket when harvested. This, an un-named Iban husband and wife said to each other, was the equivalent of not farming at all, and they took their case to Samerugah. Samerugah set off to ask a spirit (*petara*), although in another account he refers the case to Pulang Gana, which illustrates the type of confusion common in mythical relationships. On his way, he met a dead tree still standing (*punggu*), which asked him where he was going. The dead tree told him the way, adding that it wished to go up itself and could not, wished to go down and could not, and asked that this too be referred to *petara*. Next Samerugah came to the deep pool which asked him where he was going. The pool directed him adding that it too wished to go down-river or up-river but could not, and asked that this also be referred to *petara*.[1] After three days he came to a house and was shown the final hills which are the abode of *petara*. He came at last to a long-house of fifty-five doors where he inquired after the room of his *petara*. The *ruai* was shown him and he sat down. *Petara* asked him whether he had eaten, and when he said 'no', prepared rice for him. After eating in the *bilek*, they sat down to talk and *petara* asked him what it was he wanted. He replied that he could not understand why when he planted one sowing basket full of seed he reaped only one. He knew of nothing he had done wrong. *Petara* asked whether he had a wife and parents-in-law. He said he had. 'How do you refer to your parents-in-law?' asked *petara*. 'By their names', he said. 'That is the reason', said *petara*, 'why you have such a poor harvest, because you have not learned to show respect for your parents-in-law (*b'entua*). And if they have brothers and sisters you must not call them by their names either;[2] if they are older, they should be addressed as "*ika*", if younger, "*adeh*".' In conclusion, *petara* explained the reverence due to the whet-stones, and said that if all these conditions were duly observed

---

[1] In other accounts, these same queries are referred to Seragunting; see below.

[2] These are known as 'in-laws of the sun' (*entua mata hari*).

there would be an abundant yield. The Iban consider themselves indebted to Samerugah for this knowledge.

Before leaving, the case of the dead tree and the deep pool were also put before *petara*. He explained that the tree could neither fall nor rise because it was supported by a jar (*tajau*), but if this were removed, the tree would collapse to the ground. The pool, he said, was tied by roots; if these were severed, it would flow away. Much the same explanations are given in the context of Seragunting's visit to Sengalang Burong, when he is asked to make similar inquiries.[1]

Seragunting or Surong Gunting and Iban Ancestry

The myths concerning Sengalang Burong are equally important. His full name is Lang Sengalang Burong (*singa* means lion, but this is a Malay not an Iban word and the animal is unknown in Sarawak or even Borneo; *lang* means kite, and is the name given to the Brahminy Kite; *burong* means bird); more often known simply as 'Lang', he is most respected in his capacity as high spirit of the omen birds, the source of Iban *adat*, and war chief.

The form in which Sengalang Burong expresses himself directly to men, *lang*, the Brahminy Kite (*Haliastur Intermedius*), is a sub-species of *Haliastur Indus*. The Kite belongs to the 'diurnal birds of prey . . . [which hunt] other living creatures, such as small mammals, birds, snakes, fish, and reptiles' (Smythies, 1960, 140). In appearance and habits Lang corresponds almost exactly to the description of *Garuda* (Dubois, 1959, 640) venerated by the Hindus. The significance of Sengalang Burong in Iban religion certainly implies Hindu influence. It is especially remarkable since Lang is not, strictly speaking, an Iban omen bird (see below, pp. 128 seq.), although he occupies a key place among the Iban spirits.[2]

---

[1] See section following. Another version mentions also the *payan* bamboo which cannot shoot because of a gong (*gong*). Both the jar (*tajau*) and the gong (*gong* and *tawak*) are prized valuables among the Iban; in this account they are incorporated into the mythology.

[2] In the *gawai kenyalang* festival (cf. below, pp. 195 seq. and a brief note by Freeman, 1960b) which is celebrated in honour of Lang, the stylized image used is, strangely enough, not that of the Kite but that of the Rhinoceros Hornbill (*Buceros rhinoceros*), which is, in fact, killed by the Iban—primarily for its tail feathers (Smythies, 1960, 317–18). The Hornbill lives mainly on wild fruit (Smythies, 1960, 313 and 318) unlike the Kite, but the image is invariably

The central myth concerning Sengalang Burong is elaborate and contains a number of variations. But although even the names vary, in outline the story is always the same. A mortal kills a bird which is changed into a woman's skirt; he marries the owner and they have a son. It emerges later that she is actually the daughter of the bird-spirit, Sengalang Burong, and her son, Seragunting, is therefore part spirit. Seragunting eventually succeeds in proving his divine ancestry to the satisfaction of his spirit relatives and is introduced by them to the mysteries governing prosperity and success. Seragunting, finally, stands at the head not only of the Iban spirit pedigree but also of their physical ancestry.

In one account Menggin was the son of Damu and Remi, the daughter of Serapoh (see below, pp. 93–4). Damu left the household after a quarrel with his father-in-law and Menggin remained in the care of his mother Remi and her brother Sampar. When he grew up Menggin was fond of using a blow-pipe and on one occasion went after an attractive bird which he had noticed from the longhouse *ruai*. The bird settled first on one tree and then on another. Both times Menggin missed it with his dart. Eventually, however, he was successful and shot it. But when he went to collect his trophy, he found the bird had been transformed into a woman's skirt. He took the skirt home with him and told no one of the incident. Three days later, an unknown girl, who was very beautiful, appeared at the longhouse bathing place and, after bathing together with the other women, came up to the house. She was invited into various rooms, but declined, asking where Menggin lived. She was shown his *bilek* in the middle of the longhouse. When she found it she went inside but refused Remi's invitation to sit down on the grounds that she was not yet properly dressed. Again she asked after Menggin and when she discovered him she requested the return of her skirt.[1] Finally Menggin agreed

represented with a snake in its claws. The Hornbill has been considered an omen bird among the Kayan (Harrisson, 1960, 37) although it 'is no longer serviceable in this way' (ibid.). Its peculiar nesting habits (Smythies, 1960, 312–13) have attracted considerable attention and it has acquired an important position in Borneo lore. Harrisson (1960, 36–7) observed a 'hornbill-headed tree of life' among the Kenyah and draws attention to its continuing importance among the Ngaju of South Borneo. It would appear that the Iban have given a Hindu name and character to a traditional Borneo bird.

[1] Skirt loss is a common theme in both Land Dayak and Malay lore (see Harrisson, 1965a, 29, n. 29. 2, who calls it 'almost obsessional'). It is a widely recurrent aspect of a myth which may have Indian origins.

to give it back, and as soon as she had put it on, the girl was entertained in his room. Later that evening, when the longhouse people asked her why she had come, the girl replied that she wanted to collect the skirt which had been taken by Menggin. But, she said, she would stay and marry Menggin if he wished. He agreed to whatever his mother and uncle should decide. After a brief discussion, Sampar said they were content with the proposal on condition that the couple stayed in the family *bilek*. And so Menggin married the girl who disclosed that her name was Endu Dara Tinchin Temaga.[1] Before long, Dara Tinchin Temaga became pregnant and in due course bore a son who was given the name Surong Gunting.

Another account[2] does not differ fundamentally from the first except in the name of the hero, here called Siu. The difference in the name of Surong Gunting/Seragunting's father may reflect the relative insignificance of his person in comparison with Sengalang Burong himself and Seragunting. As mentioned, Surong Gunting and Seragunting are variant pronunciations or variations of the same name.

In this account an Iban warrior called Siu proposed to the young men of his house that they should all go bird-hunting with their blow-pipes to see which of them would be the most successful. They went off in different directions, each with a bundle of food for the day. Siu failed to find a single bird until, towards evening, he came upon a wild fig tree,[3] which was covered with more birds than he had ever seen together on any one tree and of all varieties. Every time he shot one bird with his dart, many fell to the ground. In a very short time, he had killed many more than he could carry. He set off homewards but could not find the way, until, after wandering through the jungle, he at last heard the typical noises of a longhouse nearby. Siu washed himself in a stream, concealed the birds and his blow-pipe in the undergrowth, and went up to the house. In the longhouse everything was silent.

---

[1] 'Endu Dara' are titles for a young girl; 'Tinchin Temaga' means 'ring of brass'.

[2] According to Freeman (1960a, 76, n. 7) this was 'first published by Gomes in 1904' but it occurs in Ling Roth's compilation of 1896 where it is credited to Perham (i. 198 seq.).

[3] In Iban *kara*, a tree to which spirit properties are often attributed. A fig tree is also important among the Hindus who consider it sacred to Vishnu (Dubois, 1959, 652).

And there was no one on the *ruai*, although Siu was sure that he had heard noises from outside. In the middle of the house he discovered a light and suddenly a girl's voice addressed him from the *bilek*. A beautiful girl, who apparently already knew his name, appeared with sireh leaf and betel nut and asked him whether he had eaten. When Siu said no, she prepared food for him. Siu began to ask the girl questions but she refused to answer, and instead asked him what he was doing. He told her he had gone astray in the jungle. Although he saw no adults in the longhouse other than the beautiful girl, Siu was easily persuaded to stay a few days. When the time came to depart, he wanted to take her with him to be his wife. She agreed to marry him on condition that he told no one of this longhouse that he had seen and would never harm a bird or even hold one in his hands. He promised. Then she told him that her name was Endu Sudan Galiggam Tinchin Mas,[1] the daughter of Sengalang Burong, and that this was her father's longhouse. The reason that there was no one there, she explained, was because the men had all gone off to obtain the head which was necessary to conclude the mourning period for many of their relatives who had recently been killed. Siu remained with his wife for a time, but some weeks later he asked her to go home with him. When they arrived, everyone congratulated Siu on his safe return and admired his beautiful wife. Siu's own mother, who had thought him dead, would not at first believe that it was really Siu who had come home. But when she saw him dressed in his own clothes, she recognized him, and made them both welcome. Endu Sudan Galiggam Tinchin Mas stayed with Siu in his longhouse and in due course bore him a son, who was given the name Seragunting.

The account of Siu's son does not from this point differ, except in detail and elaboration, from the story of Menggin's son.

Sengalang Burong: Augury and the Social Order

It is told that Siu was invited to inspect some beautiful birds which had recently been shot by one of the people in the longhouse and he, without thinking, touched them admiringly. The other version does not mention the birds. In both, however, Seragunting/ Surong Gunting is said to have been laid to sleep by his mother

[1] 'Tinchin Mas' means 'ring of gold'.

while she went to fetch water. Menggin (or Siu) then heard the child crying and endeavoured to soothe him, but he refused to be comforted and kept pointing towards the river. At long last, Menggin picked up his son and went out to look for Dara Tinchin Temaga.[1] But at the river she was nowhere to be seen, and they could find no trace of her anywhere around the longhouse. Since the child continued to cry and kept pointing towards a track in the jungle, Menggin after a time decided to follow this. They went on until it became dark. The night was spent in the jungle, and in the morning a small bundle of food appeared mysteriously. After they had eaten this, Surong Gunting started once more to cry and point, so again they followed the track. Similarly the next day and the next night, and every morning a bundle of food appeared from nowhere. Menggin went on and eventually they came to the seashore. In one account boats were heard and they hailed the oarsmen but these refused to stop, pretending not to hear. Eventually, however, they were, as by a miracle, able to wade across: in one account it was said they were guided to an unknown sandbar by the giant spider Emplawa Jawa. At the other side they travelled through the (hornbill) country known as Tansang Kenyalang, and came at last to a bathing place. It transpired that this was the bathing place of Dara Tinchin Temaga's longhouse. When they eventually found her, she explained to them very carefully that the path leading up to the longhouse was beset with spikes and knife-blades but a fly would alight on selected points and on these they could safely tread. She then told them that on entering the longhouse they had also to be extremely careful. They must only sit on her father's *ruai* and, when eating, they should eat only from the plate on which the fly first settled. When the time came to sleep they should go to the mosquito net on which there was a firefly. Dara Tinchin Temaga then returned to the longhouse. Menggin and the child followed and were punctilious in obeying her instructions.

Although the longhouse members refused to consider Menggin and his son as relatives, they lived with Sengalang Burong, the father of Dara Tinchin Temaga, until Surong Gunting could both walk and speak. The very day following this achievement, Surong Gunting went up and seated himself immediately beside Sengalang Burong. His grandfather asked how he had the temerity to do this without so much as being invited. Surong Gunting replied

---

[1] This is the most generally accepted name for Surong Gunting's mother.

that, since it was his own grandfather, an invitation was unneces-
sary. Sengalang Burong at once denied that Surong Gunting was
his grandson. When the boy insisted, he was given a number of
ordeals to prove his ancestry. The description of the ordeals varies
considerably. In some accounts they include a competition for
spinning-tops, wrestling, hunting (in this connection Surong
Gunting was offered only weak old dogs with which to hunt, but
was successful in bringing back a huge boar which he alone dared
kill, doing so with a small knife). There are also versions in which
Surong Gunting was required to walk on the edge of a knife, to
gather up a mass of tiny beads from under the longhouse, and to
recover oil from round about. When he proved himself successful
in all these, he was finally instructed to raid a bees' nest in a tall
tapang tree in broad daylight. He returned with the honeycomb.
When Sengalang Burong still refused to recognize his grandson,
Surong Gunting called on the bees to sting Sengalang Burong and
chase him up into the loft, and only summoned them away after
being granted full recognition of his status. Having accepted him,
Sengalang Burong loved his grandson dearly and devoted much
of his time to conversation with him. However, it so happened
that not long after these events, news came that Ketupong, the
true husband of Dara Tinchin Temaga, and son-in-law of Sengalang Burong, was returning from the warpath. Dara Tinchin
Temaga told Menggin to take Surong Gunting away to their own
country.

On his return Surong Gunting participated actively in farming
and head-hunting expeditions, but was not especially successful.
He decided, therefore, after a time, to visit his grandfather again
in order to seek advice. On the way he met, among others, the
seven stars (Bintang Tujoh) who asked him where he was going
and why. Surong Gunting replied that when he farmed he consistently had mediocre harvests, and in head-hunting raids he was
not very successful, hence he was going to Sengalang Burong.
The stars explained their function in guiding humans through the
farming cycle. They told Surong Gunting their positions in the
sky which would indicate when it was time to begin clearing and
the season for sowing. Afterwards he came across the three stars
(Bintang Tiga) who explained how they too could be used for
assistance in timing. Finally he met the moon who told him of the
regard appropriate to the lunar phases.

When he reached the longhouse of Sengalang Burong, Surong Gunting went straight to the *ruai* of his grandfather and introduced himself. His mother, Dara Tinchin Temaga, came out of the *bilek* and took her son to meet the youngest of Sengalang Burong's daughters called Endu Dara Chempaka Tempurong Alang. For years Surong Gunting lived and farmed at his grandfather's house before explaining the purpose of his visit. Sengalang Burong then, on inquiry, expounded the nature and importance of taking omens (*beburong*). 'Fetching water and defecating apart,' he said, 'in all that men do, they must heed the omens' (*samoa utai dikreja orang enda tau enda beburong*). In answer to Surong Gunting's question as to which bird omens were good and which were bad, Sengalang Burong explained that the only birds which truly counted were his sons-in-law: Ketupong, Bejampong, Embuas, Pangkas, Papau, Beragai, and Nendak, and he pointed them out. 'On the left of my *ruai*', he said, 'is your uncle Ketupong, then Beragai, and then Pangkas who has the nickname Kutok. On the right is Embuas followed by Bejampong, then Kelabu nicknamed Papau and also called Senabong. At the end is Nendak.'[1] Sengalang Burong proceeded to name the birds appropriate to the various phases of the farming cycle (see below, pp. 136–7, 161 seq.). Two or three days later, Ketupong led a head-hunting expedition and Surong Gunting was invited to learn the significance of bird omens on the warpath. Upon the expedition's successful return, Sengalang Burong taught his grandson the correct procedure for the major festivals (*gawai*) and some key verses of the *pengap* incantations.

After a time it was discovered that Dara Chempaka Tempurong Alang was pregnant. Sengalang Burong was furious when his youngest unmarried daughter disclosed that Surong Gunting was the father.[2] Sengalang Burong summoned a meeting at once and reminded all that it is a most serious offence for relatives of adjacent generations to marry (see above, pp. 39–40); this could cause

[1] Although Nendak is not married to a daughter of Lang and does not have a proper *bilek* in the longhouse, but a *langkau* hut attached to the *tanju*— which is the customary residence of those who are not (yet) full longhouse members—he is, for most practical purposes, grouped together with the others, who are known collectively as Lang's sons-in-law (*menantu Lang*).

[2] In no account is Dara Tinchin Temaga blamed for being unfaithful to Ketupong her original (bird) husband by whom she had no children according to most accounts although a son, Gom, appears in one recorded genealogy (see below, p. 96).

the land to become barren, erosion of the soil, fouling of the water, and the failing growth of many different plants. For full propitiation the offender should be sacrificed on a stake of bamboo (*bunoh pantang enggau aur*) but in the circumstances it was agreed that a pig-offering might be made together with the traditional valuables: beads, ornaments, and woven cloth. In conclusion Sengalang Burong expounded the prohibited degrees of marriage and the expiatory payments required of offenders and he told Surong Gunting to instruct the Iban on his return home. It was of course impossible for him to marry Dara Chempaka and the child, if born, would not be allowed to live.

Eventually Surong Gunting returned to his own longhouse where he taught his people (the Iban) about the stars, the bird omens used in farming and on head-hunting expeditions, he explained the prohibitions governing marriage and the punishment for offenders, and led the others in ritual festivals as he had been instructed.

Details about the residence of the 'birds', their nicknames and poetical honorifics occur only occasionally in *jerita tuai* and to some extent in *tusut* tables, but information is common and extensive in *pengap*. Although the names are broadly familiar to any senior Iban versed in his tradition, there are many reputable *tuai burong* (Dadup for example) who could not repeat the full names of Sengalang Burong's daughters and who would not consider this in the least important. But in the *pengap* journey which goes to the spirits above (*nimang ka langit* or *ka'atas*), it is customary to pass the birds' domain (*mansa burong*), and any *lemambang* who has learned this particular journey knows the detailed mythological description of the birds, although he is not necessarily expert in augury or the other ritual activities. Since they occur mainly in *pengap*, the full names, nicknames, titles, and honorifics are poetical in form and usually have internal rhymes:[1] ...Temaga... China, ...Ngembai...Entekai, ...Midong...Ketunsong, ...Pengabas... Mas, and so forth.

The wife of Sengalang Burong is called:

Endu Sudan Berinjan Bungkong
Endu Diu Tiong Menyelong.

[1] Although some of the names comprise ordinary Iban words, most cannot be meaningfully translated.

Her name had been changed because of an illness; this is standard practice after serious sickness, since it is thought to deceive evil spirits who may continue in pursuit. Originally she had been called:

> Indai Kachendai Bepantak Jirak
> Dara Sentaba Balun Kupak.

Lang's daughters are:

(1) Endu Dara Tinchin Temaga — the wife of Ketupong
    Endu Cherebok Mangkok China

(2) Endu Langgu Ketunsong Ngembai — the wife of Beragai
    Dayang Kumang Bunga Entekai

(3) Endu Kechapah Dulang Midong — the wife of Bejampong
    Endu Kumang Bunga Ketunsong

(4) Endu Bentok Tinchin Pengabas — the wife of Pangkas
    Endu Letan Pulas Mas   (Kutok)

(5) Endu Kechapang Dulang Mas — the wife of Embuas
    Iyak Ketupang Bunga Libas

(6) Endu Moa Puchong Pengabas — the wife of Kelabu
    Pinggau Besai Nadai Meretas   (Papau)

and finally,

(7) Endu Dara Chempaka Tempurong — who, subsequent to
    Alang   Seragunting's visit,
    Endu Langit Dayang Kumang   became the wife of
    Kunding Burong
    Malam[1]

Sengalang Burong and *Gawai* Celebrations

According to another important myth, the Iban still did not celebrate the *gawai* rites correctly. Consequently, when the legendary war leader Dempi invited another, Maripat, to celebrate at his longhouse their joint success on a head-hunting raid against the Bugau Dyaks (who inhabit the Ketungau and other northern tributaries of the middle Kapuas), Sengalang Burong confused the date by causing the moon to be invisible to the real Maripat.

---

[1] Burong Malam is a locust or cricket. As Richards, 1968, 132, points out, the special role of Burong Malam is peculiar to the Saribas.

Instead, on the appointed day he himself and his retinue arrived at the longhouse disguised as Maripat and his followers, but refused to enter the longhouse because there was no appropriate ceremony to welcome them. Dempi admitted that he knew of no such ceremonies. It was then agreed that 'Maripat' and his party should take over the longhouse temporarily. They divided themselves into two groups: one to act the part of hosts, the other guests. The host group first constructed *pandong* 'altars' on the *ruai*, made ready *piring* sacrifices and offerings, then came down from the longhouse to greet the guests with fowls, and a pig by way of expiation (*ginselan*), as well as food and brewed rice (*tuak*). Both Dempi's and 'Maripat's' people joined in cock-fighting, in drinking, and feasting, and that night the first long incantations, *pengap*, were intoned round the *pandong* on the *ruai*. In a different version, the spirit visitors cure their hosts of a strange illness which suddenly befalls the longhouse, and subsequently teach them the correct ritual practice. Common to both, however, is that 'Maripat' and his party are at last revealed as Sengalang Burong and his relatives who then fly away towards the spirit world in the form of Lang, the Kite, and the omen birds.

In all the myths which relate to Sengalang Burong and his relatives, he shows himself well disposed toward the Iban. But the spirits are not simply benevolent, superior beings, able and willing to guide the Iban. They are actually kin (*kaban*). The essence of the Surong Gunting myth lies in the 'proof' of his ancestry, that he belongs partly to the world of men, through his father, the mortal Menggin (or Siu), and partly to the spirit world, through his mother, the daughter of Sengalang Burong himself.

Sengalang Burong most commonly reveals himself through Lang. When he himself is described in the Surong Gunting myths or from dream experiences, it is invariably as an aged, venerable Iban—a typical grandfather. The inhabitants of Lang's longhouse look like and lead a life similar to that of ordinary Iban with the exception that they are immortal and free from the uncertainties and sufferings of life on earth—but not, evidently, from the un-certainties of married life. Lang's spirit insight enables him to advise and direct men: he foresees the consequences of their behaviour because he knows the correct order of things. The Iban do not consider themselves subject to his arbitrary caprice. They view him more as an all-seeing, aged *tuai*, who wills the best for his kin and enforces the code because he knows it is for the ultimate benefit of all.

Serapoh and Burial of the Dead

Another myth relates to the legendary Iban hero Serapoh. After a spate of deaths in his longhouse, on one particular morning Serapoh's own father died, at noon his mother, and in the afternoon his brother. No one understood the reason for the tragedy. But next day, while everyone was in tears, Serapoh heard a voice from outside asking him the matter. He explained, and the voice then inquired what arrangements the Iban were making to care for the dead (*ngintu pemati*). When he answered none—they simply disposed of the bodies—the man said it was only to be expected that people continued to die.[1] Serapoh asked him what was to be done, and the voice replied: 'When a man dies after breathing his last, he must be washed and then touched with three smears of turmeric (*kunyik*) on his forehead. After he has been dressed and his belongings put aside for use in the after life (*baiya*) the corpse should be carried to the *ruai* and placed with the property inside a partition. A wooden pestle (*alu*) must be set crossways at the head of the steps leading into the house at both ends to prevent the spirits from Sebayan, the land of the dead, from entering the longhouse; to them the pestle appears to be a cobra (*tedong dipeda mata sebayan*). That night there may be wailing and chanting (*sabak*) for the dead man, and in the morning, after he has been given food (*dibri makai*), the corpse should be taken to the burial-ground (*pendam*).' A tree is then felled for his coffin (*santubong*), and after the corpse has been placed in this, the coffin is buried.

Once the body is in the ground the window opening in the roof of the dead man's *bilek* must be closed to make the *bilek* dark, since what is light in this world is dark in Sebayan; conversely darkness in the *bilek* here means his *bilek* in Sebayan will be light. The period of mourning then begins and that evening a light must be left burning outside. This light is left burning for three, five, or seven nights, according to the status of the dead man and his

---

[1] Harrisson, 1962, 14, *et al.* attributes certain rites to Serapoh's instruction by Puntang Raga in the course of his general argument concerning (secondary) burial practices in Borneo, but note the reservation regarding Saribas use expressed above, p. 58. See also Hertz, 1960a, 54 and *passim*.

family. For the same period the bereaved are in deep mourning, and may only eat their special mourning food (*makai pana*); they must eat black rice as a sign of their wretchedness, because black rice here corresponds to white rice in Sebayan and wretchedness to joy. The wife or husband of the dead is said to be widowed (*balu*) and is not allowed to remarry until the widowhood has been properly abrogated (*dikupas*, which means 'cleaned' or 'cleared'). While widowed, a man or woman is not permitted to wear clothing which is brightly coloured (*mansau*, literally, red), shiny (*bekilat*), florid or ornate (*bebunga*). And while the mourning prohibitions are in force it is a serious offence to have sexual relations or to go to live with anybody.

Finally, the spirit addressing Serapoh disclosed that his name was Puntang Raga, and disappeared.

Spirits and Demons

There are innumerable other myths or legends which describe the origins of various, sometimes local, beliefs and practices, events in the spirit world, and spirit dealings with men. Many of these concern the adventures of lesser spirits and mythical heroes, of which Kling and his circle are the most important. Although these have nothing like the prestige and influence of Sengalang Burong and Pulang Gana, they are considered helpful: Tutong, for example, is the patron of blacksmithing. The lesser spirits are regularly invited to participate in ritual celebrations.

It is believed that the greater and lesser spirits all originally lived together at Temaga Gelang. But Lang, Kling, Ribai, and Sabit Bekait were involved in a dispute about a rambutan fruit-tree and they separated. Lang and Sabit Bekait each went to different parts of the sky (*langit*), Ribai to the shore (*tasik*), while Kling remained at Panggau. For a time Panggau was common territory to both Kling's group and the ancestors of human Iban. Specific localities in both Sarawak and Indonesian Borneo are actually associated with their exploits, such as Mount Tiang Laju near Engkilili and an *ensurai* tree at the mouth of the Lemanak (see below, p. 129). But the division between the two groups took place in the Kapuas, before the Iban migration to Sarawak. A myth tells that Kling's father, Chang Chelawang, acquired invisibility from a cobra. His own family and part of the longhouse decided to share his invisibility, but fifty families chose to remain visible, and they constructed a new longhouse in the Ulu Merakai, near the present border, under the leadership of Belayan Lelang and Buntak, and from there they subsequently migrated to Sarawak.

Finally, in the spirit world, are the evil *antu* demons who, like Girgasi, hunting in the jungle with ferocious hounds, or metamorphosized into voluptuous women, lead men to an evil fate. Some of these are connected with the spirits of the dead who have met with misfortune or have received inadequate treatment at or after death. *Antu koklir* are a common example: these are believed to be the spirits of women dying in childbirth, who attack, in particular, the reproductive organs of men, which they hold responsible for their untimely death. *Antu* are associated in stories with fear of the dark, fear of being alone or lost in the jungle, fear of being attacked by ferocious animals, snakes, and the like— these are the shapes in which *antu* most commonly appear[1]—and fear of the dead returning for revenge or in spite. They are also told simply as horror stories.

Tusut Genealogies

Iban genealogies (*tusut*) preserve the record of their ancestry from the spirit world.[2] The average number of generations remembered is slightly over twenty from Sengalang Burong to the present day, although one old man at the Simanggang conference, Mujah,[3] claimed there were over thirty. The tables are learned by rote; because of the use of internal rhyme and the poetic form, a block of several names is more easily omitted than an isolated individual.

[1] Of the other known varieties of *antu* one of the commonest is *antu buyu* which is thought to assume any form it pleases (commonly a snake or orangutan) and take possession of women.

[2] They are extremely important to the Iban. Freeman was seemingly unaware of this since he writes (1957a, 53, n. 24) '. . . the longest line of succession that I collected was one of five generations, including the *pun bilek* who was still living. The Iban, in their bilateral society, are much more interested in the spread or scatter of relationships . . .'. It may be true that the Iban are interested in the 'spread and scatter', but they are also concerned with their antecedents, not least their spirit ancestry.

[3] Not to be confused with the principal informant of Harrisson and Sandin, 1966.

As the record approaches the present day, the speaker in his presentation strives to conform to remembered history, but for the distant past he is content to establish the main lines of the pedigree. Much of the importance of *tusut* for the Iban lies in the 'documentary' evidence of their ultimate descent from the spirit hierarchy and, where relevant, their relationship to Sengalang Burong.[1] In reply to a question at the Simanggang conference (see above, pp. 56 seq.), an Iban said that while it was difficult for him to believe that he was directly descended from a spirit, there appeared to be no mistake in the record—although he conceded that there might be some omissions.

A typical example, which illustrates the poetic form, use of internal rhyme, mythical names, and honorifics in the remoter passages changing to a direct pedigree in the more recent generations, is Limbang's *tusut*, recorded in the Delok.

Layang Langit gave birth to Kumang Chiremang Bintang
Who took to husband Jumban Bulan
Whose child Aji Kunding Kansuwi Sang Kensima Maling Brani
Married Dara Kumang Bericha
Whose son Lang Sengalang Burong Sangkut Lang Lik Perintik Rekong[2]
Married Dara Taba Malun Kupak Kechandai Lawai Pantak Jirak
Whose daughter Mangkok Encherebok China Dara Linsin Salin Temaga
Took to husband Bekubu Burik Bulu Burong Ketupong Labang[3]
Whose son Gom
Married Sarani Bunsu Tedong Chenaga Umbang
Whose child Tumbai
Married Dimit Indu Di Bukit Beringgit Mayang
Whose son Ngimbong Julok Kukok Manok Labang
Married Dayang Mapong Indu Digupong Orang Lulong Arang
Whose child Langkop, leader of the Undup
Married his namesake
Whose child Kindin
Married Nyala
Whose child Berangka

[1] Sandin's genealogies, 1967, 96 seq. and elsewhere evidently serve this purpose. Most of them trace the origins of (prominent) Saribas Iban to the spirit hierarchy.
[2] The honorifics and soubriquets vary although there is no doubt that this is the same Lang Sengalang Burong.
[3] Similarly, Dara Tinchin Temaga and Ketupong are given additional names.

Married Dayang Ilam Kumbai Orang Nyabak Sahari Samalam
    Pechah Ayam Butul Pemandang
Whose son Nading Kling
Took to wife Dayang Sinak Indu Ditugak Langgong Lawang
Whose daughter Mawas Indu Diteras Titi Nunggang
Married Rasoh, the leader of the Kumpang,
Whose child Sumbang Orang Meran Ka Wong
Married Awa
Whose child Mawan
Married Laja
Whose child Dina
Married Bendong
Whose child Lungan
Married Liba
Whose child Daru
Married Tagaya
Whose child Rai
Married Gila
Whose child Beredai
Took to husband Rengkang
Whose daughter Sutai
Married Melaka
The father of Limbang.

This genealogy traces Limbang's descent through his maternal
grandfather and eighteen generations in a direct line from Sengalang Burong and the Iban spirit hierarchy. As is to be expected
in the bilateral Iban society, *tusut* do not follow rigidly either the
male or female line.

Limbang was even able to recite an alternative version of his
ancestry. The other line, which also goes through Limbang's
maternal grandfather, leads back to overseas connections and Rajah
Tindit.

Bungkong Menalu took to wife Ribut Nyipu
Whose daughter Dayang Sapuntang Benang
Married Demang Nutop
Whose son Guntor Bebaju Bindu
Married Sirau
Whose daughter Seribangi
Married Mentri Bandar
Whose son Rajah Tindit Tau Nidit Langit Mesai Kepit Tanggi
    Simelang
Took to wife Seriam Bungai Gumbang Lelangan Anjong Pasang

Whose daughter Chala
Married Nga Pandai Nanga Bukit Rabong Ringang
Whose daughter Beradai
Married Brauh
Whose son Bedana
Married Ganggong
Whose son Jampi
Married Uni
Whose son Awan
Married Bulan
Whose son Rampai
Married Sati
Whose son Rundang
Married Enchi
Whose son Basan
Married Perada
Whose son Bada
Married Sanggu
Whose son Gui
Married Juntut
Whose son Rengkang
Married Beradai
Whose daughter Sutai
Married Melaka
The father of Limbang.

The genealogy of Endawie anak Enchana, a Saribas Iban and the first Minister for Local Government in Sarawak, who is about twenty years younger than Limbang, has twenty-one generations to Seragunting (see opposite).

Tusut genealogies not only establish the spirit pedigree of human Iban,[1] they also recall the origins of important varieties of animal and vegetable life—rice plants and certain fruit trees, for example. The ancestry of the durian fruit is traced through Simpang-Impang to the same *antu* spirits which sometimes appear in the mythological passages of human-spirit *tusut*. To this extent spirits and men, animals and even plant life are, in a remote sense, interrelated.

---

[1] Sandin, 1956 (repeated, with others added, in Sandin, 1967), gives further *tusut*. These are examples of personal pedigrees mentioned above.

Beji
|
Nisi Bunga Besi
|
Antu Rambayan Bulu
|
Telichai Tuai Kitai = Endu Dara Sia (f)

Berenai Sugi	Retak Daai
Kumpai Benai	Serapoh
Tali Bunga	Remi (f)
	Menggin
Seri Ngiang (f) =	Seragunting

Sera Kempat
|
Ridoh (f)
|
Gupi (f)
|
Garaman Ensoh
|
Beragai (f)
|
Beti Brauh Ngumbang
|
Talak
|
Badas (f)
|
Blaki
|
Penyut
|
Sudan (f)
|
Blaki
|
Bayang
|
Jabat
|
Amba (f)
|
Melaya (f)
|
Minggat
|
Chenggit (f)
|
Sa
|
Rinya (f)
|
Endawie[1]

[1] The genealogy appeared in the *Sarawak Gazette*, No. 1280, Oct. 1964, and was confirmed by Endawie.

VIII. WORLD-VIEW[1]

The Spirits

To say that 'the mythology of these people has little relation to their religion' (Hose and McDougall, 1912, ii. 136) is to miss entirely the meaning of the myths. From the myths a view emerges of the universe and its inhabitants, which explains the basis for Iban social behaviour, moral conduct, and ritual. The mythology provides Iban religion with its dramatic personalities and terms of reference.

The universe of Iban experience underlying and expressed in the myths is essentially one. To describe it the Iban use words which are largely common to the Malaysian peoples or of extraneous origin. *Petara* comes from India, *adat* is said to be an Arabic word, *antu* occurs throughout Malaya and Indonesia, so do *samengat* and the ordinary words *dunya*, *langit*, and *menoa*. But although the words occur commonly, the meaning which the Iban give them is not always the general one, and it is necessary to establish the content and implications of these concepts for the Iban.

The universe is inhabited by two types of divine or demon-like spirits: *petara* and *antu*, the spirits of dead men (*antu*) as well as of the living, animal and vegetable: men (*mensia*), mammals and other animals (*jelu*), reptiles, i.e. snakes (*ular*) etc., birds (*burong*), fish (*ikan*), insects (*indu utai*), trees (*kayu*), and plant-life—leaves and grasses (*daun, rumput*).

Petara is most likely derived from the Hindu word, *batara*, meaning 'lord', and is not, as has been suggested, a corruption of *avatara*.[2] Wilkinson's Malay dictionary (Reprint, n.d., 132) traces *betara* to a Sanskrit word for 'holy' and describes it as a title ('lord') given to major Hindu divinities and assumed by the rulers of Majapahit. Among the Iban, *petara* is used as an honorific for important spirits, in particular as a general title for Sengalang Burong, Pulang Gana, and other prominent members of the spirit

---

[1] This chapter in a slightly different form has been published as 'Some Iban Concepts' (Jensen, 1968).

[2] This possibility is discussed in Skeat, 1900, 86 seq., n. 3.

hierarchy. It is actually pronounced *batara* in many areas, and so spelled in some early accounts (e.g. St. John, 1863, i. 69).

That 'the name of God amongst them is Battara . . .' (Keppel, 1846, ii. 175, quoting Brooke) impressed most observers and they concluded that the Iban had been exposed to Hindu influence in this, but only this, respect.[1] With the main exception of Chambers —a missionary—who considered 'their religion . . . a species of polytheism' (St. John, 1863, i. 70), most Europeans (including Johnson (Brooke), Gomes, and St. John) attributed to the Iban a 'very satisfactory' belief in 'one Omnipotent Being who created and now rules over the world . . . Batara'.[2] Even Sandin (1957, 117) says in an early paper: 'The animist Sea Dayaks believe that God is one who created all things visible and invisible. He is known as *Petara* . . .'. He treats the names Selampandai, Selampetoh, and Selampeta as functions of *Petara* which 'riddle' he compares to the Christian Trinity. This, however, is a view which does not recur in Sandin's subsequent writing,[3] nor in his Iban publications.

Wishful thinking apart, there is little reason for crediting the Iban with an almost monotheistic belief in one supreme god called *Petara*. The word is used by the Iban as a title for spirit(s) much as it is by the Hindus. Although it is true that the word can be either singular or plural, it occurs most commonly in the plural. The standard prayer, which begins: *petara apai, petara indai, petara aki, petara ini* ('spirit of my father, spirit of my mother, spirit of my grandfather, spirit of my grandmother'), may be ambiguous and open to interpretation, but a phrase often heard makes the intention clear: *petara nadai enda manah; bisi utai ditulong sida*, which means '*petara* cannot fail to be good; they are helpful in many ways', where *sida* ('they'), invariably plural, is in apposition to *petara*.

Antu, on the other hand, is emphatically Malaysian. *Hantu* in Malay means 'an evil spirit, a ghost or goblin' (Wilkinson, 1902, 690). And *hantu* of all varieties occur among Malay peoples everywhere. *Antu* among the Iban are quite often evil. *Antu* are thought

---

[1] As Low, 1848, 174, says, this 'appears to be the only relic left them of their former intercourse with the Javan Hindus'. He notes elsewhere, 203, that the Iban did not practise cremation nor abstain from animal flesh.

[2] See similarly Perham's comments, Ling Roth, 1896, i. 169.

[3] Harrisson and Sandin, 1966, 121, for example, speak of 'Selampandai, Selampetoh, brother of Sengalang Burong' with no suggestion that these are persons of a triune *Petara*.

to be responsible for illness and death. Illness is caused when an *antu* passes close by (*pansa utai*; the Iban even use the euphemism 'something' (*utai*) to avoid saying *antu*) (see below, pp. 147 seq.). The *manang* cures the very sick by killing the *antu* (*bunoh antu*). Noises in the jungle are sometimes said to be the bark of *pasun*, the dogs with which *antu* hunt the spirits of men; when these are heard an Iban is sure to die. And when he is dying, it is believed, *antu* take away the spirit/soul (*samengat*) of the dead man while his relatives clamour for him to return to the land of the living. As soon as he is dead, he himself becomes an *antu*, and the expression for taking a corpse to burial is *nganjong antu* ('take' or 'escort' an *antu*). So *antu* among the Iban comes also to mean a corpse.[1]

Antu are not invariably evil. In practice 'the line of demarcation between *Petaras* and *antus* is altogether indistinct' (Ling Roth, 1896, i. 182). In the myths, *petara* and *antu* often occur as if the words were interchangeable. Even Perham, after describing Sengalang Burong as a leading *petara*, is quoted[2] as saying of him 'he is a great *antu*'. In brief, when called *petara* the spirit is presumed well disposed towards men; *antu* can be both good and evil, though evil and unfriendly spirits are always called *antu*. Both *petara* and *antu* look, in 'real' life, much like the Iban. Sengalang Burong is described as a venerable Iban and his longhouse community is composed of spirits who hunt and farm, behave, and appear like the Iban themselves. Terrifying *antu* resemble human beings also, but they are gigantic in stature, hairy, and ferocious. Spirits have the additional attribute of being able to reveal themselves in different forms; they can also appear as animals.

The myths, legends, and ancestral tables express the manner and extent to which *petara*, *antu*, the Iban, and other life are all related. By assembling the myths it is possible to create a network which establishes, although remotely and sometimes in spite of apparent discrepancies, the relationships which exist not only among the spirits and between the spirits and the Iban, but also between spirits, men, and the animal and vegetable world. These relationships are not all significant in the literal sense. But the

[1] As *hantu* means among the Ngaju (Schärer, 1963, 50); the word is related to *anutu* and *anitu* meaning deity.

[2] Ling Roth, 1896, i. 183, although in another context, 179, he says 'the *antu* indeed causes . . . sickness and wants to kill and so has to be scared away; but *Petara* is regarded as the saving power'.

myths and *tusut* do demonstrate to the Iban that all facets of life interact and are at some point actually interrelated. The names of men and spirits—in their various manifestations, which occur like cross-references in different mythical sequences—are sufficient proof that they all inhabit the same universe. Where generation levels are confused or details obviously inaccurate, the Iban attribute this to faulty memory, not to a mistake in the record.

Appearance of the Universe

The appearance of this universe which all inhabit is not consistently described. In spite of interaction between the various inhabitant groups, the universe is divided into distinct regions, but how these regions relate to each other is not always clear.

In the mythical past it would appear that all once shared the same territory, Temaga Gelang (see above, pp. 94–5), from which the different spirit groups and the ancestors of the Iban subsequently moved. The heroes, Kling and his entourage, became separated from the higher spirits like Sengalang Burong, who departed to the sky, to the shore, and to the earth. Mortal men in their turn moved away from the company of Kling who remained in what seems to be a 'real' geographical area. Surong Gunting, however, in the myth, travels to join his mother by crossing water, although Sengalang Burong is said to live in the sky and makes his appearances from above. In another myth,[1] a mortal called Beji tried—unsuccessfully—to reach the spirit world by setting up a ladder on earth; a curious rock formation near the Sarawak–Indonesian border bears witness to the disastrous collapse of his project. There is no doubt that contact occurs constantly between the various regions, but the Iban have no precise geographical/topographical concept of their spatial relations. The territories are distinct, yet in touch. The commonest image used to describe the universe (and which accords to some extent with accounts of the creation) is of two bowls, one inverted upon the other, with a flat area between the two. The Iban also say that the universe is something like a three-tiered (*tiga ringkat*) food-carrier, having—one above the other—three layers which meet at the edges.

---

[1] The myth of Beji occurs widely in various forms and was published as early as 1910; this version is included in the Borneo Literature Bureau compilation, 1963, 125, and attributed to Howell.

Dunya, the ordinary word for the earth experienced by men, is relatively flat and lies in the middle. In accounts of the creation, mountains occurred when the earth had to be compressed to fit under the sky. *Langit*, the ordinary word for the sky, is like a vault above the earth and is thought to join the earth at the edges: the sun travels daily over the surface of the curved sky, rising from the remote horizon in the morning and returning in the evening to the opposite edge. *Langit* itself is inhabited by Sengalang Burong and the other major spirits associated with augury, head-hunting, and success in general.

The view of the universe is less clear with regard to the spirits who live elsewhere. Pulang Gana, spirit of growth and fertility, is approached through the 'earth gate' (*pintu tanah*); in the myth, Pulang Gana came upon Samerugah by chasing a porcupine into a hill-side hole, from which he emerged eventually as into another land beyond the mountain. The region of Pulang Gana, which is invariably associated with the earth, is not identical with Sebayan. But Sebayan, land of the dead, lies below the earth. It is approached by river from a specific geographical point, the Mandai river,[1] which is situated in the upper reaches of the Kapuas (beyond the point where the Iban originally entered Sarawak). The inverted bowl analogy helps to explain the apparent opposites which characterize Sebayan. Night, for example, for the living on earth, is day in Sebayan; consequently the spirits of the dead are most commonly encountered in dreams, at night, when Sebayan is awake and abroad.

But the notion of complementary or opposite concepts goes beyond the rather obvious phenomena of night and day, which the Iban in any case relate to the circular journey of the sun. Blindness on earth may signify sight in Sebayan, which is commonly associated with the phenomenon of blind *manang* who, in healing the sick and dying, enter the world of (dead) spirits. The inverted world below helps to maintain the balance between disparate forces, a balance which lies at the centre of Iban thought. Harrisson and Sandin (1966, 223) speak of the 'fundamental topsy-turvy of universalism', and Harrisson (1965a, 4) of the 'Upside-downess . . . of Iban theology'. But to describe their understanding of the

---

[1] According to Richards, 1962, 409, 'The Mandai is supposed to be connected underground with a very deep pothole in the Ulu Ai called Lubok Kelebuai, the abode of Genali, King of the Waters.'

universe—not merely Sebayan—as a series of divisions 'here and not here, this world and another(s)', a 'mystical' system where 'Black is white, live dead, beauty ugliness, silence an uproar, your sister a brother' (ibid.) is to distort the complementary nature of the world which is made up of physical and spirit elements and the essential balance which the Iban discover in this (see below, esp. pp. 109 seq.).

Menoa Territories

Within the one universe each group has its own *menoa* or territory. The word *menoa* does not belong to Iban religious vocabulary in the strict sense; in ordinary usage it means quite simply a geographical area, as in the phrase 'our district' or 'territory' (*menoa kami*) or 'in somebody else's territory' (*di menoa orang*), where a group of Iban have farming, hunting, or other rights. But it can also be used to signify an area of spirit authority. Sometimes it is not possible to draw a hard and fast line between the two. Kling for example, in the myth which describes how half the longhouse chose to be invisible (and became spirits) while the other half decided to remain visible (and became the ancestors of men) begins with a geographical territory and moves to a spirit *menoa*. Many *antu*, which belong to a spirit *menoa*, are thought to inhabit areas of real jungle.

With the exception of the river Mandai which has a recognized mouth in the human world thus providing a geographical link with Sebayan, most spirit *menoa* cannot be located geographically like Iban areas. The *menoa* of the spirits are at one and the same time present and remote from human *menoa*, in the sky, for example, or infinitely deep in the jungle, or below the ground. It is not only in the accounts of Kling that the spirits appear to inhabit the same world as men. The constant interaction between men and spirits is evidence of the belief that spirit *menoa* actually coincide with Iban *menoa* but on a different plane of experience.[1]

[1] Schärer's analysis, 1963, 158 (in the original text, 1946, 178) of Ngaju concepts of interlocking areas reflects one aspect of Iban thought. 'The Upperworld (in most ceremonies the Underworld is placed in the Upperworld, since together they form the entire universe) is no image of fantasy, it is this world, i.e., it is the tribal area, and all the places, rivers, tributaries, lakes and riverbends are named in the *basa sangiang*, in the sacred and poetic language. The

To forestall possible conflict between rival interests in the same *menoa*, the individual Iban indicates the area which he wishes to use, and in recognition of spirit rights, not by way of purchase, he makes an offering to the spirit(s), who may, or may not, already consider this their territory. The account of Pulang Gana provides the basis in myth. Sacrificial offerings are invariably made at all times in which the Iban stake a claim to the use of land, whether for a short or long term purpose. Success of the undertaking implies that the arrangement has been satisfactory to all parties. When, however, events occur which are undesirable—bad harvests, sickness or death—it is assumed that something has proved unacceptable to the spirits who then express their dissatisfaction by the calamities which they have the influence to inflict. A calamity is something which in the perfect and natural order of events does not occur: serious or chronic sickness, a wound which refuses to heal, or death in early or middle age (death in old age when there are children and grandchildren to uphold the *bilek*'s existence is considered natural). The behaviour of the spirits is essentially the same, when they effect calamities of this nature, as that which is expected among men when one man has infringed the rights of another, territorially or otherwise. In such circumstances there are two conceivable courses of remedial action. In milder cases it may be possible to satisfy the spirits with further offerings and sacrifices, but when the consequences are really serious or continue to recur, the only solution is to abandon the farm, longhouse, or project which has disturbed the *menoa* rights or interests of another party.

The *Samengat* Spirit

It is not only the spirits who move on two planes, living in their spirit *menoa* and wearing various physical forms in the world of men. All life has two parts, all life which is essential to the Iban,

Upperworld is the world of the *sangiang*. Each group possesses its own area or areas. The supreme deities, with their highest servants (personified functions), reign over this world. They do not live in their own world of lakes and rivers and tributaries. Their houses rest on a sacrificial rack and are the formal representation of human society and the human world elevated to the supernatural and transcendental.'

human, animal, and even vegetable, has a physical and spirit side. The physical, mortal, visible body (*tuboh*) is one part; the other is the spirit counterpart or spirit/soul, the *samengat*.[1]

First, the possession of *samengat* is a characteristic of human beings; in fact, the possession of it is a measure of their humanity. During the initial three months of pregnancy (called by the special word *nyera*), the embryo is said 'still to be blood' (*bedau darah*), 'it does not yet have a spirit/soul: it is not yet a true human being' (*empai bisi samengat, empai nyadi mensia*). From the third month the embryo has a spirit/soul, is human, and much greater importance attaches, for example, to abortion.

The *samengat* is intangible, of a shadowy substance; some say 'like a shadow' (*baka kelemayang*). The *samengat* is sometimes considered to be a small-sized[2] or insubstantial replica of the living man.[3] The *samengat* is also spoken of as if it had an identity of its own. In life the *samengat* of man is confined to his body, except when, in dreams, he seems, in the person of his *samengat*, to move and have experiences independently of his body.[4] Thus it is the spirit/soul of man which meets the spirits in dreams. And in serious illness the *samengat*, the life-giving force which animates a man, is thought temporarily to leave his body. Consequently, the *manang* healer has, as his principal aid in treating the sick, a *batu ilau* charm stone, or crystal, in which he 'sees' and locates the *samengat*, with a view to recapturing it and bringing it back to the body (see below, pp. 146 seq.). Finally, at death, the *samengat* leaves the body permanently. When an Iban is dying, the *samengat* is in the process of leaving the body but may still be within earshot—so to speak. Before death is an established fact,

[1] This belief is not peculiar to the Iban. It is common to the peoples of Malaya and Indonesia (see, for example, Landon, 1949, 15 seq.) and survives among Muslims. For example, Wilkinson, reprint, n.d., 419, in defining 'Samengat' says that 'Malays believe that this spirit of life is found in all nature, even in things that we consider inanimate. Thus the "soul of iron" . . . is responsible for the special merits of iron. . . . This animistic belief underlies the special reverence paid to certain weapons . . . and comes out clearly in the harvest rites associated with the "rice soul".' See also Skeat, 1900, 47 seq.

[2] Richards, 1962, 410, records an account of an Iban woman, that is, her *samengat*, shrinking to 'the size of [a] thumb'. Her husband kept her 'soul' and was able to bring her back to life.

[3] In recent years photographs have occasionally been compared with the *samengat*, though this is not general.

[4] The same belief occurs among Malays and Indonesians, Wilkinson, reprint, n.d., 419.

the assembled relatives commonly shout 'come back, come back' (*pulai, pulai*), calling on the *samengat* to return to the body.

When an Iban dies he is said 'to become an (*antu*) spirit' (*nyadi antu*). His life-giving spirit/soul abandons the body but continues to have a spirit existence. Although the spirits of dead men have their own *menoa*, Sebayan, the spirit of the man who has recently died does not immediately settle down in Sebayan. Until the final burial rites have been performed,[1] the spirit is thought to be without an established territory and is likely to come searching for food and firewood; consequently surviving relatives leave offerings and gifts in and around the longhouse to placate the spirit of the dead which might turn aggressive if thwarted, frustrated, or left hungry. The *samengat* remains as an *antu* spirit in Sebayan for an indefinite period until eventually dissolving into dew. The dew is taken up into the ears of rice which are eaten by living men who in their turn die. Some Iban say that a man has seven *samengat* spirit/souls and these die one by one till, finally, the last *samengat* dies and becomes dew. Other Iban interpret this as seven stages in the continued existence of the *samengat* after death, which are related to the seven divisions (*serak*) of Sebayan. Like most Iban thinking which concerns first origins and ultimate destiny, the ideas are obscure and a little confused. The Iban are concerned principally with life as they experience it and the immediate fate of the dead—especially as this affects the living. The existence of the spirits in Sebayan is, for the most part, believed to resemble life among the living. The spirits of the dead also inhabit longhouses and plant rice.

The *samengat*, however, is not restricted to humans, living and dead. Many animals and some aspects of vegetable life also have a spirit/soul. In particular, those animals which are considered dangerous—like snakes and crocodiles—unusual, or important as a source of food, have their *samengat*, so do birds, specific insects, certain plants and trees, and even some inanimate objects (see above, p. 107, n. 1). These are all significant in Iban experience. Only animals, insects, vegetables or inanimate matter, which have no significance for the Iban, have no *samengat*, like cockroaches for

---

[1] It has been suggested that temporary burial preceding the later conclusive (secondary) burial was once widely practised in Borneo, see Hertz, 1960a, 34 seq., and Harrisson, 1965a, especially 10, who associates this custom with the Iban. (Cf. ref. above, p. 93, n. 1).

example. The 'human' emotions and behaviour associated with the *samengat* do not mean that the Iban, as at first might seem the case, confuse the nature of animal and vegetable life by attributing human qualities to reptiles and insects. Nor do the Iban expect animals to behave in a human way in their natural form.[1] The belief means that the *samengat* of animals and other life has an existence of its own, in a sense distinct from the body it mostly inhabits. The *samengat*, or spirit counterpart, exists on the same plane and corresponds to the *samengat* of men. *Samengat* of men, as might be expected, act and feel much like human beings without a physical human body.

None matters more than the personified spirit/soul of rice, *samengat padi*, to which human emotions and responses are regularly attributed and with which the *samengat* of man is ultimately identified. But even certain inanimate objects may have a spirit counterpart with the usual *samengat* qualities. This is true, for example, of the treasured jars (*tajau*) which play a significant role in Iban economic and social life, as well as some of the implements used in rice cultivation, in particular iron implements and knives.[2] It also applies to *baiya* burial property, which includes clothing, jewellery, weapons, tools, cooking utensils, and heirloom valuables left for the use of a dead person in Sebayan. Since it is the spirit counterpart which counts in this context, *baiya* items are usually broken or damaged to render them worthless in the physical world.

Both the spirit and physical worlds are aspects of the same order. They are not in conflict but are characterized in many ways by opposite and complementary facets of existence as the Iban see it; nor is this merely a question of the opposites associated with Sebayan like night/day and seeing/blind. The balanced dualism of Iban thought lacks the strong antitheses elsewhere associated with right and left.[3] Left (*kiba*) in Iban does not as a rule have 'sinister' or unclean associations, in spite of Iban contact with the Muslim Malays. Iban thinking is based on a complementary scheme in which both aspects are of comparable value. On the one hand the

---

[1] The *ensera* concerning *plandok*, the mouse deer, for example, are stories like Brer Rabbit or Winnie the Pooh; they are usually told for the entertainment of children and have little relevance to the Iban interpretation of animal life; see above, p. 70.

[2] See above, quotation from Wilkinson, p. 107, n. 1.

[3] See Hertz, 1960b, 99 seq., and, later, papers by Beidelman, Needham, etc.

world of physical experience, on the other the spirit world, and under each head the properties associated with it—in complementary pairs:

(living) men: *mensia*	spirits and the dead: *petara* and *antu*
the body: *tuboh*	the spirit/soul: *samengat*
mortal	immortal
visible	invisible
substantial	insubstantial
the ordinary and profane	the sacred
the earth	the sky.

Associated with these pairs are prohibitions: *pemali* on the one hand and universal order: *adat* on the other; the state of *angat*: heated, feverish, infected over against *chelap*: cool, tranquil, healthy; even numbers and odd—especially 3[1] and 7[2]; and the colorations: dark, dull, or of no particular hue as opposed to light, bright, and especially red.

The scheme of complementary associated properties can be extended to include certain other relationships.[3] For example, there is a correlation found principally in Iban augury (see below, pp. 132 seq. esp. pp. 136-7) between the columns:

[1] The number three is associated with the thrice repeated 'Oha' which accompanies the *biau* ceremony and precedes invocations. The creator called three times in bringing man to life. The *piring* is commonly threefold. The universe can be divided into three parts: *langit*, the sky above; *dunya*, the earth; and Sebayan, below the earth. Its inhabitants fall into three principal categories: *petara*, *antu*, and *mensia*, human beings.

[2] The number seven is even more important in Iban religion (as it also is in Malay traditional belief; see, for example, Skeat, 1900, 50 *et al.*). Sengalang Burong and Pulang Gana belong to seven siblings; the daughters of Sengalang Burong are seven, so are Samerugah's daughters—and, above all, the omen birds. *Langit* is sometimes thought of as divided into seven layers, and Sebayan has seven *serak*. The 'best' *piring* sacrifice is sevenfold and there are seven *samengat*. This list is not exhaustive, but gives some indication of the constant recurrence of the number seven in Iban lore. Harrisson, 1965a, 32, n. 35. 1, refers to eight as 'lucky' and 'even semisacred', but this is not borne out by more usual Iban belief and practice, although an eightfold *piring* is not unknown. The apparent emphasis on eight in Harrisson and Sandin, 1966, 284, may be due to an assumption derived from the seven daughters of Sengalang Burong and the seven omen birds, who are not exactly paired off: Nendak is married to someone other than Sengalang Burong's daughter and Burong Malam is not a true bird (above, p. 91, n. 1 and below, p. 132, n. 1)

[3] Cf. Needham, 1962, 96, who says of Purum social organization that it is 'ideologically part of a cosmological conceptual order and is governed identically by its ruling ideas'.

man   woman
right   left
mimpin; 'stronger' flight,   *raup*; 'weaker' flight, from left to
  from right to left   right
ruai[1]   *bilek*[1]
up-river   down-river

and to some extent also:
hard soil   soft soil

The *Adat* Order

Each member part of the universe, be it spirit, human, animal, or vegetable, belongs to the universal order and has its normal and appropriate way of behaving according to its nature. When it follows the order, it follows its particular *adat*. And this is the basis for Iban *adat* law.

Adat as a concept has been widely used by both English- and Dutch-speaking writers. Ter Haar (1948, 5) gives credit to Snouck Hurgronje,[2] the Dutch-Indonesian Arabic scholar and statesman of the nineteenth century for pointing out that 'since customary practices among most of the peoples of the archipelago were denominated by the Arabic word "*adat*", or custom, it would be fruitful to speak of "adat that has legal consequences"—"adatrecht" in Dutch, or "adat law" in English.' Ter Haar (1948, 5) says further that 'the term was not introduced into statutory enactment until 1929, but today the concept has been thoroughly explored and its contents carefully defined.' This refers to *adat* as customary law. Further, although *adat* has been said to include a man's personal habits, the ways of the world, the conventions of society, the operation of natural laws, rules governing sports or games, the laws of war, court etiquette, fines, fees, and penalties, the Malay term *adat* 'does not in its strict sense cover religious law (*shara 'hukum*), statute law (*undang-undang*), conventions (*muafakat*) or European laws'.[3] *Adat* is actually distinguished from

---

[1] When Selampandai, the 'god of creation' (Freeman, 1958a, 413, calls him 'Sempandai'), whose earthly manifestation is a species of locust, is heard at night, this is thought to signify that a woman has conceived. 'If Selampandai is heard from the *bilek* [the child] is likely to be a girl, from the *ruai* a boy' (Jensen, 1967, 166).

[2] The reference is to *De Atjeher*, 1893, i. 357.

[3] Wilkinson, reprint, n.d., 5–6, see also Richards, 1963, 1.

religious law which among most Malays and Indonesians is Islamic; its meaning is restricted to that indigenous customary law which has no direct connection with (Muslim) religion.

The Iban, however, have not in the past been subject to Muslim law, which they do not recognize. Among them, *adat* retains the traditional sense, which is far wider than law as understood in the west and much deeper and more binding than mere custom or convention. As with the Ngaju in South Borneo, 'the notion has a double meaning. Firstly, that of divine cosmic order and harmony, and secondly that of life and actions in agreement with this order. It is not only humanity that possesses *hadat*, but also every other creature or thing (animal, plant, river, etc.), every phenomenon (e.g. celestial phenomena), every period and every action for the entire cosmos is ordered by the total godhead, and has to live and act according to this ordained place' (Schärer, 1963, 74–5). '*Hadat* rules the whole of life and thought, and all relations between man and the cosmos' (ibid. 98).

The *adat* as revealed to the Iban by Sengalang Burong is designed to ensure a mutually satisfactory relation between men and the other inhabitants of the universe. Although in his instinctive response to life around him the Iban may see himself as standing at the centre of the universe, he knows that he does not control it. He recognizes that he is part of a whole which encompasses other people and other levels of existence. He believes the universe to be inhabited by various groups, human, spirit, animal, and vegetable, which have some interests in common but also have diverging and conflicting interests. *Adat* exists to ensure harmony in this universe and to promote the well-being of all its inhabitants, among them the Iban.

The *adat* of plants is to grow, of fruit trees to bear fruit. Animals also have their *adat*, their natural way of behaving within the total order. The *adat* of an Iban involves the observation of innumerable rules governing social behaviour and ritual acts, and to explain alien behaviour the Iban say 'that's their *adat*' (*nya adat sida*). Although the differences in *adat* between different groups are recognized and the occasional conflicts which occur as a result, the consequences of 'following *adat*' (*niteh (ka) adat*) are expected to be harmonious relations, good harvests, health, and general prosperity, a state which the Iban call cool and tranquil, *chelap* (see above, p. 110, for its place in Iban thought). The complement to *adat* is *mali*, that which is forbidden, prohibited, or restricted.[1] *Adat* is upheld and defended by a series of *pemali* (the noun derived from *mali*), *penti*—strictly the 'compensation' required for certain transgressions, or *pantang*, which literally means 'what is driven in' and established.

An offence against *adat* disturbs the universal order, producing disorder and the undesirable 'heated' or 'feverish' state, *angat*. The results of disorder range from minor sickness to epidemics and crop failure. Lesser transgressions may affect only the *bilek* concerned, although this is not necessarily so since an offence against *adat* disrupts the total order. The consequences are more the result of this disturbance than punishment inflicted on the guilty. Serious transgression of *adat* invariably touches the whole community. Particularly blatant offences result in *kudi*, the state of sterility where the natural order ceases to function. As already mentioned (see above, p. 40), incest provides the most important example, murder another. One area in the Lemanak was considered 'sterile land' (*tanah kudi*) because it had at one time been the site of bloodshed at a head-hunting encounter. During Confrontation with Indonesia *Penghulu* Rangga of the Undup was most concerned lest fighting and bloodshed should similarly make *tanah kudi* of the upper Undup.

Since *adat* represents the order of the natural universe, *kudi* is the consequence of disrespect, ridicule, or actual interference with the natural order. An Iban who had witnessed pigs being induced to copulate at an agricultural station was convinced the *menoa* would become *kudi* in consequence. It is a serious offence even to mock natural behaviour, as, for example, the sight of copulating dogs which invariably appears comic to the Iban. Many are the stories told of Iban men and women who laughed rashly at animals or fish and brought calamity on the area. Some were themselves turned to stone, and petrified formations, called *batu kudi*, serve as perpetual reminders.[2]

What is 'bad', that is, what constitutes a transgression of *adat*, is essentially that which produces undesirable results. It is bad for that reason and to that extent. *Adat* is not an absolute ethical

---

[1] Cf. Ngaju concepts of *pali* which are similar, Schärer, 1963, 75–6.

[2] As already mentioned (see above, p. 76, n. 2), the conviction that the mockery of animals (like incest) will cause natural catastrophes and lead to petrification occurs widely in the Malaysian region; see, for example, Schärer, 1963, 99.

standard. If, for instance, an offence has been committed and someone in the longhouse subsequently dies, the expiatory fine is increased (called *tungkal*)[1] since the death is regarded as a 'consequence' of the disorder created by the offence against *adat*. However, the badness of an act is not always immediately apparent and it may have consequences in the long-term for others in the community or *menoa* rather than, or as well as, the offender. Therefore, while it is true to say, as Evans-Pritchard does of incest among the Nuer,[2] that the badness lies in the consequences, it is equally true that although the consequences are unpredictable, *adat* provides the essential yardstick for behaviour, a rule for social conduct which becomes a 'moral' standard. Ultimately the prosperity of a *bilek* and a community provides the true criterion for the correctness of their *adat* observance.

Hence when the Iban encounter difficulties, or calamities occur, they conclude that the *adat* has not been correctly observed. The 'trial' of presumed offenders is not a trial in the western sense, nor does the punishment necessarily have to 'fit the crime'. When the guilty person is known or suspected, his case is heard by a 'court' of longhouse members and, if found guilty by consensus, he is fined by the community. Unlike *ukum* fines to government this is not so much a fine with the meaning of a punishment imposed, as compensation offered to the offended (spirit) party. The Iban do not use the word 'pay' (*bebayar* or *mayar*), they say that they 'meet', 'complete', or 'fill' (*ngisi*) such a fine. In circumstances when the guilty person is unknown, cannot be found, or cannot afford the fine, it is possible for the *tuai rumah* to 'fine' himself and restore order in the universe of man-spirit relations. Similarly, the *ngampun* ritual endeavours with offerings and sacrifices to appease those spirits who may have been unwittingly offended at critical times in connection with rice planting, sickness, and, in particular, epidemics.

When the *adat* is disturbed, the Iban, his *bilek* and his *menoa* are 'heated', 'feverish', or 'infected', *angat*. The *adat* is designed to

[1] For example, Richards, 1963, 21. 'An unmarried woman who is pregnant and has not named the father [thus implying the suspicion of incestuous intercourse] is fined if she goes up to another house. If anyone dies in that house because of the offence, the fine is greater.' See above, p. 40, n. 1.

[2] 'Nuer do not reason that incestuous congress with a kinswoman is bad and therefore God punishes it but that God causes misfortune to follow it and therefore it is bad.' 1956, 194.

safeguard that 'state of grace' in which all parts of the universe remain 'healthy', 'tranquil', and 'cool', *chelap*, and the Iban are 'content', *lantang*, physically and in spirit. This hope is summed up in the lines with which most prayers conclude, when the Iban ask to live 'a full life-span in contentment, health and comfort':

> *gayu*[1] *guru*
> *chelap lindap*
> *grai nyamai.*

[1] The word *gayu* meaning 'long life' may be related to the notion of *ayu*; they share a common indicative verb form (*ngayu*). *Ayu* is used of an other world spirit image of living Iban which is believed to grow in clumps like banana shoots. The plant dies when the *samengat* leaves man on the death of his body.

IX. MEN AND THE SPIRITS

Dreams

SINCE in the complementary realms of men and spirits the sun lights Sebayan at night, the spirits (of Sebayan) see clearly during the hours of darkness. To them it is daytime. Dreams, therefore, provide an obvious setting for spirit encounters. In dreams, the *samengat* of man has experiences which are independent of the sleeping body. While the body remains asleep in one place, the *samengat* may wander abroad and in doing so it frequently encounters non-human spirits. In dreams, the *samengat* which has the properties of a spirit moves in the spirit world.

Dreams as a whole can be divided into three categories: first, personal encounters with members of the spirit world who convey a (direct) message; the second and most common category consists of those dream experiences not involving a direct encounter with a spirit but concerning events in Iban life which are interpreted as referring to current or projected undertakings. The third type are those dreams relating to daily experience which are considered too ordinary to have any significance.

The appearance of a spirit in a dream may, on occasion, correspond only to a social call—this applies especially to the appearance of the spirits of dead (and contented) relatives. But from time to time a spirit reveals itself in a dream to pass on useful information—where, for example, a charm (*pengaroh*) is to be found. Sometimes the two occur in conjunction. Lensi, for instance, had a dream in which she saw her grandmother who had recently died; as the grandmother was leaving, she told Lensi that if she looked at the foot of a particular banana palm she would find a charm (*pengaroh*). Next morning Lensi discovered a small, smooth, black pebble by the banana.

The spirits do not only appear to present charms, they also come to demand attention. Within one month, Lanchai of Rh. Sa in the Lemanak, had two dreams. On the first occasion he saw a woman as beautiful as Lulong (one of Kling's group) who spoke to him and said she wanted him to hold a celebration (*mai iya gawa*); she was both hungry and thirsty, she said. Lulong's mother, who accompanied her in the dream, carried a small bottle and a man was seen to spread out a mat for recovering harvested rice. The next day Lanchai prepared the usual sacrificial *piring* with *tuak*. Two weeks later, another—this time unidentified—spirit appeared to Lanchai and asked for a food offering. The next day he offered a sevenfold sacrifice and performed a *biau*: two plates were prepared, the one placed in a basket covered with a woven *pua* cloth, and suspended over the *ruai*, the other taken to his farm. Both were left for three days. A dream such as this is not necessarily thought of as specifically good or bad; the reaction on the part of the Iban makes it either one or the other. To ignore an encounter with a spirit in a dream or to pay no attention to a request for food would antagonize the spirit, who could then be expected to seek retribution. Lanchai, for his part, felt that if he had not performed the sacrifice the harvest would have been a poor one for the longhouse, but that after the appropriate sacrifices had been made, all were certain to have a good yield; he deduced this from the mat for recovering rice.

Whereas the spirits usually make their meaning clear when encountered in dreams, the interpretation of non-spirit-encounter dream sequences may pose problems, although, according to Iban notions, the interpretation of dreams is for the most part analogous. The majority of everyday dreams concern ordinary human activities: running, swimming, climbing fruit trees and so forth, and the familiar dream activity: flying. While the intepretation depends on particular circumstances and varies from individual to individual, it is never devious. If the dreamer is involved in no special undertaking at the time, the dream is interpreted as referring to his life in general. Flying (*mimpi trebai*), for example, means that the dreamer will have a long life, as does running away (*mimpi rawan*), except the dreamer be fleeing from an evil *antu* spirit which is decidedly inauspicious. To swim across a river (*ngemerai ai*), when the dreamer is at first afraid then overcomes his fear and reaches the other side in safety, means that there will be a plentiful harvest (*bulih padi*). Bad dreams (*jai mimpi*) in general, but particularly dreams of shame or embarrassment (*mimpi malu*) in which the dreamer is made to feel inferior because he is unsuccessful, for example, in farming, or finds that he has insufficient food, are treated with great concern. It is thought unwise to work the following day, since this could be expected to result in an undesirable occurrence like a cut or snake-bite. A watch which had been stolen in the Lemanak was returned after three days because the thief had had a *mimpi malu*, although he refused to say precisely what it was. On another occasion, Gaik of Rh. Melintang in the Lemanak, was genuinely frightened by a dream in which he was spattered by a colourless liquid, which he took to symbolize worms going at his corpse.

Dreams which have no immediate meaning are often interpreted in the light of subsequent events. Temonggong Jugah at the Simanggang meeting dreamed of a turtle being reeled in, having its throat cut and then put in a pot by his wife. At first he thought this sounded promising, but when the following day he was unexpectedly recalled to Sibu, he interpreted the reeling in in relation to his recall and the throat-cutting as symbolizing his being prevented from speaking further. Similarly, Jabah had a dream in which she was shown a fruit tree heavy with fruit, but she decided to put off the gathering, and when she subsequently returned, the fruit had been eaten by squirrels. Later she interpreted this as referring to her relationship with Megong, who had wanted to marry her, but when she hesitated, had married her cousin instead.

The most important dreams in Iban thought are those which precede or occur during a major undertaking. Dreams provide the essential spirit endorsement before the Iban dare embark on a new, important, or difficult project, be this a new longhouse, a new farming season, a festival, enlisting in the Rangers or other expedition, migration, or even a wild-boar hunt. Since the interpretation is direct, a standard 'good' dream is one which offers an obvious parable of the proposed undertaking without depicting the activity itself. Before the farming cycle begins it would be propitious to dream that the whole longhouse went tuba-fishing (fishing with the poisonous derris root) and had so good a catch that when the fish were divided there was plenty for all. Before leading the tuba-fishing in the Lemanak in June 1961, the leader (*tuai nubai*) Kilat dreamed that, during the course of a feast, he entered a longhouse where he saw a great many people lying drunk all over the floor. This he interpreted as an auspicious dream representing the many fish floating stunned to the surface of the water. But to dream of the actual project is inauspicious. If, for example, an Iban dreams of the precise animals he proposes to hunt, he considers this a bad omen, since the spirit of the animal in question is thus somehow aware and warned of the hunt. Similarly with other ventures. Analogous dreams do not reveal the Iban's intention to those who might wish to frustrate him. Most satisfactory are, therefore, those dreams which, with good outcome, suggest an analogy or parallel to the project in question.

Where the project concerns only one or more individuals it is the dreams of these individuals—and those of their *bilek*—which count. Young men who are about to enlist in the Rangers or Police Field Force, for example, hope that they or their *bilek* family will have dreams similar to those desired before head-hunting expeditions. To dream that the longhouse is on fire predicts defeat and misfortune, but to dream of putting out a fire is interpreted as overcoming the enemy, and felling a tree implies taking a head. Individual dreams may always be considered more widely important and the whole longhouse community will, in special circumstances, respect the dream of its lowliest member. Certainly within the *bilek* the dreams of all, even children, may have significance. But nothing matters as much as the dream of a community leader before a project which involves the whole longhouse.

The start of an undertaking may be postponed, should the leader have a dream giving rise to frustration or anger (*mimpi ringat*). If, for example, he dreams that during tuba-fishing, fish were seen but only a few were successfully speared or caught, or alternatively, he dreams that while gathering fruit, although there appeared to be plenty on the trees, the party collected only a small quantity and many of the fruits had been gnawed by monkeys, he would not have the confidence to begin. The leader would probably forgo leadership entirely if he had a decidedly shaming dream (*mimpi malu*): if, for example, he dreamed that, although his was a large farm and the burn had been good, while everybody else had an excellent rice crop his own was a poor one. In no circumstances could he remain the leader if he had the worst dream of all, dreaming that he was killed (*mimpi parai*). In this event another would be found to replace him.

Leadership is commonly associated with a flair for constructive dreaming. This means that the dreamer regularly has dreams which appear relevant, secondly, that he is able to interpret their meaning—the advice of the spirits—and, that, acting on this interpretation, he is successful. This proves him a man of insight, discrimination and judgement. Auspicious dreams are, of course, also a prerequisite of leadership, since the candidates for 'office', *tuai burong* as well as *lemambang* or *manang*, must be confirmed by the spirits in an appropriate dream before assuming their roles. A *tuai burong*, first and foremost, is said to be chosen by the spirits (*petara milih tuai burong*), and since the spirits communicate much of their advice as well as warnings through the medium of dreams, these become an important basis for selection. It is common when a new *tuai* is required, for the prospective candidates to await the verdict of the spirits in a dream. Next day the Iban accept as *tuai burong* the man who has had the 'best' dream. This selection is subsequently confirmed by bird omens. The initiative may also come directly from the spirits. Sara of Silik,[1] for example, was visited in a dream by spirits and summoned to be a *manang* (see below, pp. 144 seq.); she was warned that if she refused, misfortune would befall her and when she replied that she had not the knowledge, the spirit offered to teach her—also in dreams.

Apart from times of crisis or before major appointments when the Iban attach significance to dreams which they would not otherwise think important, the Iban consider irrelevant or meaningless the remaining category of dreams. If, having had a dream to which he attaches no importance, the Iban wishes to stress the fact, he may emerge in the morning holding his ear-lobe. This signifies that the dream 'has not been heard'. The Iban are essentially pragmatic, and when spirit advice is not considered desirable or necessary and nothing unpleasant ensues, all is well. The emphasis remains on the apparent consequences of dream experiences as borne out by subsequent happenings.

Dreams can even be willed to serve a personal purpose. Since marriage is considered invalid if either party has an unpropitious dream during the first week and divorce is then automatic, dreams are sometimes used as a pretext to escape from an unwanted alliance. The Iban themselves recognize and laugh at this. But although the dreamer is granted his divorce, he is liable to forfeit respect for his dreams (and views) on this and other matters, unless later events endorse his interpretation.

---

[1] An area in the Kumpang.

Pengaroh Charms

Pengaroh, the name given by the Iban to 'charms' or amulets of stone, wood, or bone, can be either positive or negative in their effects. They may serve as protection against wounds or against illness, or to make an Iban brave and healthy. They may be designed for specific ends (making a man attractive to a particular woman, for example), or 'general purpose'. The value of any individual *pengaroh* stands in direct relation to its apparent effectiveness. As is to be expected, *pengaroh* receive special attention in times of stress and danger, during illness, or on the warpath, but many Iban have one or two favourite *pengaroh* which they always carry with them.

Pengaroh may be inherited or acquired personally. Most common are the cases of *pengaroh* presented gratuitously by a spirit in a dream,[1] but apart from these, new *pengaroh* are usually sought when the available *pengaroh* have proved ineffective in coping with a current difficulty, or novel, exacting circumstances are likely to find them insufficiently potent. If, in this event, no help is revealed in a dream—that is, the spirits do not choose to approach the Iban—it is possible for the Iban to approach the spirits in quest of a *pengaroh*. The hearth (*dapur*) has associations with the spirit world and if a man or a woman dares to put an arm deeply into and around the ashes of the hearth, it is said that he may feel it drawn or pushed (*narit sama matak*) or suddenly chilled (*jari berasai chelap*). If this experience frightens him and he withdraws his arm, the spirit will refuse to help. If the Iban has the courage to withstand the trial of the spirit and continues to push his arm through the hearth all the way to the corner post (*tiang dapur*), he may well be rewarded by discovering a *pengaroh*. The actual *pengaroh* in this case is usually a small stone with some distinctive quality of colouring or texture.

Nampok

For most purposes, spirit guidance is expressed in dreams and through bird omens, future prospects foretold by pigs' livers, and tokens of spirit assistance, when forthcoming, offered in the shape of *pengaroh*. Occasionally, however, an Iban remains seriously ill,

[1] As in the case of Lensi, see above, p. 116.

continues to suffer from a chronic disease or defect, or believes himself the victim of recurrent misfortune, even after trying the efficacy of charms, making the appropriate *piring* and offerings, or being treated by a *manang*. In these circumstances he may attempt to provoke a direct confrontation with the spirit world. On rare occasions a young man does this also to prove his resourcefulness to himself and to others. If the Iban shows himself equal to the experience, he can expect to be rewarded. The recognized procedure is called *nampok*. This is the culmination of Iban intercourse with the spirit world (*pengambis pengawa Iban*) and is thought to require great courage and resilience. Although a meeting with the spirits may produce beneficial effects, it is always liable to 'backfire', and has to be handled with the utmost caution.

The spirits are thought to inhabit in particular hill-tops and graveyards, places where the jungle has never been cleared and wildlife commonly occurs. Spirits are also found in a leopard's lair and in pools where crocodiles live. Consequently when an actual confrontation with the spirits is sought, the Iban goes to one of these places. Although *nampok* may occur in any of them, it is commonest to choose either a forest-covered hill-top (*tuchong bukit*) or a graveyard (*pendam*). Graveyards are considered especially suitable because of their greater concentration of spirits —in ordinary circumstances not many Iban like to walk more than a few yards into a graveyard even in broad daylight.

Nampok follows an accepted procedure. Friends and relatives may escort the Iban (*nganjong*) to near the *nampok* site, but they must then go off elsewhere. For the actual encounter it is essential that the Iban be entirely alone, nor must he take with him a weapon for his own defence. Before dark he prepares the *nampok* site (*pangkalan nampok*) and sees that the *piring* sacrifice and cock which he has with him are in readiness. The *piring* should be ninefold, or at the very least sevenfold, and must not have been touched by any other person, or by poultry, dog, or pig. The fowl for the *biau* must be a cock; a hen is not acceptable. At dusk the Iban performs a *biau* either sitting or standing. Three times he calls on the spirits and challenges them:

Antu Gerasi, Tuah Tui,
Buau Nyada, Gerasi Papa,
Tau ka urar, tau ke ngemayar,
Tau ka tedong, tau ka remaung,

Aku tu nadai guna, nadai kedayar,
Aku minta ampit, minta gigit,
Minta kunya, minta tekah,
Nyadi samoa kita sampal ambis, sampal lengih,
Ari wong, ari tuchong, ari langit, ari bukit.

Gerasi Spirit, Tuah Tui,
Buau Nyada, Gerasi Papa,
Whether serpent, whether dragon,
Whether cobra, whether leopard,
I—of no value and no standing—
Call on you to strike me, bite me,
Chew me, fright me!
Come every one of you, all of you,
From the waterfall, from the hill-top, from the sky, and from
the mountain!

After this, the Iban kills the cock with a small knife, and touches
himself with its blood. He sits down, if he is not already sitting,
and places the *piring* on his thighs with the dead cock on top.

Before a spirit appears in person, the Iban is tried. Versions of
the trials vary, but inevitably involve encounters with animals of
which an Iban is normally frightened and which are considered
spirit manifestations: snakes, especially, and bears. Before these,
however, comes the *geranyan* fire-ant which is particularly large
and vicious. The fire-ant seems about to bite the Iban, but the
Iban may in no case try to kill it or brush it away. After being
tried, and when he is ready for the spirit confrontation itself, the
Iban beats out a summons for the spirit to appear (*sepepat*).[1] The
spirit may choose to manifest himself in animal form, or like Antu
Belabong Dilah (whose name means that his tongue is long enough
for a head-cloth) make his appearance first as a snake which grows
to enormous size and is then miraculously transformed into an
antu in person. Antu Belabong Dilah is so powerful that he has
only to point fiercely at a tree for it to fall. If the Iban runs away
in fear at this juncture, he is cursed (*ditepang*) and would suffer
consistent misfortune (*pulai ka hal*): he would be unsuccessful on
expeditions, a coward in head-hunting raids, and have poor rice

---

[1] A special rhythm is beaten which is thought to be particularly effective in
summoning the spirits. This rhythm is never used unless spirit presence is
deliberately sought and the appropriate sacrificial offerings are in readiness.
For reference to the effects of rhythmical drumming of a particular sort, see
Sturtevant, 1968, 133–4; see also Needham, 1967.

harvests. If, on the other hand, the Iban stands his ground and addresses the *antu*, who, when not in animal likeness, resembles an outsized, ferocious Iban, the *antu* is expected to reward him by revealing a *pengaroh*. The *pengaroh* itself usually consists of a polished or distinctive stone (*batu*), a tusk or tooth (*ngeli*), piece of antler (*tandok*), or other bone; sometimes, in exceptional cases, a knife (*duku*), more rarely a ring (*tinchin*), or even a spear (*sangkoh*) or a shield (*trebai*).

Before departing the *antu* explains how the *pengaroh* must be cared for (*ngintu*), the number of sacrificial offerings needed for it to prove efficacious. The required *piring* is generally ninefold or sevenfold, never less, but unless instructed in a dream to repeat the *piring*, it is offered once only. On returning to his *bilek* the Iban reports to his wife the instructions of the *antu*. If she, without question, endeavours to meet the requests and at once makes preparations for the *piring*, the *pengaroh* may become valid not only for the Iban himself, but also for his children and his children's children (*sampai ka uchu*). If, on the other hand, the Iban's wife at first refuses or begins to raise objections, the *bilek* may be cursed by the spirit to the extent that the *pengaroh*'s efficacy is strictly limited to the person of the man himself (*tuboh iya empu*).

Ngarong

The acquisition of spirit support through *nampok* is associated in the Iban mind with possessing a *ngarong*, described by Hose and McDougall (1912, ii. 90) as the 'secret', and by Hose (1926, 201) as the 'Unknown Helper'. Hose calls it 'one of the most extra-ordinary and rarest beliefs . . . held by the Ibans' (ibid.), but does not seem to recognize the way in which the concept of *ngarong*, or more usually *tuah* (or *tua*[1]), fits naturally into the Iban scheme. Nor was he the first to note its existence; St. John (1863, i. 84) was aware of the concept though he did not use the term,[2] and Perham (Ling Roth, 1896, i. 188) cites the case of an Iban who had a python for his *tuah*.

Whereas the *pengaroh* provides a tangible memento of the

---

[1] This is the spelling used in another early reference (1922 and 1923), re-printed Anonymous, 1963, 149.

[2] Similarly, Freeman, 1958a, 414 (in his review of Scott's dictionary) refers to *antu nulong*, which he calls 'familiar spirits'.

spirits' favour, it sometimes occurs to 'only one in a hundred men' (Hose and McDougall, 1912, ii. 92) that an individual spirit consistently favours an Iban (and his *bilek*). Where this happens, the guardian spirit is known as *ngarong* or *tuah* and usually associates itself with the form of a potentially dangerous animal—commonly a species of snake. The normal order of events includes a dream, a spirit encounter, a particular animal, and subsequent success. In such circumstances the animal in question is venerated with *piring* and never killed or eaten. Sometimes the guardian animal spirit is also identified with a dead relative. Nuli's uncle, for example, in the Ulu Entebar, Undup, encountered a dead ancestor in a dream at his farm. Next morning he discovered a cobra by the hut. The season was an excellent one, and from then on he allowed a cobra to live in his storage loft and considered it as the earthly manifestation of the spirit who had brought him good fortune and whom he also identified with the dead ancestor. He expected both living and subsequent *bilek* members to respect the cobra in order to ensure the continued favour of his *tuah* or guardian spirit.

Augural Birds, Animals, and Insects

Low, writing in 1848, did not find that the Iban 'hold in superstitious dread any species of birds',[1] but Bock (1881, 222) says explicitly that 'the flight of birds is keenly watched by the Dyaks in all parts of Borneo, the movements of the hornbill and hawk, and the manner and direction of their flight, being especially regarded as emblematic of future events'. Over the years the majority of Sarawak travellers have noted that augury plays an important role in Iban life and have remarked on it, but there have been few attempts at a serious commentary.[2]

A story is still widely told which explains why the Iban practise augury. Although it was recorded in one form as early as 1887[3] and aspects of it also occur elsewhere in Borneo—for example,

[1] 276, although he mentions 'faith . . . in omens' (275)—principally insect noises.

[2] Only one systematic study exists, Freeman, 1960a (included as a chapter in Smythies, 1960, and also published in *Bijdragen*, 1961) criticized by Harrisson, 1965a, 6, n. 15.

[3] In a paper read before the Manchester Geographical Society, see Dunn, 1963, 22–3.

among the Maloh people of the Kapuas (see Harrisson, 1965b, 317)—it may be relatively recent, since in most versions it refers not only to Chinese and Malays but even to Europeans. The story goes that once upon a time all races had the secret of writing. When, during a flood or on coming to a river, the European put the secret of writing securely in his hat, it was perfectly preserved on arrival at the other bank. The Malay, dressed according to the style of his race, tucked it into the collar of his blouse and this was only a little damp at the far side. The Chinese put the secret into his shirt while swimming across the river and the writing ran (which is why the Chinese have such curious characters), but he was able to decipher it. The Iban, however, had on only his loin-cloth and when he reached the other bank the secret of writing had become completely soaked and was illegible. He tried to dry it in the sun, but before it was quite dry the birds came down out of the sky and carried it away. This is why the Iban do not know how to write and must depend on bird omens.

One speaker at the Simanggang conference suggested that that was how the birds had acquired the knowledge which Sengalang Burong later revealed to Surong Gunting. But even he considered this a conscious attempt to accommodate the story within the familiar mythological framework. The myths concerning Sengalang Burong and Surong Gunting do not explain the origins of augury, but how the Iban acquired their knowledge of omen birds from the spirit world. Their grasp of the principles of augury is closely associated with the kinship ties between the Iban and the spirit birds. Freeman (1960a, 76) does not mention this fundamental point in his account of the mythical charter: that the spirits, revealed in omens, are relatives (*kaban*) of the Iban, not unconnected outsiders, strangers, or 'other people' (*orang bukai*). In all accounts of Surong Gunting's visit to Sengalang Burong's longhouse, he finally proves himself the child of a mortal Iban father and Sengalang Burong's own daughter. Thus the spirits show concern to advise and assist their own kin through the established code of social behaviour, augural advice, and ritual practice, which are intended to benefit all and ensure harmony between varying interests.

The Iban consider augury to be characteristic of them and basic to their *adat* and way of life. Augury is one way and one of the most important in which the spirits communicate with men. The spirits, it is true, reveal themselves in dream experiences, but as often they express their advice and warnings to men through natural phenomena. Augury is called *beburong*, a word derived from *burong*, root meaning 'bird', and, secondly, 'omen'.[1] But Iban augury is not restricted to bird omens. In its secondary meaning, *burong* may apply to an animal or event, and in this sense it refers not so much to the object itself, as to the situation in which it occurs. Both Freeman (1960a, 74) and Richards[2] choose Homeric comparisons for their descriptions of the Iban.[3] In the context of augury a closer parallel might be the mocking comment of Aristophanes:[4]

> Unlucky or lucky, whatever has struck ye,
> An ox or an ass, that may happen to pass,
> A voice in the street, or a slave that you meet,
> A name or a word by chance overheard,
> You deem it an omen, and call it a Bird.

Although almost all occurrences can be considered significant in certain circumstances, generally speaking the meaningful is that which does not conform to a 'normal' behaviour pattern or lacks an obvious (natural) explanation. Since all aspects of life have their *adat* or code of normal behaviour, special meaning is attributed to departures from *adat*.

Whereas it is the *lemambang* who knows and recites the full honorifics and nicknames of the birds and omen animals when he passes the birds in intoning the *pengap*, detailed knowledge of the principles of augury is the *tuai burong*'s domain. It is the augur, or *tuai burong*, who enjoys a reputation for attracting appropriate omens, is able to interpret these correctly, and proves this by the success of his undertakings. Before and during all major projects he and the longhouse community look to the omen birds and animals for guidance.

Those animals and insects which, apart from the birds, most

[1] This double meaning of 'bird' occurs widely; see the Aristophanes quotation (below) from classical times and, for example, Beidelman, 1963, 46, for a modern parallel.

[2] 1959, 9, although this is a general comparison which does not refer specifically to the practice of augury.

[3] James, 1950, draws attention to the close similarity of Iban augury and that practised in Etruscanized Rome.

[4] Lowes Dickinson, 1958, 19, quoting Frere's translation of *The Birds* 717, stresses the importance of these beliefs to the early Greeks.

commonly serve as omens are the deer—*rusa*, the sambhur deer; *kijang*, the barking deer; *plandok*, the mouse deer; the larger mammals—*remaung*, the leopard; *bruang* or *jugam*, the honey bear; the snakes—*tedong*, the cobra; *belalang*, the hamadryad; *sawa*, the python; also *ingkat*, the tarsier, and *tengiling*, the anteater; the insects—*(re)rioh*, *(re)rejah*, *burong malam*—all locusts; as well as *aji*, moon rat; *sandah*, bat; bees, *manyi*; and vermin, *chit*. But this list is neither definitive nor exhaustive. Animals other than these may become omens in special circumstances. On the other hand, where an omen insect, such as the *rioh*, or *rerioh*, locust in the Delok, becomes too common for its appearance to be considered meaningful, it may lose its force as an omen. There are also birds and others, which carry messages from the spirit world without being omens proper. *Bubut* (the bird *centrococcyx*) is said to be one of these. When *bubut* is heard calling at night, it implies that somebody is dying: it is thought that the bird is summoning the *samengat* of the dying person.

The most important omens are those birds, animals, and insects which express the persons of Sengalang Burong's sons-in-law, and the other spirits. To ask the Iban for a precise definition of the relation between the spirit and the 'bird' in which it manifests itself is as futile as chemical analysis of the host after Roman Catholic Mass. The spirits are ethereal (sometimes invisible) and associated with the sky; birds also inhabit the sky, are frequently heard without being seen, and they are, to the Iban, the least earthly of creatures. The other omen animals, snakes and bears in particular, are associated with wild undergrowth where *antu* spirits also live. Some omen insects are peculiarly vociferous and difficult to locate, which may give them the impact of a disembodied voice—the call of a spirit.

The Omen Birds

Undoubtedly, those which matter most are the omen birds. It has been suggested (Hose and McDougall, 1912, ii. 87) that only thirty-three members of each genus are, in fact, true omen birds, but since these are impossible to distinguish from the others, the genus as a whole is credited with full omen status.[1] The actual

---

[1] This may, on rare occasions, be used to explain an 'inaccurate' omen.

birds known by the names of the *bilek* holders in Lang's longhouse are:

Pangkas	(Maroon Woodpecker)	*Blythipicus rubiginosus*
Beragai	(Scarlet-rumped Trogon)	*Harpactes duvauceli*
Ketupong	(Rufous Piculet)	*Sasia abnormis*
Embuas	(Banded Kingfisher)	*Lacedo pulchella*
Papau	(Diard's Trogon)	*Harpactes diardi*
Bejampong	(Crested Jay)	*Platylophus galericulatus*
Nendak	(White-rumped Shama)	*Copsychus malabaricus*

Since the birds are the earthly manifestations of the spirits, who in their own world look and behave much like human Iban, the birds themselves are commonly spoken of as though they were people. They are occasionally called 'a person' (*orang*). Bejampong has a top knot (*bejugu*) because, the Iban say, he is a 'real man' (*amat lelaki*). In general, however, it is the call and not the appearance of the bird which counts, and the birds are, therefore, characterized primarily by their calls. Three of the birds have two distinct 'voices' (*dua iti nyawa*). This is the way the Iban describe the alarm calls of Ketupong, Pangkas, and Papau. Two stories account for their extra voice. The one[1] says that the birds had a dispute about an *ensurai* tree. According to a Lemanak informant this was Bunga Nuing's and stood at Nanga Lemanak (see above, p. 94). Ketupong, Papau, and Pangkas said the tree would fall towards the river, and the other birds said away from it. When it actually fell towards the river, Ketupong, Papau, and Pangkas shouted in triumph (*manjong*) and this became their second voice.[2] *Senabong*, the alarm cry of Papau, is said to be 'like someone shouting in triumph' (*baka orang manjong*). Since, in another account, Ketupong—Sengalang Burong's senior son-in-law and leader of the birds when they go on expedition—was thought to have inadequate status and to be insufficiently respected (*orang enda bechaya ka iya*), he found an additional voice necessary. The alarm calls are often spoken of as if they emanated from separate birds; they have distinct characteristics and a different interpretation in Iban augury.

The bird-calls, as commonly the birds themselves, are most

---

[1] Also recorded by Freeman, 1960a, 83, n. 21.

[2] A dispute as to which way a tree will fall also occurs among the Maloh, Harrisson, 1965b, 250. This too establishes the dominant role of *Sasia abnormis*, here known as Antis.

usually described in terms of human speech and emotion. For example, Beragai is called the happy, pleased bird (*burong gaga*) because he 'laughs like an Iban' (*ketawa baka kitai Iban*, which simply means that he laughs like a human being) and the others are commonly characterized by similar analogies.

Ketupong, often known as *burong tengklak* ('one-word bird') is described as *baka orang tunggal jako, jako siti aja* ('like a man of a single utterance, who speaks one word only').

Embuas, often known as *burong sinu* ('pitying bird') or *burong kasih* ('kind bird')[1] is also called *burong brat* ('heavy bird') in the sense of being loaded with success. If Embuas is heard after the ritual clearing (*manggol*), the call is known as *burong chelap* ('cool bird') signifying that although the burn may not be particularly good, the rice is likely to grow well.

Beragai, often known as *burong tampak* ('bright bird') is also called *burong gaga* ('happy' or 'pleased bird') and *burong ketawa* ('laughing bird') because the bird 'laughs like one of us (Iban)' (*ketawa baka kitai Iban*).

Papau (who has the additional name Kelabu) is often known as *burong rabun* ('unseen bird'). It is also called *burong bula* ('bird of deceit') since it deceives or blinds the enemy or the quarry. Papau (the Diard's Trogon) in fact inhabits remote, thick vegetation and is rarely encountered by the Iban.

Bejampong, usually known as *burong jampat* ('quick-moving bird') and *burong gegar* ('excited bird') can also be referred to as *burong gaga* ('happy' or 'pleased bird'). The call is sometimes described as *baka orang dras bejako* ('like someone speaking quickly').

Pangkas, often known as *burong panjong* ('bird who shouts out') is described as *tegar laban nya* ('powerful because of it').

Nendak, almost invariably known as *burong chelap* ('cool bird') is described as 'like someone whose words give comfort and shade' (*baka orang ngelindap jako*).

The names representing the alarm cries are spoken of as if they were distinct birds with their own characteristics:

Kekih, the alarm cry of Ketupong, is known as *burong mangah*

---

[1] Freeman, 1960a, 83, describes Embuas as *baka orang mentas jako* ('like someone speaking kindly'), which as Harrisson, 1965a, 6, n. 15, observes is not much like the actual sound, described by Smythies, 1960, 299.

('fierce, angry bird') and sometimes *burong gegar* ('excited bird'). The call 'uses venomous language' (*jako bisar*) and is described as 'like an Iban angry with someone' (*baka (kitai) Iban ka nganu orang*).

Senabong, the alarm cry of Papau, is known as *burong darah* ('blood bird') and also *burong panjong* ('shouting bird'): the call is described as 'like someone shouting out' (*baka orang manjong*).

Kutok, the alarm cry of Pangkas, is called *burong tampak kitai* ('we clearly seen'), which is bad when hunting or on the warpath, and the call is described as 'like someone always angry and bothersome' (*baka orang slalu nganu, ngachau*).

Like the comparisons with human speech and emotions, the descriptive nicknames emphasize certain qualities normally associated with the omen. For example, Nendak, known as *burong chelap* ('cool bird'), is a good augury since coolness, the opposite of heat, fever and so forth, signifies health and comfort. But to hear Nendak (cool and opposed to heat) immediately before firing a farm would be likely to imply a poor burn although the harvest might eventually be good. The nicknames, however, are only descriptions. Because they are appropriate to the sound and significance, they have acquired wide currency. They satisfy the Iban fondness for repetition and alternative ways of saying the same thing. But there is no categorical objection to describing a bird call in a new way relevant to a particular situation or individual. Although general principles certainly apply, the birds may have differing significance for different people at different times. Individual Iban are permitted their own interpretation and the validity of this is borne out by the subsequent failure or success of their undertakings.

Some Iban feel that they have a special relationship to one or other of the omen birds. This may or may not be associated with the semi-serious adoption in childhood of a particular bird. It is said that a boy who chooses Ketupong as his own special bird could become very important, a *Penghulu*, perhaps, since Ketupong is the senior son-in-law and 'their leader' (*tuai sida*). Children who choose Nendak, Embuas, Bejampong, etc., look for the special qualities of these birds, with which they hope to associate themselves.

Interpretation of Omens

The relative importance of the bird spirits in Lang's longhouse has comparatively little to do with their significance in practical augury. The order for hearing does not correspond to the arrangement and status of the spirit *bileks*. All experts assembled at the Simanggang conference were agreed that the first bird to be heard on most occasions is Nendak, who is the least in Lang's longhouse since he is not married to one of Lang's daughters nor does he have a proper *bilek* of his own.[1]

Omens can be divided into two categories: those which occur unexpectedly and those which are deliberately sought. Of the first group there are omen birds which are seen by chance and not heard. As a rule the mere appearance of a bird is not important, since a bird which does not speak, a dumb bird (*burong agoh*), obviously has no message to convey from Lang (*enda ngasoh Lang bemunyi*), although in exceptional circumstances it could mean that the bird deliberately refuses to speak and thus withholds approval of a project. Sengalang Burong himself, however, sometimes appears in sight, in the form of the Kite, and although he does not have a specific part in the augural system, his presence is invariably noted, and, in this case, it is the appearance, not the voice, which matters.

When the bird utters a call and appears in sight, this is meaningful. The interpretation, however, depends on the direction of its flight. This may be either from right to left, called *mimpin* (which also includes passing on the right), or from left to right, called *raup* (also including passing on the left). *Mimpin* counts as a stronger omen (*kring agi*) than *raup* and is more important. In usual circumstances, if the bird flies in the same direction as the Iban is himself progressing, this is a good sign. If it flies in the opposite direction, the Iban is more likely to consider it a bad omen. When the bird flies both ways across the Iban's track

[1] Harrisson and Sandin, 1966, 283, contend that Nendak is 'low class' and 'a minor omen bird' but this is hardly so in practice. Similarly, Harrisson and Sandin's reference to 'eight omen birds', 284, infers a position in practical augury from the liturgical importance (in *pengap*) of Burong Malam, a spirit/ locust who, after Surong Gunting's visit, married the youngest daughter of Sengalang Burong. As stated above, p 91, n. 1, Burong Malam is not a bird but an insect, and although important along with other insects and animals for certain types of augury, he does not generally count as a true 'omen bird' (see also Richards, 1968, 132).

(*mimpin raup*) it lacks confidence; it is said to be *malu* (shamed) and the prospects are not encouraging.

Jaloh, *Jeritan*, and *Laba*

Jaloh, which Howell[1] translates simply as the 'cry of an omen bird', is generally used of an inauspicious omen. When heard by chance this is interpreted as a warning. It is not confined to Ketupong, as Harrisson and Sandin (1966, 264) seem to imply. In fact *jaloh* is used of any bird, animal, or other omen which is understood to advise the Iban against his intended occupation for the day. This applies, in particular, to work at the farm or other activities which have religious significance. It is assumed, should the Iban choose to ignore the warning, that either some harm will befall him or his *bilek* or, at best, the project will not succeed. Consequently, it is usual after hearing *jaloh* not to work that day. Work in this sense does not include non-farming activities like gathering or chopping firewood and other jobs which need to be done in or about the house. The implications of *jaloh* apply also to *punggu* (meaning literally, 'a dead tree which remains standing'). When a dead tree suddenly falls on a windless day or without some apparent reason, the Iban react to this as they would to *jaloh*.

An omen which is accidentally observed at or before the beginning of a specific major undertaking has the name *jeritan*, and is especially important. Of the birds only Nendak does not function as *jeritan*. This omen acquires a special significance if it is the first bird-call heard when setting out to initiate a new important project or just as the project is about to begin. The Iban respond to *jeritan* with an offering which includes a farming knife (*duku*). Like a *laba* omen at the farm, the ultimate significance of *jeritan* may depend largely on the Iban reaction. If this is correct and adequate, the results will be beneficial—otherwise not.

Finally, there are the instances of omen birds, animals, or insects (more usually animals or insects) encroaching on the farm area or entering the longhouse. Omen birds or animals which appear at the farm during crucial stages of the cycle are often called *laba* (see below, pp. 169–70). *Laba* are essentially good omens, but the

[1] 1900, 63. The word does not appear at all in Scott, 1956.

benefits likely to ensue depend on the Iban reaction. If the Iban response is inadequate, the 'effect' of the *laba* will be harmful; on the other hand, a *laba* duly respected with the appropriate offerings and ceremony is likely to mean good fortune. Whereas omen birds and animals commonly appear at Iban farms, it is comparatively rare that they actually enter a longhouse. It does, however, occur, and the event is vested with considerable significance. If Lang, the Kite, comes into a longhouse, this is considered a good omen and he will be welcomed with ceremony. But the appearance of the birds Ketupong, Beragai, Bejampong, Embuas, Kutok, for example, or animal omens like *kijang* (the barking deer) require the Iban to abandon their longhouse temporarily. For three days they stay away from the house and during this time they offer *piring* sacrifices and seek auspicious omens. In extreme circumstances, where the omen is considered wholly negative and subsequent augury and ritual have proven themselves insufficient to restore the correct man–spirit relations, the longhouse would have to be abandoned entirely. I heard of one such case. In one other the Iban compromised by inverting the entire longhouse, the *tanju* at the opposite side with the *bileks* replacing the *ruai* and vice versa.

To ignore major omens in the longhouse means sickness and death (*mali angat*). Even lesser omens in such a context are significant. For example, in July 1961, a kingfisher (*ensing*) entered Rh. Sa in the Lemanak. The Iban called it 'spear of the spirits' (*sangkoh antu*) and assumed that if the appropriate *piring* were not offered the consequences might be death or a longhouse fire. But no action beyond the *piring* was thought necessary. When the locust (*re*)*rioh* appears in a longhouse, as happens not infrequently, a response is also required. The Iban offer a *piring* and refrain from farm (or other significant) work for a day; they also observe prohibitions against basket-fishing (*mansai*) and rice-drying (*nyembi*). Even a firefly (*sempepat*) in the house is thought by a few to have meaning, but it is not a true omen nor generally recognized.

Deliberate Augury

The other major class of omens consists of those deliberately sought. The process of seeking auguries is known as *beburong* (the verb derived from *burong*). For many practical purposes, the initiative in augury rests with the Iban themselves. In day-to-day life the Iban turn constantly to the omen birds for advice and guidance. In these circumstances they do not wait for the birds incidentally to make known their views; the Iban go out consciously to seek auguries.

Although any Iban may *beburong*, it is usually done by more senior and experienced *tuai bileks*, and where community undertakings are concerned, the *tuai burong* invariably takes the lead (see above, pp. 60–1). The very early morning is the preferred time and the augur and other participants observe two restrictions (*pemali*). They are not permitted to eat (*nadai tau makai*), lest 'the birds should not come down since they have already had enough' (*burong enggai laboh, udah kenyang*) and they are not allowed to bathe (*nadai tau mandi*) because 'the birds will have wet feathers and might fall ill' (*burong basah bulu, ka sakit*) (see below, pp. 159 seq.).

The site varies. Usually it is not excessively far from the longhouse, but it ought not to be too close. Ideally it is near to old jungle, and for some important augury it should be on the true right bank of the river. The place, however, matters less than the bird-calls heard. Each time he hears a relevant call, the augur pulls out of the ground or picks up from those he has placed in readiness a small shoot or twig, using either his left hand or his right hand according to the side of the omen. These are called *kayu burong*, 'bird omen-sticks', sometimes *paung burong*, and serve as the tangible expression of an augury. Ideally they should be of *kamuntin* or *engkrebai*, but they can be of any wood which does not ooze sap or latex (*nadai begetah*). Neither should the twigs used have any water in them; consequently they are always shaken a little before plucking. The size varies slightly but the sticks are normally smaller than a pencil, although they may on occasion be up to 'the size of a toe' (*mesai tunjok kaki*); they are most often about eight inches long—the Iban use the measure *sa-jingkal*, a hand span. When the augural series is complete *piring* sacrifices are offered on both the left and right sides of the site.

No important undertaking may begin before the spirits have been consulted. Auguries are therefore essential at all key stages in the farming cycle, before house-building, migration, marriage, head-hunting expeditions, and so forth. Even the (bird) spirits themselves, when described as embarking on a journey, are said to *beburong*.[1]

In this area of deliberate augury, the birds play a dominant, almost exclusive role. The desirable omens vary between individuals and with the circumstances, but certain general principles are valid. The usual order for hearing, when an extended sequence of omens is required, begins with Nendak, followed by Ketupong, Beragai, Bejampong, Papau, Pangkas, Kutok, and, finally, Embuas. The sight of Lang may also be added in conclusion. However, as *Penghulu* Narok of the Upper Skrang said at the Simanggang conference: 'At the beginning, all say Nendak; but for the remainder, each man seeks his own' (*Pun Nendak magang; ujong ngiga ka diri*).

In seeking auguries those heard on the left and on the right are clearly differentiated. This does not seem to bear any relation to the assumed *bilek* arrangement in Sengalang Burong's longhouse, where Ketupong is said to live on the right side, presumably up-river, of Sengalang Burong[2] and Bejampong on the left. The residence arrangement is of liturgical interest and has no apparent relevance to practical augury. In almost all augury the left side omen should precede the right (*kiba dulu*). Left and right side omens are spoken of as couples, 'bringing husband and wife' (*mai laki bini*); while the number heard on each side is not usually the same, in a sense they correspond to each other as a series.

Since a greater number of calls heard on the left is believed to soften the soil (*maioh kiba ngasoh tanah lemi*) before farming, and more calls on the right are believed to harden it (*ngasoh tanah kring agi*) (see below, p. 161), the consequent emphasis in augury depends on local soil conditions. A study during the 1963 and 1964 farming seasons showed that the following combinations were sought before initiating clearing of farm-land:

Nendak on the left	9	5	9	5	3	5
Nendak on the right	9	3	3	7	5	5
Ketupong on the left	2					1
Ketupong on the right	1		1	1		
Embuas on the right	1					

These series were in most cases associated with a single Beragai

---

[1] Freeman, 1960a, 70, n. 10, notes this also.

[2] As Harrisson (1965a, 7, n. 16) stresses, there is not much evidence for Freeman's contention (1960a, 77, n. 9) that Ketupong actually lives with his wife in Sengalang Burong's *bilek*; on the contrary, this would appear improbable in the light of certain myths and *pengap*.

call on either side—here called *burong basah*, 'moist bird', as an omen for rich, moist soil. Before setting off on a journey or expedition the combinations were:

Nendak on the left	2	2
Nendak on the right	3	5

plus Ketupong on the right if the direction were up-river; on the left, if down-river. Where expeditions go deep into the jungle, Beragai, left or right, is auspicious, and Bejampong on the right. During head-hunting, Pangkas on the right, Bejampong on the right, and Kekih on the right could be considered good omens. In this context Ketupong on the left, Kekih on the left, and Embuas on the left would be bad. Nendak, left and right, usually suffices before building, although Ketupong, Beragai, and Pangkas may be used also.

Only in connection with the birds sought before moving longhouse to another district (*burong pindah*) is there a conscious association between women and the left, men and the right. The bird is usually Nendak, although some Iban use Ketupong too. The number of calls differs with the place and circumstances, but these combinations were recorded in the Delok, Undup, and Lemanak:

Nendak on the left for the women	9	7	5
Nendak on the right for the men	9	9	9

The *kayu burong* symbolizing these calls were divided between the *ruai* for the right-hand calls (for the men) and the back of the *bilek* for the left-side calls (associated with the women) (see above, pp. 110–1).

With the exception of a general pattern and certain characteristics usually associated with a particular bird, there are few hard and fast rules in Iban augury. Much inevitably depends on the circumstances and situation. The 'cool bird' Nendak, almost always a good omen, since coolness implies health, is not equally good before the burn. Papau which 'blinds' can have opposite interpretations according to which party suffers the blinding. Experience provides the ruling criterion. For example, a particular series successful in one farming season might well be repeated annually, provided external factors remained more or less the same. Interpretation in Iban augury is only partly *post hoc, propter hoc*, where the 'consequences' of remembered bird-calls in the past may be applied to new situations.[1] The bird calls do not themselves produce an effect. The call is a message of advice or warning from Lang, conveyed with a purpose, although sometimes only subsequent experience may reveal its true meaning. Again, the omen itself cannot hurt the Iban (*nadai tau nganu*). If he chooses, he may ignore Lang's advice, in which case he takes on his own head (and perhaps others') the consequences of his behaviour. The true significance of an omen lies in how the Iban responds and whether he and his *bilek* prosper.

Divination

As a means of establishing man's general relationship with the spirits and in divining future prospects and events, the Iban also use the liver of a young domestic pig. (Wild boar, although regularly hunted and eaten, is not considered suitable for this purpose.) Having been ceremonially fed, washed and combed, the pig, which may be either male or female, is speared to death by cutting the jugular vein, and the stomach neatly opened with a sharp knife. The liver, still warm, is extracted by hand and placed on a *sabang* leaf for inspection. The pig itself is eaten afterwards, except in connection with the less usual rites in which it is offered to the spirits. Divination by pig's liver is used most commonly to foretell either the course of a serious illness or farming prospects, although it is not confined to these ends and may be intended to divine the future of any activity related to the relative standing of men and spirits. The interpretation varies with the circumstances.

The Iban see the liver as divided into various parts and each of these parts is identified with the territory and/or interests of men on the one hand and spirits on the other.[2] When viewed from the ventral side, the liver divides into three lobes: the right lateral, right central, and left lateral lobes. The gall-bladder lies between the last two. The relative condition of the lobes and gall-bladder,

[1] Freeman, 1960a, 79, n. 15, says *post hoc ergo propter hoc.* It is, however, relevant to remember that the Iban do not regard the birds as 'causing' the events and circumstances they predict.

[2] Hose and McDougall, ii. 63, identify different parts of the liver with actual human territories and interpret these as significant for inter-human relationships. This does not at present appear to be usual Iban practice, although in the context of head-hunting the *antu* lobe may be associated with the enemy.

ligaments, fissures, and prominences, colour, spots and nodules, all have significance for the Iban interpretation. The gall-bladder, called *empedu*, is particularly important. The meaning depends on its length, colour and the direction in which it lies. It divides the left central lobe, *dulang gayu*, which represents the *menoa* territory of men (*mensia*) from the right central and right lateral lobes (*teresit*) which are associated with the spirits, *antu* (central) and *petara* (lateral). The caudate lobe is called *terentong* and this may also be significant in divination.

The basic division is between the side of men and the spirit side (including the spirits of the dead). A sinew at the base of the gall-bladder (*empedu*) which apparently links the lobes at either side, becomes a bridge (*andau*) between men and *petara*. In illness this provides the benevolent spirits with an approach to the sick man (*jalai petara ngabas iya*), without which they cannot attend him and the patient will die. In farming it signifies that what is good in the current season will be good in the following one also.

If the gall-bladder (*empedu*) itself is full and bloated (*kenyang*), this may mean a good harvest, but in divination for the sick it is a bad sign. Especially if it is also dark in colour (*chelum*). On the other hand, a thinner, paler gall-bladder is considered good in cases of sickness, particularly when the base is strong and firm (*pun iya ganggam*). All will then be well with the patient: 'even if he is already half dead, he will recover' (*stengah nyawa iya ka mati ka pulai ka grai*). If the gall-bladder is particularly long, this means in farming divination that he who has had plentiful harvests in the past will continue to do so and, similarly, the man who regularly has a poor yield will have poor seasons in future as well. It may also be associated with long life. In sickness, however, it has a very different interpretation. If the gall-bladder is long it implies that the spirit of the sick man is 'already a long way from us' (*udah jauh ari kitai*), which is tantamount to saying that he has left the territory of the living. If, however, the gall-bladder (*empedu*) is pointed (*tajam*) and lies directed towards the lobe associated with men, this is a bad sign in all circumstances. It signifies that other forces are against us (*masih ka ngelaban*). In illness this means a very slow recovery; in farming it is certain that there will be setbacks and misfortunes.

The condition of the right lobes is also important. Since these 'belong' to the spirits, it is not a good sign if they are marred by sinews or fissures. In particular, if the right central lobe is prominent it could be understood to mean that 'the *antu* are too close and liable to fall upon the Iban' (*antu kelalu damping lalu ninggang Iban*). This would be the interpretation during sickness or before a dangerous undertaking like a head-hunting (*gayau*) or similar expedition when the Iban confront the *antu*.

If the first liver examined is equivocal or suggests an undesirable interpretation, it is usual to kill a second pig or even a third. If, after that, the significance continues negative, the Iban would, if possible, abandon the proposed undertaking entirely, or else abandon hope. Although the Iban have assured me this has been known to happen, it did not once occur in my experience, although the liver of a second pig was not infrequently examined.

Most adult Iban have some knowledge of divination and study the livers which are presented for examination. Real experts (*orang pandai*) are few; there is not always one in a longhouse. These offer their opinion only when specifically asked. Limbang, for example, explained once that, to judge by the liver he was shown, it was quite obvious to him that a sick Delok child would die, but since the others seemed satisfied with it, he said nothing. The child died.

X. SICKNESS AND HEALING[1]

WHILE *adat* in the broad sense constitutes the norm of universal behaviour, particular groups, be they human, spirit, or animal, have their particular *adat* (see above, pp. 111 seq.). In theory, were all to observe meticulously their own *adat*, there would be less sickness and mishap, but sickness and undesirable happenings would not vanish entirely since the *adat* of one group may conflict with that of another. Thus sickness and death among the Iban may be the outcome of legitimate *adat* behaviour on the part of an animal or spirit only very loosely, if at all, related to Iban conduct. More usually, however, these states result from breaches of *adat* on the part of those afflicted, members of the *bilek*, or others in the community, who have disturbed the universal order and caused a 'heated' or 'feverish' condition (*angat*).

Minor ailments are a partial exception. Unless they become serious or recur, colds (*renga*) for instance, headaches (*pedis pala*), or ordinary stomach upsets (*pedis prut*) are not attributed to the spirits or thought due to breaches of *adat*. The treatment of such complaints is usually medicinal. Blood-letting is also practised in cases of localized aches and pains, such as headache and backache (*pedis blakang*), and to cure bruising. To take an example of headache treatment at Rh. Ancheh. One temple, the right, where the pain was said to be worse, was pierced parallel to the eye and as soon as the blood flowed freely a piece of paper was rolled, placed against the wound, and lit. This was then covered with a bottle and the suction created within the bottle drew blood. The process was repeated three times first on one then on the other temple. In a case of backache blood was let from below the shoulder blades. Both men and women without specialist qualifications were seen to administer the treatment. But with these minor exceptions, sickness and sudden or early death are believed to follow from a disturbance of the *adat* order. Apart from death in old age when the grandchildren are growing well and the continued identity of the *bilek* has been secured—and to some extent death in infancy— death is the ultimate calamity. Serious or chronic illness, consistent

---

[1] This chapter has been published in slightly different form (Jensen, 1972).

lack of success in farming, hunting and fishing, a portentous
or disturbing dream, or other experience are similarly seen as the
work of the spirits. All are thought to require a response to determine the reason for spirit involvement and, if necessary, propitiation for a breach of *adat*, satisfaction for infringing a spirit's rights
or the meeting of a spirit's demands. In this the *manang*, or healer,
(see above, pp. 63–4) has an important role to play.

Morris (1967, 197 seq.) describes the Oya Melanau counterpart,
a-bayoh, of the Iban *manang* as a 'shaman'. To the extent that he
sometimes goes into a trance, thus moving into another psychic
state, the Iban *manang* can also be called a 'shaman' in accord-
ance with a common definition. Harrisson and Sandin (1966, 38
and *passim*) say 'doctor'; Harrisson (1965a, 33) states that he
would 'prefer "shaman", though on some narrow definitions he is
not exactly that; and he is often a lot more. . . . It would be nice
if we could call him "Doctor" and use this as a name prefix,
leaving obscure . . . whether he is medico, philosopher, ethno-
botanist or abortionist.' The *manang* have also been called 'priests'
in early accounts;[1] and in recent ethnography Wulff (1960, 130)
speaks of the Ngaju *basir* as 'priests' and relates these to the Iban
manang. But they do not function as priests in any normal sense
of the term and shaman or simply 'healer' is probably the best
description in English.

The person of the *manang* in Iban society has been the subject
of considerable interest from the time that travellers first described
the Dyaks[2] to recent anthropological accounts. The *manang*'s role,
however, is more limited than has sometimes appeared to be the
case from early descriptions and to judge by the contemporary
emphasis; Howell and Bailey's dictionary, for instance, has more
than three full columns on *manang* (1900, 99–100) while, as already
stated, the entire entry under 'lemambang' reads 'a patron saint'.[3]
It is, none the less, extremely important, and was perhaps still
more important before the Iban became superficially aware of
European medicine.

The *manang*, as someone capable of intercourse with the spirit

---

[1] For example. St. John, 1863, i. 73, as quoted above, p. 63.
[2] Low, 1848, 175; St. John, 1863, i. 73, etc.; Perham's writings (included in
Ling Roth, 1896); Gomes (largely quoting Perham's material), 1911 and 1917;
Howell, 1900, and in contributions to the *Sarawak Gazette*. See also the
anthology of papers on Sarawak subjects published by the Borneo Literature
Bureau, 1963.   [3] Howell, 1900, 92; see above, p. 61.

world may be a person of some power in the locality where he operates. Usually his influence is confined to a limited area, though the reputation of certain exceptional *manang* may extend more widely. But although known for his achievements when effective, the *manang* is not otherwise a man of consequence or status in the community. Nor did I come across an instance of a *manang* who was also an augur (*tuai burong*) or headman (*tuai rumah*). On the contrary, the expression 'to be like a manang' (*baka manang*) is derogatory since it implies that a man grows insufficient rice for his *bilek*. Children are scolded for imitating a *manang* lest they become like one; and children themselves poke fun at a *manang* in the open when he is disadvantaged in the bright light and they have the security of numbers and the option of an easy escape. In the terms of normal Iban values, the *manang* is not a success. Success is measured largely in plentiful harvests, and the *manang*, who has frequently to be absent from his farm, is rarely a successful farmer, although his own farm-work may be supplemented by the labour of others given in lieu of payment for his services. Since a good name among men is also associated with physical prowess and skill in felling, hunting, and on expeditions, the *manang* is seldom a man of standing. The majority of *manang* suffer or have suffered from a physical handicap of which blindness or poor sight is by far the commonest, and a characteristic associated with the *manang*. While the *manang* may not enjoy the prestige of a respected position in Iban society, he is nevertheless likely to be widely known and feared by many. This is partly because the Iban acknowledge their need for a *manang* in certain circumstances, and partly because a human being at times so intimately associated with the spirits carries some of the attributes of spirit power or has the aura of it.

It is not unknown for an Iban to aspire to be a *manang*. The aspirant is likely to be a person of some intelligence and sensitivity —those I encountered were—and, while this is not invariably the case, he or she may suffer from a physical handicap or disability. To aspire to be a *manang* is one thing; it is another to be called. Mandoh of Rh. Sa in the Lemanak had for some years hoped to become a *manang* but he never received the necessary authority from the spirits. Others may be chosen against their will. To refuse would mean taking the consequences of spirit disapproval upon oneself, one's *bilek* and one's community. As mentioned above (see above, p. 120), Sara of Silik in the Kumpang was called to be a *manang* although she claimed she did not wish it. It is a vocation. The Iban is summoned in a dream which is said to involve experiencing himself in a new way, commonly in the dress of the opposite sex. A man, for example, dreams that he is wearing a skirt (*bekain*) and has his hair in a chignon (*besanggol*). In the dream he is summoned perhaps in the form of a riddle to perform certain tasks. Assuming his initial response is correct the aspirant is taught, principally through dreams, the functions of his office under the supervision of Menjaya Raja Manang, spirit ruler of the *manang*. The spirit calling the Iban remains his familiar spirit, his contact, guide, and helper in the spirit world. This is the only recognized apprenticeship; an Iban cannot 'make himself a *manang*' (*manang ngaga diri*). However, the novice may supplement his spirit training by receiving practical instruction, and even the tools of his profession, from an established *manang*. In this case the senior *manang* is likely to be a relative. Although the activity has been claimed as hereditary, there is little recent support for this beyond the common Iban disposition to follow in the footsteps of his father or a close relative (*purih*) in exercising special functions where his own proclivities coincide with the nature of the office.

Earlier accounts laid particular stress on the different grades of *manang*. There are three of these: *manang mata* literally 'unripe', in other words an apprentice not yet fully qualified, *manang mansau*, the 'ripe' or qualified *manang*, and finally *manang bali*. This distinction is now less important, although certain rites may be performed only by specifically qualified *manang*. The highest grade of *manang* is the *manang bali* for which exceptional qualifications and elaborate and costly initiation offerings are necessary. This state, described as man transformed into woman, is now virtually unknown, but it may have been commoner in the past. Low (1848, 176 *et al.*) obviously regarded the phenomenon as usual among the Iban and St. John (1863, i. 73) mentions it also; Gomes (1911, 180) on the other hand, encountered it only once in seventeen years among the Iban. The tendency apparent in Gomes's experience half a century ago is borne out by recent enquiries.

The *manang bali* is sometimes described as a hermaphrodite,[1]

---

[1] There is, however, no specific suggestion other than Low's report (1848, 177)

sometimes as a transvestite, a man who has adopted female dress, lives like a woman, and may even take a 'husband'. The sex-change element has long fascinated those writers who described the *manang*. It is apparently not exclusive to the Iban; a similar phenomenon occurs in South Borneo among the Ngaju (Wulff, 1960). The vocationary dream which is said to involve a trans-vestite experience is relevant. Equally significant may be the myth which concerns the spirit ruler of the *manang*, Menjaya Raja Manang, who is the antecedent of all *manang*. Menjaya Raja Manang was originally the brother of Sengalang Burong but on becoming the first *manang* and curing the wife of his/her brother, changed sex, and was called Manang Bali Menyadi Aki Sengalang, Raja Menjaya ke Betalaga Baroh Rekong. Changing sex roles may serve the purpose, although not articulated or per-haps even recognized, of granting the transvestite, homosexual, or hermaphrodite a legitimate social place, but more important in the present context is its significance in spirit terms. The Iban recog-nize the *manang bali* as a man, but he lives like a woman. In a society where the sexual roles are clearly, if not dogmatically, defined, this sets the *manang* apart from normal people. As such he observes the characteristics of neither sex; he is neither true man nor true woman, implying that he does not belong fully to the world in which Iban men and women live. While exhibiting some aspects of male and female human behaviour, he also belongs partly to another world, the world of the spirits.

This ties in with the other characteristic attribute of *manang*: their physical disability, in particular, their blindness or poor sight. The world of men and the spirit world are associated with certain opposite values: visible and invisible, light and darkness, and so forth, a list which includes seeing and not seeing. Men, for example, see during daylight, but cannot see at night when the spirits see. Thus the blind man who cannot see by day like an ordinary Iban is credited with spirit sight. The physical handicap of blindness in this way becomes an asset in dealings with the spirit world, indeed enables the *manang* to see the spirits where others cannot. There is a basic difference between the properties of a *manang* and those of a *lemambang*, the other Iban religious practioner to move among the spirits (described above, pp. 61–3).

that the *manang* be physically incapable of fatherhood—a view which Low himself did not share.

The *lemambang* performs his role only during occasional major rituals and may exercise other important functions in the community. Since they would incapacitate him in his day-to-day existence, he assumes the opposing properties associated with life in the spirit world only symbolically when intoning the *pengap*. The *manang*, on the other hand, practises regularly and often at short notice. His daily life, his place in the community and his own person are identified with being a *manang*.

While divination by pig's liver may serve to indicate the prospects of a patient, it is not thought to further actual recovery. The *manang*'s role is to make the correct remedial action possible; to achieve this he must establish the spirit cause of sickness, spirit motives, and spirit involvement in the case. Thus his basic function is diagnostic. The *manang* has first to determine the nature and site of a complaint, the condition and whereabouts of the patient's *samengat*, and, by entering the spirit world, discover what is required to re-establish the right relationships, thus restoring the *samengat* in health to its owner.

The *manang* is equipped with a 'medicine box' (*lupong*), which contains a variety of objects including pieces of tusk, wood, root, stone, crystal, and glass. Some are thought to be fossils and they look as if they are. Perham mentions the use of imported glass marbles (quoted in Ling Roth, 1896, i. 272–3); this is not improbable since any object might serve which had been revealed in a particular way and was believed to be vested with spirit properties. The most important is undoubtedly the quartz crystal *batu ilau* or 'seeing stone', in which the *manang* perceives the *samengat*.

A *manang* may inherit much of his stock-in-trade from a relative, if he was heir to the business, or from an older *manang* who instructed him during his novitiate; he obtains other items from his fellow *manang* during the initiation ceremony, and, finally, he may himself acquire additional items for his *lupong*. These are normally revealed in a dream, as is the case with *pengaroh* and similar articles or charms (see above, p. 121). The revelation is usually in the form of a riddle: the *manang* may be instructed to look for river snails (*ngiga tekuyong*) or bamboo-shoots (*tubu*), but instead of snails or bamboo-shoots he finds a fossilized stone or other distinctive object. Next day at the place in question the dream is confirmed by what he discovers. These dreams and discoveries which lead to the formation of his medicine box are all part of the *manang*'s apprenticeship. The *manang*, incidentally, is not expected to carry his own *lupong*. When he is called for any but very minor rites, he is fetched by a member of the patient's *bilek* and his *lupong* is carried for him.

The rites which the qualified *manang* may be asked to perform vary greatly in relation to the gravity of the circumstances and the patient's stature. The lesser rites are by far the most common: commonest of all are those undertaken after a disconcerting or bad dream (*jai mimpi*), such as when an Iban experiences a landslide, is divorced, capsizes in his boat, is crippled or wounded, or, worst of all, dreams of his own death or the death of one of his family (see above, pp. 117 seq.). A bad headache or other pain on waking or during the following day confirms the implications of the dream, which is seen as a confrontation with a spirit. The spirit may merely intend to give a warning, to express a wish, or it may have evil intent. To avert the consequences of ignoring the spirit's intentions, advice, or desire, the *manang* is summoned to discover the meaning of the dream, and this enables the Iban to take appropriate action or precautionary measures.

Almost as common are the rites at time of sickness vaguely attributed to the crossing of a spirit, euphemistically called *pansa utai* ('something passed by'), which refer to an *antu* spirit encounter (see above, p. 102) of which the Iban may not be consciously aware. The *manang* is expected to effect a cure by identifying the cause and determining the site of the complaint in his *batu ilau* before removing from the patient's body the physical token deposited by the spirit. The token may be almost anything: a piece of wood or cloth, perhaps translated as a squirrel's hair (*bulu tupai*) or the sting of a bee (*butoh manyi*). The rite itself is simple. The *manang* bites the blade of a knife for strength; he also puts to his mouth the objects from his box with which he strokes the patient to discover the place of the illness. A mixture of blood from a fowl, turmeric, and spittle is prepared as ointment. The same treatment is used in other straightforward cases or where the cause is believed to be similar: when, for example, a child does not grow normally, or imprecise symptoms are experienced over a period of time.

When simple rites fail in their objective, the *manang* is asked to perform more elaborate ceremonies like those used in instances of serious or recurrent sickness. Although these vary, the principle remains the same. It is based on the belief that in grave cases the *samengat* leaves the body; the gravity of the illness relates directly to the distance that the *samengat* has gone. The *manang*'s task is to discover the whereabouts of the *samengat* and return it to its owner; this he attempts in various ways. He may use a small effigy (*pentik*) of the Iban fully dressed with a headcloth and ornaments to draw back the straying *samengat*. He may try to entice it back with the promise of offerings. But if, as is commonly believed to be the case, the *samengat* has been led away by a spirit, the *manang* has first to identify the spirit which has the *samengat* in its power, then cajole, coax, persuade, or force it into surrendering the *samengat* to its human owner. Sometimes he merely wills the spirit off, sometimes he barks at it, or endeavours to frighten it away, ultimately he may attempt to kill it: *bunoh antu* (mentioned above, p. 102)—the name often given to an important *manang* rite—and in this process he invokes the aid of his friendly and familiar spirits.

The pattern of the rites is essentially the same, revolving, as they do, around the pursuit of the *samengat*. The central feature is the *pelian* chant intoned on the *ruai* of the *bilek* afflicted. The rite begins after dusk; the *manang* always operates at night when the spirits are believed to be abroad. The accessories sometimes differ in detail but they consist principally of a spear (*sangkoh*), blade up, tied with leaves, and the *lupong* box set out below. Above is a plate, at the foot a cup upside down, and midway a basket containing rice, tobacco, and chewing ingredients. During the course of the rite the *ruai* and *bilek* and the objects found in and around them are all given symbolic significance in relation to the *manang*'s journey in search of the errant *samengat* (which invariably involves crossing a stretch of water between this world and Sebayan). The *tempuan* passage part of the *ruai*, for example, signifies the reach of a river (*rantai*), the space where the women pound rice (*lubang indu nutok*) a waterfall (*wong*), the door of the *bilek* is a great stone (*batu*), the *bilek* itself a lake (*danau*), a plate (*pinggai*) becomes a vessel or boat (*prau*), the bush-knife (*duku*) a paddle (*sengayoh*), the poultry-feed cup (*jalong manok*) a bailer (*penimba*), a bead (*marik*) on a string the line to tie the boat (*tali prau*), and so forth. The *manang* may pursue the *samengat* in a *prau* over water or try to catch it with a cloth, as if he were net-fishing (*nyala*).

The *manang* begins the *pelian* itself by describing parts of the house—by way of preliminary orientation. Then with increasing speed, he moves towards the spirit world. Amidst the lavish, decorative verbiage of the *pelian*, much of which is incomprehensible to the ordinary Iban, the *manang* articulates his moves first to identify the spirit which controls the *samengat*, and then his efforts to obtain its release. Walking round and round, and becoming faster and more voluble as he intones the *pelian*, the *manang* may in difficult cases fall suddenly to the floor in an apparent state of trance (*luput*). When he does, he is covered with a *pua* cloth. In these circumstances it is believed that the *samengat* of the *manang*, exercising its special relation with the spirit world, travels in pursuit of the patient's *samengat*. The *manang* finally revives as if waking and rises with his right hand clenched. He appears to be holding something. This is the *samengat* which he returns to the sick man through the crown of his head. When the *manang* does not go into a trance, the *samengat* may be discovered on a part of the patient's body—a toe, for instance—but it is invariably returned through the crown of the head. The climax, when the *manang* recaptures the *samengat* (*nangkap samengat*) occurs towards dawn. The rite concludes with the waving of a sacrificial fowl over the sick Iban, accompanied by an appropriate invocation. A pig is sacrificed in the most serious cases.

These rites begin on the sick man's *ruai* and only if the *manang* fails to find the *samengat* here, does he enter the *bilek* (*tama ka bilek*). To enter the *bilek* represents a much deeper penetration into the territory of Sebayan and exposes the *manang* to considerable risk. It is said that a *manang* may die if he ventures that far. His position, reputation and power, however, rest on his special relation with the spirit world which grants him access where others would not be admitted or dare to go. When the *samengat* is only a short distance into the spirit world, it can easily be recalled, but its recall becomes progressively more difficult when the *samengat* is said to be in the tomb (*sungkop*) or, ultimately, housed among the spirits (*udah berumah ka antu*). In easy 'cures' the *manang* removes the cause of illness without going into a trance, as he does in the more difficult cases; in the most serious he is unable to function alone and more than one *manang*, even three or four, take part in the rite. In extreme cases, when it is obvious that the patient cannot live, the *manang* will refuse to act. And he has no role in mortuary rites.

Whether or not a cure is effected, the *manang* is paid for his services. The fee (*upah*, also called *sabang*) varies from a small plate (*pinggai*), a piece of iron (*besi*), and one dollar or its equivalent for a minor rite, to a *mandoh* jar, a piece of iron and the equivalent of two dollars for a somewhat more elaborate rite, to an Iban woven cloth (*pua kumbu*) used as a door covering, a better quality *mandoh* jar, iron, and the equivalent of at least five dollars for a major ceremony, to still more for the most demanding occasions.

The very elaborate rites, although recognized and named, are extremely rare. During three years in the Lemanak only one took place to the best of my knowledge. This may have been partly due to the presence (at a distance of one or two days' journey) of a qualified medical practitioner, although at times of serious illness or in circumstances which they found disturbing the Iban preferred to be at home in the setting of their own *bilek* family and longhouse community.

3a. *Biau* fowl-waving ceremony

3b. Examining a pig's liver

4a. *Piring* sacrifice offered in a raised support

4b. Harvesting rice

PART 3

XI. ATTITUDES TO RICE[1]

The Rice Cult

RICE to the Iban is not just a crop. Hill rice cultivation is their way of life, and has become, for the Iban, their hallmark. In the first place, rice cultivation distinguishes men from animals (*jelu*). Iban folklore includes a story about Manang Gagak who once held a meeting with representatives of the animal world to plan the approaching season, but although the animals all admitted that they enjoyed eating rice, they were unwilling to accept the discipline of planting and to contribute the necessary labour. In the second place, rice cultivation also distinguishes the true Iban from his remote predecessors who lived in the jungle like wild beings (*baka antu*, literally, like '*antu*', that is, not entirely human) or 'primitive tribesmen' (*baka Punan*, literally, 'like the Punan'—nomadic hunters who do not cultivate crops). In the third place it sets the Iban apart from other tribes and races who do not farm hill rice according to the same conventions and beliefs. And, finally, the Iban believe their agricultural methods confirm their spirit pedigree, since their faith in the cult and knowledge of the techniques of shifting hill rice cultivation are derived from the spirits.

It is not merely that the Iban prefer the taste of hill rice which they frequently refer to as 'sweet-flavoured' (*bangat manis*) or 'delicious' (*nyamai*) in distinction to swamp or imported varieties —they consider these tasteless (*nadai asai*). It is not merely that they find working in a jungle clearing more congenial than swamp cultivation—and Iban terrain is more suited, also, to dry rice farming. It is not only the fringe benefits of readily available firewood,

---

[1] The substance of this and the following chapter has appeared in a preliminary paper: 'Hill Rice' (Jensen, 1965).

timber for house-building, timber for boats, wild vegetables, fruit, fish, and game, all of which occur more commonly in interior jungle areas than they do in the permanently settled, developed, and intensively cultivated districts down-river. These factors contribute to the Iban preference, but the underlying reason for their attachment to hill rice culture is the inherited way of life. As the Iban frequently say: 'Our *adat* is hill rice cultivation' (*adat kami bumai*).

For generations rice has meant the difference between eating and going hungry, between health and sickness, prosperity and deprivation, even life and death. It was and is to the Iban his very existence (*pengidup*—'life itself') and the focus of his activities. This is reflected in the elaborate vocabulary associated with all aspects of rice cultivation. Not least interesting, although similar to expressions found throughout South-East Asia, are the distinct words used to describe rice in its various forms: it is called *padi* when unhusked and as a plant in general, *brau* (or *bras*) when husked, and *asi* when boiled; puffed rice is *rendai* and sweet glutinous rice *pulut* or *puli*. Numerous distinct stages in the growth of the rice plant also have their special terms (see below, pp. 184–6), and even rice storage bins are classified in fifteen or more categories.[1] Farming land too has its own terminology,[2] and

---

[1] Names of bins, classified by diameter:

(1) *Engkabai*—from the shoulder (where the pack strap goes) across the chest to the finger tip.

(2) *Penigong antu*—from outside the shoulder across the chest to the finger tip.

(3) *Simpai ibang*—from the top of the upper arm (where people used to wear armlets) across the chest to the finger tip.

(4) *Simpai*—from (just above) the elbow across the chest to the finger tip.

(5) *Penyiko*—from the elbow itself across the chest to the finger tip.

(6) *Tumpa umang*—from the middle of the forearm across the chest and to the opposite finger tip.

(7) *Tumpa raja*—(bracelet of wealth) is slightly larger than (6).

(8) *Dekoh*—from the wrist across the chest to the finger tip.

(9) *Pemalit insak*—from the hollow (*sirang*) at the base of the thumb across the chest to the finger tip.

(10) *Lilih minyak*—from the outside edge of the palm or fist across the chest to the finger tip (this is the part where oil on one's hand always runs to).

(11) *Tinchin*—from the finger, where a ring is worn, across the chest to the finger tip.

(12) *Sapemantok burong*—(the bird's beak), from the middle joint of the finger, across the chest to the opposite finger tip.

(13) *Sapemeda*—a fathom, from finger tip to finger tip with the arms stretched out sideways.

[*Notes 1 (continued) and 2 opposite*]

bamboo varieties,[1] for example, are elaborately distinguished partly in relation to their uses, but partly also as indicators of soil and growth conditions.

Reverence for Rice

The spirit of rice (*samengat* or *antu padi*) which is 'just like one of us' (*baka kitai tu samengat padi*) is accorded the utmost reverence and respect. The spirit of rice has almost human responses and is consistently sensitive to human behaviour. Rice is described in terms of human moods and attitudes: it is 'unhappy', 'feels unwanted'—Iban women 'take pity' on small grains while harvesting,[2] it 'catches cold', 'needs company', and 'likes attention'. It is not merely that the *samengat* of rice constitutes a parallel concept to the *samengat* of man, but, in the last instance, a question of actual identification with the Iban since the human *samengat* when it eventually dissolves into dew, is taken up into the ears of rice.[3]

It is forbidden at all times to 'hurt' rice and this is interpreted psychologically as well as physically. In most areas, until recently, the Iban refused to allow government officials to measure or survey (*nyukat*) farmland lest the rice resent the intrusion. A similar reason has often been given for not planting rubber trees: for fear the rice spirit should take offence and go away (*enggai ka samengat padi nyau*), which would have disastrous consequences for countless generations (*enda ulih utai brapa penurun*). It is thought inadvisable even to express satisfaction or take personal pride in an abundant harvest; instead of saying, as he might of another, that he has had a rich harvest (*bulih padi*), the Iban says

(14) *Sapengayak*—big enough to stretch out both arms and turn about without touching the sides.
(15) *Tau enggau betenun*—big enough for weaving in; the largest size.

There are also named categories to indicate the height of rice bins, defined by the corresponding part of the body of an Iban of average height.

[2] Virgin jungle is called *kampong*. After felling and farming, the progressive stages of regenerated growth are known as: *jerami, dijap, kakah, krukoh* or *pangkal, temuda, damun, pengerang*, and finally *rimba*, which is like 'old jungle' again. The words relate to the size and circumference of the growing trees.

---

[1] To name only some: *betong, buloh, payan, aur, muntih, gangging, temiang, engkalat* as well as the distinct 'striped' (*surik*) varieties.
[2] Freeman, 1955a, 53, para. 113, mentions an Iban woman taking pity 'on such small and imperfect *padi* plants'.
[3] See above, p. 108, also below, p. 189, where the wax-burning ceremony is described.

modestly of his own crop that there is 'enough to eat' (*chukop makai*). It is expressly prohibited (*mali*) to tread hard (*nujah*), kick (*ngindik*), strike (*maloh*),[1] or break (*matah*) rice on the farm or in the longhouse, except in the actual process of reaping (*ngetau*), treading out the ears (*ngindik*),[2] threshing (*nungkoh*), pounding (*nutok*), and milling (*ngisar*).

The fear of *puni*, which requires an Iban always to take a little or at least to touch any food or drink which he is offered, is especially potent with regard to rice. An Iban who is offered rice will invariably take some whether or not he has already eaten or is hungry. Rice in any form—unhusked *padi*, husked *brau*, boiled *asi*—may never be thrown away. If it is not eaten by the Iban, it is fed to the dogs, the pigs, or the poultry. Even the rice from an area of land which for some reason has become taboo to the Iban themselves is used as poultry feed. The Iban are particularly careful not to spill rice. Should this happen, they gather up the individual grains at once. If, however, rice is spilled where it cannot be retrieved, underneath the longhouse, for example, there is a special ritual to recall the spirit of the rice. A piece of firewood from the hearth (*papong lutik*) and water (*ai*) are offered through the floor to symbolize the rice spirit's path of ascent (*jalai antu padi niki ka rumah*). Simultaneously the Iban utters an invocation:

> *Niki di, antu padi, antu puli,*
> *Tu tangga undah di, lalau undah di.*
> *Niki ka rumah,*
> *Tansang, gelanggang, penepan, pencharan,*
> *Ngagai penindok, ngagai penudok di empu.*
> *Pulai ka tibang penampang,*
> *Ka sadau, ka dangau kitai empu.*

> Come up, spirit of rice, spirit of sweet rice,
> These are your steps and the rail for your crossing.
> Come up to the house,
> Your nest and your roost, your perch and your coop,
> Where you sleep, where you sit.
> Come home to the rice bin, bin of increase,
> To the storage loft, to our dwelling.[3]

---

[1] This is given by Freeman, 1955a, 67, para. 151, as a reason why the Iban refuse to use flails.

[2] *Ngindik*, to step, tread upon or kick, is also used in the specific, technical sense of treading out the ears, which is not forbidden.

[3] Freeman, 1955a, 29, para. 61, records a similar prayer.

Stellar Lore

The Iban were taught by Pulang Gana the rites and sacrifices appropriate to the initial stages of the agricultural cycle; and by Sengalang Burong they were instructed in the code of augury as an aid to agriculture. But although these assured them of the spirits' favourable attention, the Iban were not conspicuously successful hill rice farmers at first, partly, it is said, because they had no knowledge of the seasons of the year (*nadai betaun bumai*).

In the equatorial rain forest environment where seasonal changes are barely perceptible and the coming of monsoon rains variable,[1] the stars provide the most reliable guide to the time of year. The Iban have names for only a few constellations, and on the whole show a limited interest in astronomy. It is forbidden to count the stars; should an Iban even try, it is believed that he will die. The Pleiades, however, occur in Iban lore as Bintang Banyak. It is generally thought that they were originally seven sisters.[2] Some accounts maintain that one of the sisters committed incest and died pierced with a stake of *aur* bamboo; others that one tripped and fell to earth where she was smashed to pieces and became the great Kapuas lakes in the interior of Indonesian Borneo, near the Sarawak border. The Pleiades are the most important of constellations in Iban agriculture, but Orion is also significant. Another myth, which provides the background for the use of stars in farming, relates that the youngest of the 'three stars', Bintang Tiga, the Iban name for Orion, came courting to earth. Before he went back to the sky, he said to the Iban: 'You appear to have no use for us. If you were to marry me, all would be well for you.' He offered to teach the Iban the number of the months in the year and how they might remember this by tying knots in bark string; he also promised to explain the significance of the constellations and their place in the sky as an indication of the month and the corresponding phase of the rice cycle.

[1] Table 1, p. 9, makes this clear.

[2] Durrell, 1960, 103, mentions a belief in Rhodes that the Pleiades are really seven in number but 'we only see six because one, Sterope, hides her face on account of a misfortune that befell her; others say that her name was Electra, and she hides because of her grief at the fall of Troy'. Anthony Richards, in a private communication, recalls that according to Greek legend one of the Pleiades lay with Sisyphus and so was left out; in this connection he has drawn my attention to an observation of Robert Graves that the seventh star in the group became extinct towards the end of the second millennium B.C. (Graves, 1957, i. 154).

Early in June when the Pleiades, Bintang Banyak, appear above
the horizon (*tisi langit*) it is known as the fifth month and this is
the time to initiate the annual cycle and to perform the rites of
manggol, which precede the clearing of new farm-land. Work continues during the sixth month when Orion emerges over the
horizon. When the Pleiades have been seen at the zenith (*prabong
langit*) before daybreak and Orion is about to reach the zenith, it
is called the eighth month and is high season for burning off the
farms (*nunu*) and planting the rice seed (*nugal*). This takes place in
September. If, because of bad weather, the burning has to be
postponed, and the Pleiades have dropped again to the horizon
(*udah nisi langit*) before sowing, a poor harvest is to be expected
(*enda bulih*).[1]

[1] Some Iban also attach importance to sirius (Bintang Tangkong Peredah),
believing that rice sown after sirius has passed the zenith will not mature
properly (see Freeman, 1955a, 40, para. 83).

XII. THE ANNUAL CYCLE

The Rice Cycle

THE cycle of traditional agriculture follows a definite pattern. There is, however, some variation not only between one season and the next due to weather conditions,[1] but from one area to another, and even between longhouses in the same area. Clearing jungle for the new season's farms theoretically begins in June, firing of farm-land at the end of August or the beginning of September, followed by planting and the harvest in the following March. Table 30 indicates the actual range found in a small area. The four longhouse communities were all farming within a ten-mile radius of each other in the middle Lemanak. Rh. Sa and Rh. Nyambar considered themselves as 'earlier than usual'. Rh. Ancheh regarded theirs as a 'normal' season, and Rh. Li were, by general consensus, exceptionally late in planting.

The *gawai* celebration which usually precedes planting is a longhouse event but the individual *bilek* decides how soon after the rites it feels ready and content (*lantang*) to inaugurate ritual clearing at the farm. While members of the same longhouse community usually farm in close proximity and many farms actually adjoin each other, the precise timing of particular phases remains a *bilek* responsibility. Families have *bilek* prohibitions (*pemali*) as well as their own 'sacred' rice (*padi pun*) (see below, especially pp. 177 seq.) and charms (*pengaroh*) to influence the timetable. Table 31 shows how the main events of the 1962–3 season were distributed among four *bileks* of Rh. Ancheh.

The Preliminary Meeting

The first event of the farming season is the preliminary or farm meeting (*baum bumai*), which is normally held while the previous harvest is still in progress. All family heads (*tuai bilek*) take part

---

[1] During the crucial months of August (firing) and October (initial growth), for example, rainfall ranged from 5·22 to 18·45 inches in the 'dry' month of August and 5·81 to 13·12 in the first monsoon month of October (period 1951–5). See Table 1, p. 9.

TABLE 30

The 1961–2 Agricultural Cycle in the Lemanak

1961

15 April	*Baum bumai*: preliminary meeting	Rh. Nyambar
18 April	,, ,,	Sa
17 May	*Gawai Batu*: whetstone festival	Nyambar
18 May	,, ,,	Sa
18 May	*Manggol* rites to inaugurate clearing farmland	Nyambar
19 May	,,	Sa
14 June	*Ngintu Jalai Umai*: farm track rites	Sa
16 June	*Gawai Batu* and *Klingkang*: whetstone festival associated with health and prosperity festival for some families	Ancheh
18 June	*Manggol*	Ancheh
26 June	*Nebas* (clearing) completed by first families	Nyambar and Sa
30 July	,, by the last families	Nyambar and Sa
29 Aug.	*Nunu*: firing the farms	Sa
30 Aug.	,,	Nyambar
2 Sept.	*Betanam*: planting of catch crops	Sa
3 Sept.	,,	Nyambar
6 Sept.	*Nunu*	Ancheh
7 Sept.	*Nugal*: planting of rice	Sa and Nyambar
13 Sept.	,,	Ancheh
19 Sept.	*Nugal* completed	Sa and Nyambar
26 Sept.	,,	Ancheh
15 Oct.	*Paung padi* rites to promote growth	Nyambar
16 Oct.	,, ,,	Ancheh
18 Oct.	*Nugal* completed	Li
22 Oct.	*Mantun* (weeding) begins	Sa and Nyambar
28 Oct.	*Nugal* repeated on part of the farm due to devastation by pests. (This was admittedly quite exceptional and the cause of local comment.)	Li

1962

18 Feb.	*Matah padi* rites to inaugurate the harvest	Nyambar
19 Feb.	,, ,,	Sa
13 March	,, ,,	Ancheh
20 March	*Ngetau* (harvesting) completed by first families	Sa
25 March	,,	Nyambar
5 April	,, by last families	Sa and Nyambar
15 May	,,	Ancheh

and anyone interested may attend. This often includes the entire longhouse with the possible exception of the very young and the very old. (*Tuai Rumah* Nyambar said once of Rh. Sa: 'It is a very long house which makes a very long meeting!'.) The established community leaders, the augur, *tuai burong*, the headman, *tuai rumah*, and the area chief, *penghulu*, if present, and, in particular, anyone with a reputation for successful farming, do the talking.

TABLE 31

*Calendar of Main Events in the Agricultural Cycle 1962–3
of Four* Bileks *at Rh. Ancheh*

	Ancheh	Entalai	Rentap	Ngalang
Gawai festival	5 June	5 June	5 June	5 June
Manggol rites	7 June	7 June	7 June	7 June
Clearing proper	14 June	11 June	14 June	11 June
Clearing and felling completed	14 Aug.	13 Aug.	10 Aug.	14 Aug.
Firing	31 Aug.	31 Aug.	31 Aug.	31 Aug.
Planting catch crops	2 Sept.	3 Sept.	2 Sept.	3 Sept.
Dibbling and sowing begin	7 Sept.	7 Sept.	10 Sept.	7 Sept.
Dibbling and sowing complete	7 Sept.	12 Sept.	10 Sept.	10 Sept.
Basoh arang rites (to mark completion of planting)	27 Sept.	27 Sept.	27 Sept.	27 Sept.
Weeding begins	14 Oct.	13 Oct.	23 Oct.	25 Oct.
Paung padi rites (to promote growth)	16/17 Oct.	16/17 Oct.	16/17 Oct.	16/17 Oct.
Weeding complete	16 Jan.	13 Jan.	21 Jan.	15 Jan.
Matah padi rites (to inaugurate harvest)	27 Feb.	28 Feb.	28 Feb.	1 March
Berangkut (carrying home the rice) begins	26 April	23 April	6 May	25 April
Berangkut complete	13 May	11 May	24 May	11 May

At the meeting, it is decided, first, which area to farm during the coming season, and secondly, what bird omens are likely to be appropriate.

Although it is essentially a longhouse community decision, the *bileks* still operate as independent units and are permitted to opt out of the general decision should they wish to do so. This occurred, for example, at Rh. Sa during the 1961–2 as well as the 1962–3 seasons when two or three *bileks* decided not to farm in conjunction with the remainder of the longhouse community.

Finding Farm-Land

The day after the meeting, the *tuai burong* and community elders (*orang tuai*) leave at dawn to seek the omens (*beburong*) which they hope will confirm their decision. As already described (see above, p. 135), there are two restrictions (*pemali*): the first, against eating before setting out, and the second, against bathing—which applies equally to those at home in the longhouse. The party are said to be seeking jungle (*ngiga babas*) for farming, and when they approach the area which has been provisionally selected they squat by the track in anticipation of the desired bird-calls. The *tuai burong* may, if he wishes, bring with him an Embuas omen-stick (*kayu Embuas*) which he has collected on an earlier occasion. Embuas, the banded kingfisher, sometimes called *burong brat* the 'heavy' or 'loaded bird', is associated with success, especially on expeditions. As and when the bird omens are heard, the *tuai burong* pulls out of the ground, or picks up from those he has placed in readiness, the appropriate omen-sticks (*kayu burong*) with either his right hand or his left hand according to the omen, and places these carefully by his side.

If the Iban do not hear the bird-calls they had hoped to, they offer a simple sacrifice of sweet rice (*pulut* or *puli*), puffed rice (*rendai*) and *sireh* leaf, etc. on the track, and invoke the aid of Nendak:

> O ini Nendak,
> Nyadi aku tu minta tulong, minta pandong,
> Awak ka aku tu munoh babas,
> Ngiga tanah paya, tanah lemak

> O Nendak,
> I call for assistance, for ritual guidance,
> That I may go to work on the jungle;
> I seek rich land and fruitful.

Should they later wish a bird, in particular Ketupong, to repeat a call, they tap the sheath of their bush knife (*natok sarong duku*) or cough raspingly.

It is sometimes said that there should, ideally, be one omen-stick for each *bilek*, but it is usual to reduce the number of omens heard to small, odd numbers. And as soon as the desired number and type of auguries have been heard, a sacrifice (*piring*) is offered on both the left and the right side. The *piring* are at least threefold on either side, and placed on supports (*tresang*); they consist of the usual ingredients (see above, p. 79).

Auguries

When the Pleiades appear above the horizon before dawn (Bintang Banyak *pansut dipeda*) this identifies the moon as the fifth month or moon (*bulan lima*) and is a signal for the agricultural cycle itself to begin. A day or more before it is hoped to start work, the *tuai burong* and elders (*tuai*) go in the direction of the new farm site to look for further omens. These are sought near a clump of trees at the proposed farm area (*tempat bumai belayan*).

There is general agreement about the appropriate bird-calls, but considerable variation in the number and side, depending on local conditions, the desired state of the soil, and personal preferences. Since left side omens are thought to soften the soil (*maioh kiba ngasoh tanah lemi*), and more calls on the right have the reverse effect and harden it (*kanan ngasoh kring agi*) (see above, p. 136), the omens are sought accordingly. On particularly parched (*rangkai*) and overworked soil (*tanah kusi*) in the Lemanak area one year (1962), nine Nendak on the left were heard and three on the right; another longhouse in the same district that year heard seven on the left and three on the right. On the other hand, in the old Ulu Ai jungle in 1963, representative Iban chose three or five Nendak on the left and five or seven on the right.[1]

As the Iban state regularly and agreed in Simanggang,[2] Nendak is the first bird sought by all (*pun Nendak magang*) and, on fertile or good soil (*tanah manah*), many consider Nendak alone sufficient. But more often to round off the augury another bird is desirable especially if the soil conditions are not ideal, and in this choice personal predilections are strong. Ketupong, Embuas, and Beragai are all used; Beragai, called in this context the 'moist' bird (*burong basah*), is thought to have an effect like fertilizer on the soil (*baka dibri baja*). A particular 'combination' will be remembered if the subsequent harvest is good. Dadup of the Ulu Ai explained that after hearing five Nendak on the left and five on the right he harvested 117 full *lanji* carrying-baskets, which he considered a very satisfactory yield. Provided external conditions remained roughly similar, he preferred to repeat this particular 'combination'. It is even possible to reuse the *kayu burong* of a previous year, and this is occasionaly done if the harvest had been outstandingly good.

Reception of the Omen-Sticks

After the *piring* sacrifice has been offered, number and size according to the bird-calls, the *kayu burong* are brought back to the village. They are deposited first in the forge hut (*langkau repun* or *putan*). Use of the forge is of no special significance; it is simply

---

[1] See above, p. 136, for a list of various combinations.
[2] Ibid.

the most convenient place to keep the *kayu burong* until they are received into the longhouse with appropriate ceremony. If the longhouse community has no forge hut, as is occasionally the case, a shelter (*langkau*) is built for the purpose.

When a mat has been laid out (*tikai dianchau*) at the foot of the steps (*kaki tangga*), the *tuai burong*, in the company of other *tuai*, collects the *kayu burong* from the (forge) hut. He wears a knife at his waist (*nankin duku*) which symbolizes his approach to the farm (*laban ngelulu ka diri empu nurun ka umai*), bears a woven blanket (*pua kumbu*) and carries a *piring* sacrifice. He is escorted by women playing gongs (*betaboh*), lest they should hear other bird-calls which might be considered unfavourable (*burong jai*) for the occasion. The *kayu burong* are swathed in the blanket and borne alongside the *piring* to the steps which lead up to the longhouse. As soon as the *kayu burong* have been stood in a container, where they are supported by sticks to prevent their falling, they are offered *tuak* to drink (*dibri ngirup*). Meanwhile, two *piring* are prepared. The first of these is put with the *kayu burong* and then covered with a *pua*; the other is placed at the foot of the steps (*kaki tangga*). From halfway up the notched log (*tengan niki tangga*) the *tuai burong* (or another) performs a *biau* ceremony as an expitiation (*ginselan* or *sengkelan*): holding a fowl by the legs he waves it over the assembly before cutting its throat. In this case he touches with the blood first the *piring*, then each of the notches on the log leading into the house.[1] The steps (*tangga*) are also fed ceremonially with sweet rice (*pulut* or *puli*) and puffed rice (*rendai*).

The *tuai burong*, followed by the others, then touches with his feet in either order the *piring* at the foot of the steps and climbs up the log to the longhouse. The *kayu burong* are carried along the *tempuan* passage, which runs the length of the longhouse. They are placed in turn before the door of each family room (*dibai dudok ninting pintu bilek*). As they pass, the women scatter puffed rice about them and at each *bilek* they are offered *tuak* to drink and given a quid of betel nut and sireh leaf (*ilom pinang*) as well as puffed *sangking* rice. These are interpreted as an offering of value, the equivalent of money (*duit*) or silver bracelets (*gurang pirak*), and are intended to identify the family's prosperity with the prosperity latent in the *kayu burong*.

---

[1] No specific attention is paid to those parts of the *tangga* which are sometimes carved to represent human heads and genitalia.

Celebration and Division of the Omen-Sticks

The *kayu burong*, which should remain upright (*enda tau enda bediri*), are carried three times up and down the longhouse *ruai*—though this is not invariably done—then placed on the *ruai* opposite the *tuai burong*'s (often also the *tuai rumah*'s) *bilek*. Each family presents *tuak* and further *piring*. The *biau* ceremony is performed again: the *tuai burong* (or another) waves a fowl, cuts its throat, and touches the *piring* and those present with the blood. Afterwards the *kayu burong* (and *piring*) are once more covered with a *pua*.

There is often an invocation intended to scare away the malicious spirit of envy (*antu kapapas*) and call upon the good:

> *Oha, Oha, Oha!*
> *Nyadi di anang ngawa, anang ngeruga,*
> *Anang ngachau, anang rerigau.*
> *Nyadi tu piring asi, piring tumpih,*
> *Piring rendai, piring salai—*
> *Nuan anang ngalangga, anang ngeluah.*
> *Nyadi samoa utai ti jai, utai ti kebenchi,*
> *Ti tusah, ti kamah,*
> *Angkat tu di.*
> *Enti di ngalui ka tu, mati meh di!*
> *Parai makai, parai nyumai,*
> *Parai tindok, parai dudok.*
> *Nyadi samoa utai ti badas, ti kemas,*
> *Ranyur ka umai,*
> *Ngagai pangkalan, ngagai temian.*

> Now don't you make trouble,
> Upset or disturb us.
> This is an offering of boiled rice and rice cakes,
> Of puffed rice and dried food—
> Don't pass or oppose it.
> All that's evil and hateful,
> Works ill and is sordid,
> Up and away.
> And if you come past, may you die!
> Die eating, die cooking,
> Die sleeping, die sitting.
> Let all that is good, that is ready and able,
> Make straight for our farms
> And the site of our clearing.

Details of the ritual vary. It may be more elaborate. This is especially so if the full festival of the whetstones (*gawai batu*) is celebrated, which occurs frequently, but is not an annual event (see below, pp. 195 seq.). When the festival takes place new whetstones are blessed by Pulang Gana who is invited to attend. Whether or not there is a *gawai batu*, the proceedings conclude the following morning when the *kayu burong* are uncovered and divided (*bedua*) among the *bilek* families of the community. Each omen-stick is broken into short lengths of up to two to three inches and distributed. Every family receives a piece of each stick and these are tied together with red thread (*ubong mirah*) in two little bundles, the left-side auguries in one, the right-side in the other.

The Rites of *Manggol*

As soon as the *kayu burong* have been distributed, the Iban are free to proceed with the rites of *manggol*, which inaugurate the actual clearing of farm-land. No family, however, begins until it feels that it has the good will or blessing of the spirits—the state called *lantang*—and spirit approval is normally conveyed in a dream (see above, pp. 118 seq.). If, therefore, the head of the family (*tuai bilek*) or one of the senior members has dreamed during the night that he inspected his fish-trap (*bubu*) and found it full of fish, or climbed a tree with fruit in abundance, or swam across a wide river, taken to symbolize the strength and extent of the rice, this is interpreted as an auspicious dream, and *manggol* begins. If, however, any member of the family dreamed that he lost his hair, for example, or his teeth fell out, or has had any dream which could be classified as a dream of nakedness (*mimpi telanjai*) or one causing shame or embarrassment (*mimpi malu*), *manggol* is postponed. Until the family has had an affirmative dream, it is said 'not yet to be confident and content' (*bedau lantang*). If one of the *bilek* members has an unusually positive dream, then he or she is the first to slash the undergrowth (*dulu mantap babas*).

Once assured that the spirits have approved the undertaking, and, in practice, this normally occurs at the distribution of *kayu burong* or a day later, the Iban go in family units to their farms to perform the *manggol* rites. On the way their ears are stopped (*besedal pending*) to avoid hearing other undesirable bird-calls.

They take with them their *kayu burong* and all that is required for sacrifices and offerings. All *bilek* members participate, even children who cannot contribute actively, since it is thought that the fortune of one is the fortune of all. Both *manggol* and the rites which initiate harvest are matters for the *bilek* and must be attended by the man and his wife as well as their children if possible and other *bilek* members. In 1961, for example, an Iban insisted on his wife leaving hospital in Simanggang in order to take part, since he was convinced that the crop might otherwise be poor.

During *manggol* a number of *pemali* or *penti* restrictions come into force (see above, p. 113). These vary slightly from family to family, but among the most important at the farm are:

(1) *mali gali*, the prohibition against lying down, for fear the rice will recline on its side and not stand properly;

(2) *mali beklambi* or *bebaju*, the prohibition against wearing a coat or a shirt, for fear that the farm will be swathed in weeds;

(3) *mali nginti*, the prohibition against fishing with a hook, for fear that the rice will not prosper and smell badly 'like a fish' (*bau lang*);

(4) *mali mandi enti bedau datai di rumah*, the prohibition against bathing before returning to the longhouse, for fear the farm will not burn well when the time comes to fire it;

(5) *mali kemi enggau bira di tanah*, a prohibition against urinating or defecating on the ground, feared to cause offence.

On arriving at the farm site (*pangkalan*) the Iban selects a suitable tree. It must be latex- or sap-producing (*kayu begetah*), ideally *pudu*, or alternatively *tekalong*, *lengkan*, or the fruiting *arak*. With his left hand he scrapes away the weeds and undergrowth from a patch of ground close to the base of the chosen tree. He does this two or three times. Afterwards, in the same way, he does it with his right hand. Although in theory any member of the *bilek* family can do this, it is most commonly performed by the *tuai bilek*, who then places the *kayu burong* on the cleared patch and says a prayer:

> *Ngasoh tanah lemak, tanah luchak,*
> *Ngasoh tanah merema, tanah paya,*
> *Ngambi padi kami nyadi begili,*
> *Enda pitak, enda bepiak,*
> *Nyadi enga kaki sampai ka punjong.*

Make the soil fertile, make the soil soft,
Make the soil muddy and make the soil rich,
That our rice may grow in profusion,
Not heaped, not halved,
From the foot of the farm to the summit.

The left-side omen-sticks (*Nendak kiba*, etc.) are placed in position at the foot of the chosen tree, which is considered especially suitable if it has buttresses (*bandir*). The right-hand omen-sticks (*Nendak kanan*) are fixed into the tree where a cut is made (*silit kayu*) at the height of rice grain when ripe (*tuntun buah padi*). At felling, this tree is left standing. The *kayu burong* other than Nendak—Embuas, for example—may be set at the limits of the farm: the boundary with the adjoining farm (*entara*), the crest (*punjong*), the foot (*kaki*) and at the side (*rusok*).

After making a first symbolic slash, called *mantap pangkalan*, with his bush-knife (*duku*), the Iban places his ritual whetstones close to the ground. The whetstones themselves are carefully screened and sheltered (*dipantar*). Were they to be damaged, this would be a sign of serious misfortune, and in no case may they be disturbed by another Iban.[1]

After a *piring* sacrifice, which comprises the usual ingredients but must be topped by an egg, the Iban performs a *biau* ceremony. As he waves a fowl, which, in this instance, is specifically required to be female (*manok indu*), he calls on the spirits:

Oha, Oha, Oha!
Ngangau ka petara aki, petara ini,
Ngangau ka petara apai, petara indai,
Ari pendam, ari pencharan,
Ari rarong, ari santubong.
Aku tu manggol ka saharitu.
Minta tulong, minta pandong kita,
Minta sa minta kroa kita,
Kita ka nulong pandong aku,
Pulang Gana, Raja Sua,
Pantan Ini Andan,
Pinang Ipong, Sengalang Burong,
Mai pemulai pemumbai,
Batu padi, batu puli,
Batu asi, batu ai,

---

[1] See below, p. 168 and n. 1, where mention is made of the penalties incurred for disturbing the whetstones of another family.

Batu lingkau, batu brau.
Ngambi padi aku nyadi begili,
Rinda beserira, beranak ngeresak,
Mansang ngeregang, sabaka sereba,
Sarantak sarebak,
Ngambi padi aku nyamai dijapai, nyamai dipegai,
Ngambi enda langkang, enda singkang,
Ngambi nyadi raja, nyadi kaya,
Penoh langkau, penoh sadau,
Penoh gentong, penoh penurong.

I call upon the spirits,
The spirits of my grandparents,
The spirits of my parents,
From the graveyards, from the death-traps,
From the coffins, from the tombs.
I celebrate the *manggol* rites today.
I beseech your assistance, your ritual help,
I ask and implore you
Assist at my altar,
Pulang Gana, Raja Sua,
Pantan Ini Andan,
Pinang Ipong, Sengalang Burong,
Come back here bringing
The rice charm stone, the sweet rice stone,
The cooked rice stone, the water stone,
The maize stone and the husked rice stone.
Grant that my rice prosper,
And grow in profusion,
Grow quickly, increasing,
Be nourished and evenly flourish.
Grant that my rice be pleasant to handle, be pleasant to hold,
That it never run dry, ne'er go away,
That I may have wealth, and have riches,
My farming-hut full, my storage-loft full,
My rice-bin full, my farming-place full.

After this he kills the hen and arranges the sacrifice in either
two or three *piring*. One he places at ground level by the foot of
the tree where the *kayu burong* are, a second one by the whetstones
(*apa batu*), and for this he constructs a little shelter (*langkau*);
the third one is set on a raised support (*tresang dipanggau*) at a
height of five to six feet. If there are only two *piring*, one is placed
at ground level and the other on a raised support. Wherever the

piring, it is carefully fenced to forestall an ill omen: a snake, for example, passing over it (*mansa ular*) would imply poor yields for at least three years (*tetap tiga taun nadai bulih*).

If, as occasionally occurs, there are no *kayu burong* to inaugurate, that is to say, the *kayu burong* of an earlier year are being reused, the earlier omens are thought to remain valid and the season is hoped to follow the pattern of the previous harvest (see above, p. 161). Instead of the *kayu burong* ceremonial, a gold object (*mas*), which could be a ring (*tinchin*) or a gold tooth-covering (*ngeli mas*), for example, is offered at the farm base (*pangkalan*) together with a *piring* sacrifice, a bowl (*mangkok*) and a small jar (*anak benda*). The gold may be recovered after the harvest.

Clearing

When the rites have been completed the Iban cuts himself a wooden hook (*pengait*) for use in clearing and slashes a little undergrowth (*nebas mimit*). Were he to hear a bird, Ketupong, for example, or the sound of wild life (*jelu bebunyi*), he would stop and go home, otherwise he carries on slashing until he has sharpened his knife three times (*tiga kali ngansah*), then he returns to the longhouse. Throughout this ceremonial clearing the Iban uses his left hand; were he not to use his left hand, he would be in danger of extravagance or waste (*mali rua*). Women and young children also take part.

The knife (*duku*), the hook (*pengait*) and whetstones (*batu*), all remain at the farm site where they are carefully protected by wood and creepers lest they or the sacrifice should be disturbed by animal or other life. For an Iban to interfere with them constitutes an extremely serious offence against *adat*, with corresponding payment of compensation.[1]

The following day (*belanggang*: literally, following the cycle), farm work is not allowed. On the third day (*ngechol*: literally, 'go to and fro') clearing may start but only for a very short time, perhaps half an hour; no food is taken to the farm (*nadai mai asi*). On the fourth day (*ngundang*: to 'visit') boiled rice is brought (*mai asi*) and the Iban work up to the time of their mid- or late-morning meal, which is normally the main meal of the day. The fifth day

---

[1] A list of offences (and maximum fines) relating to rice farms (*pemali umai*) is found in Richards, 1963, in Iban, 54–6, and in English, 16–18.

they are said to 'work on the farm' (*turun*), and spend at least a full half-day. From the sixth day on, they work all day (*apus hari*). While the prohibitions apply to work on the farm, they do not exclude other work, and it is customary for the Iban to employ these days in catching up on other tasks which need doing in and around the longhouse in preparation for the season.

Farm Omens

During this period and for the first three full days of work, that is up to the ninth day, omens are thought particularly potent. Should a scaly anteater (*tengiling*), honey-bear (*jugam*), barking deer (*kijang*), mouse deer (*plandok*), or tarsier (*ingkat*) come into the cleared area while the Iban are sharpening their knives (*ngansah*) or eating (*makai*) or for that matter at any time, this would be considered a *laba* omen. As already mentioned (see above, pp. 133–4), the good fortune which this is normally thought to bring is in direct proportion to the Iban response.

The *laba* requires an offering, which may be eaten, but the heart and the liver must be burned by an Iban of another *bilek* who also cuts the flesh into small pieces (*krat*) according to the number of persons in the owner's *bilek* and hands these to the family, saying:

> *Tu meh orang mai tuah*
> *Ari tuan Selutan Laut Bunut,*
> *Ari Pulang Gana, Raja Sua,*
> *Ari Lang Sengalang Burong;*
> *Nyadi tu nuchoh di*
> *Bumai bulih padi,*
> *Ngayau nyadi brani,*
> *Nyadi raja, nyadi mensia.*

> This is the one who brings good fortune
> From the ruler beside the water,
> From Pulang Gana, Raja Sua,
> From Lang Sengalang Burong.
> Grant that you
> May harvest rice in plenty,
> May have courage on the warpath,
> Become rich, a man indeed.

This is accompanied by a *piring*.

The response to an omen (or dream) and the appropriate sacrifices, known as *ngintu burong*, are thought particularly difficult to judge in the case of a *laba*. Assuming that the Iban assesses accurately the wishes of the spirit, and responds to the omen correctly, it may lead to his flourishing exceedingly. Jalin, the father of Hermanus Assan,[1] for example, credited his becoming *penghulu* the same year to a particularly good *laba*. It is possible also to *ngintu* an omen just sufficiently to ward off the potential evil consequences. If, however, the *laba* has negative implications, or the response is not satisfactory, the consequences can be extremely grave. I was told of a man and his wife who both died seven days after two Tajai hornbills (*Rhinophlax vigil*) had fought at the new farm. They found the omen impossible to *ngintu* adequately.

If the Iban finds a dead omen bird or animal on the site of the farm before *manggol* has taken place, he must perform the *manggol* rites at that precise spot. If he finds a corpse afterwards, especially during the first days, it requires extremely careful ritual attention. He must then prepare three elaborate ninefold *piring*, and all *bileks* farming in the immediate vicinity take part in the rites. This could mean a plentiful harvest; but if the Iban ignored the implications of the omen and failed to show due regard, the consequences would be serious.

Although more important in the early stages, the arrival of omen birds, animals, and insects on the farm is significant throughout the season. Apart from the birds, and the animals mentioned above, vermin (*chit*), snakes (*ular*), bees (*manyi*), the locust varieties (*re*)*rioh* and (*re*)*rabi*, and *engkujut*, a hairy caterpillar, can all be taken as auguries, especially when the insects occur in large numbers, although they may lose their force if they become excessively common.[2] Whether these are good or bad omens again depends mainly on the response. 'The omen creatures appear because they want to be fed' (*kabuah burong pansut laban ka minta makai*) and events develop accordingly.

Apart from omens on the farm itself, there are *jaloh* omens which advise the Iban when not to work. Should he, for example, hear the call of a barking deer (*kijang*), sambhur deer (*rusa*), or honey-bear (*jugam*) while it is still dark, he does not go to work on the farm that day (*diau hari nya*); if he hears the call at dusk he does not go to work the following day (*diau hari siti*). These could be interpreted as warnings that there are evil spirits out hunting for men (*antu ngasu mensia*). The restriction, however, is not obligatory. The omen advises the Iban that if, in spite of it, he goes to work—in particular to his farm—something is liable to go wrong. The Iban might be bitten by a snake, cut himself, or fall ill, or his rice may fail to prosper. Similarly, if an upright dead tree (*punggu*) falls on a day when there is no wind (see above, p. 133), it is believed that ten times the strength or number of persons could achieve nothing, and no work is done that day.

Ngintu Jalai Umai

Special rites are also associated with the path which leads from the longhouse to the area chosen for farming. These occur at the beginning of the season when slashing is already under way: Rh. Sa, for example, performed the rites on 14 June in 1961, some three weeks after *manggol* (see above, Table 30, p. 158).

Augury in the early morning initiates the proceedings and the birds sought are Nendak and, usually, Beragai and/or Embuas. The rites at Rh. Sa were conducted by Lanchai, *tuai burong* for the season, and on that occasion he heard to his satisfaction seven Nendak on the left and nine on the right, as well as one Beragai call on the right and one Embuas on the left. The *kayu burong* are taken together with a *piring*, a pig and a fowl, to the point at which the new farm track leads from an earlier established path. Women beating gongs accompany the procession of longhouse members; as on other occasions, the gongs are intended to prevent further inauspicious omens being heard once the tokens of good omens are already in hand. Gong-beating ceases on arrival at the path intersection, and preparations for the sacrifice begin. The *piring* are arranged in three portions: one for the Nendak omens heard on the left, one for those heard on the right, and a third for the Embuas call. The seven Nendak calls on the left were, on this occasion, accorded a *piring* divided into two sets of seven each; the nine on the right received two sets of nine. The *piring* for Embuas was subdivided into one triple portion. Beragai was thought to be covered by the others and did not receive a separate *piring*.

The fowl was used to *biau* and waved over the *piring* in the usual manner. Then the pig was killed and its liver inspected. An unsatisfactory liver would have been thought to imply a poor harvest, pests or sickness, and had the liver been poor, the *tuai burong* would have tried a second pig. After examining three livers and finding all inauspicious, the longhouse community might have decided to change the farm site (see above, especially p. 140). On this occasion the liver proved satisfactory, and the carcass of the pig was buried beside the *piring* as an additional offering before the party returned home, once again to the accompaniment of gong-beating.

Felling

For a number of weeks the Iban clear undergrowth (*nebas*; in old jungle the clearing of low growth is called *tasau*, vb. *nasau*). The precise time varies with the age of the jungle, the size of the farm, and the number of active workers. When everything which can be cut with a bush-knife (*duku*) has been slashed, work begins on felling the larger trees: the usual word for this is *nebang*, but for virgin jungle it is called *berimba*. The Iban prefer to use a traditional adze (*bliong*) in primary forest and an axe (*kapak*) in secondary forest. During felling a *kayu burong* representing Beragai, which may be either a left- or a right-side omen, is sometimes affixed to the sheath of the Iban's bush-knife. Since Beragai is known as the bright, clear bird (*burong tampak*), it is thought that the omen-stick will ensure that falling trees are seen in time, thus preventing accidents.

Special rites are used when the Iban attempt to fell particularly large or hard trees in old jungle. In order to 'make the tree hollow' and therefore easier to fell, a blow-pipe (*sumpit*), which is hollow and hard, is set beside the tree. This is the focal part of a rite in which a *piring* is offered. Subsequently the stump of the tree is shown respect (*ngintu*) and covered with a *pua*.

Minta Panas

When the undergrowth has been cleared and felling is complete, the battlefield of dead trees and bushes is left to dry out in the sun before firing. Clearing and felling may be finished weeks before burning and this is the time when the Iban work on their farm huts (*langkau umai*) and make other preparations for the planting season. It is also a period of suspense because so much is known to depend on the weather. Ideally it is a time of little or no rain, when the hot sun acts like blotting paper on the fallen vegetation, leaving it dry and brittle for the burn. A good burn offers the best guarantee of a good harvest; as the Iban say, 'if the farm burns well the rice grows well' (*enti angus ka amai nyadi padi*). It is, however, not uncommon for rainfall to be relatively heavy during August, the crucial month. In 1955, for example, 18·45 inches fell at Lubok Antu[1] and most communities had poor or late burns. Early September is said to be the best season for firing and it is generally believed that if the burn is long delayed there will be a poor harvest. For good yields the burn should occur between the time that the Pleiades (Bintang Banyak) reach the zenith and the time that Orion (Bintang Tiga) does, usually when the two constellations are in balance, that is, equidistant from the zenith (see above, p. 156).

During wet seasons when the time for the burn is approaching or has arrived and the fields are still far from dry, special rites take place to petition dry, hot weather (*minta panas* or *minta ari*), which in Sarawak means the absence of heavy rain. These usually take place at the farm in the subsidiary longhouse (*dampa*) or most suitable of the farm huts (*langkau*). A jar (*tajau*) from a *bilek* other than the *tuai*'s is placed on the *tuai*'s *ruai* where it is dressed like an Iban woman. The jar is decorated with beads (*sementing, marik, rantai*) and an ornamental silver corset (*rawai*) and covered with a skirt of Iban cloth (*kain kesumba*) which must be red. The dressing is done by a virgin who has not yet menstruated (*indu bedau datai kamah*, literally, 'a woman to whom dirt has not yet come') and it is essential that she be considered pretty. During the rites no one in the community may wear black or white clothing lest clouds appear in the sky and cover the sun, nor should they wear darkly dyed materials for fear of rain.[2] When the jar is ready, each

---

[1] See above, Table 1, p. 9. The average for August over five years (1951–5) was 9·89 inches. 1949 was also 'exceptionally wet' according to Freeman, 1955a, 45, para. 94; more examples could easily be given.

[2] Another example of Iban 'homoeopathic magic'. Freeman, 1957b, 156, uses the expression when discussing the prohibition against breaking wind (*pemali kentut*, which he spells *kentuat*) while engaged in pottery; the noise is said to resemble breaking pots and is, therefore, forbidden.

bilek prepares and offers a *piring*. Where bamboo containers are used, these are inscribed with representations of the sun, moon, and stars. They are placed all together in one large plate on top of the jar before the *biau* ceremony when a fowl is killed and its blood smeared on the jar in expiation (*ginselan*). This is followed by a *pengap* incantation which continues throughout the night and the two nights following.

The Iban may not spend long bathing in the river and in no case may they wet their clothing during the three-day period in which prohibitions remain in force. Outsiders are not allowed up (*enda tau ditiki orang*), nor are longhouse members allowed to converse with visitors (*enda tau bejako enggau temuai*). It is forbidden even to wander about for fear of meeting someone by chance. Women are not permitted to look for vegetables (*ngiga lauk*), neither are they allowed to spread out rice for drying (*nyembi*) nor to pound it (*nutok*). The restriction on black clothing is especially potent if anybody emerges on to the *tanju*, into the open. The Iban threaten during the rites that if the weather is not dry and hot the jar will be broken. When the weather has been sufficiently sunny for three successive days, it is the custom to burn the farms and only then is the jar undressed and returned to its *bilek*. This is accompanied by a small celebration attended exclusively by longhouse members.

In an alternative ritual, the Iban use a large tree which is also treated ceremonially and offered a sacrifice.[1]

Firing

If four hot days follow each other, this is called *ari indu*; if there are six successive days without rain, *ari laki*, and the fire is expected to be fierce (*mangah*). The number of hot dry days is carefully counted and as soon as the fields are considered sufficiently parched the Iban take the decision to burn and advise each other accordingly. This is most important since contiguous farms must be carefully watched or fired together. It is a serious offence, involving payment of heavy compensation, to lose control over a

---

[1] Freeman, 1955a, 45, n. 2, records the use of an open-weave fishing basket in a ceremony designed to achieve the same end. The 'Rain Spirits' were invited to fill it, but if they failed to fill it, they were asked to stop the rain completely.

burn and accidentally set fire to a neighbour's farm, especially if
the flames reach his ritual whetstones.[1]

It is propitious on the night before burning to dream that the
spirits have given their approval. And there are certain restrictions.
Before firing it is forbidden to bathe (*mali mandi dulu*) lest the
field be cold (*enggai ka reban chelap*). Even those back at the longhouse may not follow the Iban practice of bathing at noon since
this could be associated with wet weather. It is forbidden to eat (*mali
makai*) lest the field already be sated (*enggai ka reban kenyang*);
and, if there is a 'skylight' opening (*silak atap*) in the hut or house,
it must not be closed (*enda tau ditutup*) lest the path of the wind
be obstructed in fanning the fire (*enggai ka nadai jalai ribut muput
ka api*). A ritual whetstone may be put out in the sun to make the
field hot so that it will burn well. To hear Bejampong before firing
is also auspicious; Nendak, on the other hand, otherwise almost
invariably a good omen, is likely to imply a poor burn because of
its reputation as a 'cool bird' (*burong chelap*).[2]

Firing itself takes place in the heat of early afternoon. As soon
as the Iban are ready to arrange themselves with torches (*sempun*)
at strategic points, a feather of the argus pheasant (*bulu ruai*) is
set alight to the words of a simple prayer:[3]

> *Nya nuan api misti trebai*
> *Baka bulu burong ruai;*
> *Jampat meh nuan makai reban tu.*
> *Chiribut, chiribut, chiribut . . .*

[1] See above, p. 168, and n. 1 reference to Richards, 1963, 16–18 and 54–6.

[2] See above, p. 131, where, however, it is pointed out that Nendak's positive
reputation in general might imply a satisfactory harvest in spite of an indifferent
burn.

[3] Freeman, 1955a, 46–7, n. 2, records a different version addressed primarily
to the wind:

Oh Wind Spirits where are you?
Oh call, oh summon your kith and your kin, your offspring, your people all;
Come from Sarawak and from Pontianak,
Come from Brunei, and the far away ocean.
Oh dash yourselves against my farm,
Fling up the debris, tear up the roots,
Roll over the logs, hurl down the buttress roots,
Devour outright, devour utterly,
Leave no remains, no stumps unburnt,
Leave not a branch, not a bough but in ashes.
Kor-r-r-r . . . Wind and fire
Do your devouring!

> Fire, you must fly
> Like the feather of the pheasant;
> Devour with haste the felled field.
> Chiribut . . .

To the accompaniment of the beating of a drum (*gendang*) which is thought to encourage the flames, they set fire to the field.

The quality of the burn varies enormously. In 1962 an Undup house, Empadi, abandoned nearly half their farm-land because of an exceptionally poor burn, which is not altogether uncommon during wet seasons. In 1963 some Lemanak longhouses had the much rarer experience of parched farms because the burn had been too fierce (*angus tekelalu*).

No work may be done the day after firing the farms. This is in token mourning (*diau ka ibun*) for the animals, birds, reptiles, and insects which may have perished in the flames—especially the snakes, *kendawang* (*Cylindrophis rufus*) and *tedong*, the cobra, which are traditionally helpful to the Iban on head-hunting expeditions and in farming. A *piring* sacrifice is offered at the farm as an appropriate sign of respect (*bebasa*). Other offerings may be made at the farm perimeter to feed and fend off the spirits of wastefulness (*antu rua*).

In the case of a bad burn the Iban sometimes try to stack the half-burnt branches and tree-trunks to clear the farm, and for re-burning. *Ngebak*, as this is called, is seldom very useful, and not a popular expedient.

Nyulap, which precedes the planting proper of catch crops, involves sowing cucumber seed. The Iban say a prayer as they do this with tightly-closed eyes (*mejam ka mata*). They call on the benevolent spirits to

> *Nampal mata chit pipit*
> *Mata ulat sempepat.*
>
> Cover the eyes of vermin and sparrows,
> The eyes of larvae and flies.

Then, two or three days after the burn, the women start in earnest to plant catch crops: cucumber (*rampu/entimun*), maize (*jagong/lingkau*), mustard 'spinach' (*ensabi*), and others. When planting maize, especially, it is thought important that they should use a basket with a close weave (*raga pisit*); if it has a wide weave (*jarang*) the maize will be sparsely covered.

Dibbling and Sowing

Within a week, normally on the fifth day after firing, planting of rice begins. Though not invariably so, this is commonly a cooperative activity (*bedurok*) (see above, p. 50, esp. n. 1); three or four closely related *bilek* families plant their own and each other's farms in turn. The division of labour is usually clear. The men dibble (*nugal*) using a dibbling stick (*tugal*) which is five to six feet long of a circumference convenient to hold but flaring out at the bottom to make a hole approximately three inches deep and from one and a half to two inches in diameter. The women sow (*menih*), carrying the seed (*benih*) in a small sowing basket (*keban*).

During *nugal*, as the Iban refer to the planting period, there are a number of *pemali/penti* restrictions. Of these, six are particularly important:

(1) The prohibition against cutting nails or hair (*mali beguntin*), which would symbolize the rice being eaten by locusts or other pests;

(2) The prohibition against plucking eyebrows (*mali mantun bulu mata*), which is understood to symbolize the rice being plucked out by birds;

(3) The prohibition against forging iron (*mali ngamboh*), which would make the rice hot and feverish (*angat*) as if exposed to intense heat;

(4) The prohibition against clearing away creepers (*mali matah akar*) which would expose the farm to vermin, monkeys, deer, and so forth;

(5) The prohibition against binding or tying (*mali ngebat*) as used in Iban weaving, which is thought to symbolize the stifling or tying up of rice (*baka padi ditanchang*); and

(6) The prohibition against barking a tree (*mali engkalong kayu*), because in taking bark, the edges are ragged or uneven as though nibbled by vermin (*dikrit chit*).

Other restrictions follow local traditions and vary between communities. For example, at Rh. Sa in the Lemanak, it was forbidden for the Iban to take a pig's tail, and consequently a pig, to the farm, since it was thought that the rice stalk would be bare like a pig's tail if they did. Some families are forbidden to eat pork or to handle a pig (which may be related to the pig's tail prohibition); some are forbidden to chew betel nut. Finally, while the Iban are

planting a farm and immediately before, no one else may put a
foot in the farm area (*ngindik tegalan*), and in no circumstances
may a passer-by ask them what they are doing—which is otherwise
the normal Iban usage.

On the first day of *nugal* the Iban set off at early dawn as soon as
Orion has come to rest (Bintang Tiga *badoh bejalai*). They are
especially careful with the baskets (*uyut* or *sintong*) containing
rice seed. Under no conditions may these be allowed to topple
over, and if the string should break it would mean dire misfortune
or death to the *bilek*. Rice spilled in this way may not be gathered
up (*nadai tau gumpol*), and should it be spilled the only possible
solution would be an elaborate *piring* ceremony in the hope that
the spirits might accept that as propitiation.

On arrival at the farm, the Iban place the baskets containing
rice seed at the centre. They are meticulously arranged with the
sacred rice (*padi pun*) in the middle. The *padi pun* is that portion
of rice seed belonging to a *bilek* family which has been set aside,
blessed, and surrounded by special ritual safeguards; it may not
be bought or sold and particular meaning attaches to its inheritance.[1] The sweet rice (*padi pulut*) is placed on the down-river (*ili*)
side surrounded by the other rice varieties. All are firmly supported, carefully guarded, and protected by a covering (*kibong padi*).
A *piring* sacrifice is prepared which corresponds in number to the
'birds' used at *manggol* and any relevant omens heard while
clearing. The *piring*, comprising the usual ingredients, is divided
into three portions. The first of these is placed below the cover
(*kibong padi*) together with the rice seed. The second is put on
a raised support above it. The third is fixed in the jungle which
borders on the farm and has been touched by the flames at burning
(*serarai*) as an offering to the spirits of greed, extravagance, and
wastefulness (*antu rua*).

A small pig is killed and the liver inspected. And a fowl is
waved over the sacrifice and party in the *biau* ceremony accompanied by an invocation (*sampi*). *Sampi nugal*, the invocations used
at planting, are normally long. The shortest of those recorded has
one hundred lines, the longest over four hundred. They vary with
the conditions and the skill of the practitioner, who is not necessarily the family head (*tuai bilek*). The pattern, however, remains

---

[1] Freeman, 1955a, 51, para. 110, calls the *padi pun* the 'plinth . . . upon which
the whole elaborate fertility cult of Iban agriculture is based'.

fairly similar: it is common first to mention important local names,
people who are known to be successful, and their guardian spirits:

Aku ngangau petara orang Gelong,
Petara apai Bungah enggau Ngadang,
Orang Titok ulu petara Li enggau Mujang,
Orang Titok ili petara Omar enggau Kudang.

I call upon the spirits, guardians of Gelong:
The spirits of Bungah's father and Ngadang;
At up-river Titok, the spirits of Li and Mujang;
At Titok down-river, the spirits of Omar and Kudang.[1]

The introduction is often followed by a section which seeks to
dispel evil spirits and those capable of cursing and harm. They
are threatened with the power of the *piring* and are told to be on
their way:

O sapa kita
Ti tau angkat di ujong mulut,
Tau telah di ujong dilah,
Tau jako di ujong kuyu,
Tau tepang di baroh rang,
Engka jai ati tau jai jari
Mansa umai, mansa empalai,
Mansa padi, mansa puli,
Suyak ditinggang tuak,
Mati ditinggang ragi,
Danjan ditinggang bram,
Rempi ditinggang tumpih,
Parai ditinggang rendai.
Niteh ka mata hari padam, mata hari tengelam,
Niteh ka mata hari parai, niteh ka mata hari sulai,
Niteh ka mata hari tumbang, niteh ka mata hari petang.

Whoever of you (with ill intent)
Can raise the point of his mouth,
Can speak with the tip of his tongue,
Can talk at the edge of his cheek,
Can curse below the jaw,
Of evil heart or evil hand,
Pass the farm and pass the garden,
Pass the real rice, pass the sweet rice,

---

[1] Gelong and Titok are Lemanak place-names; the other names are those of
locally known leaders and successful farmers.

May you be broken by the *tuak* brew,
Killed by the leaven from the rice beer,
Crushed by the rice cakes,
Die victim of the puffed rice.
Follow the sun in its setting, the sun in its sinking,
Follow the sun in its dying, the sun in its death,
Follow the sun into burial, follow the sun into darkness.

Then, usually, the invocation follows the pattern of a journey to advise other Iban, other races (including Chinese and Europeans) and the spirit world of the project in hand. Eventually, it reaches the 'territory' of Pulang Gana:

> *O kami tu nugal saharitu*
> *Nugal ka emperan, nugal ka tegalan* . . .
> *Kami ingat ka jako smaia dulu, ingat ka pekat,*
> *Ingat ka smaia, ka Pulang Gana,* . . .
> *Meda nuan empu bukit* . . .
> *Meda nuan empu tanah* . . .
> *Meda nuan empu dunya* . . .

> We are here today to plant rice,
> Plant rice on the flat land, rice on the farm-land,
> [Plant different kinds of rice].
> We remember the words of the ancient promise,
>   we remember the agreement,
> We remember the promise and Pulang Gana.
> Yours are the hills . . .
> Yours is the land . . .
> Yours is the earth . . .

There is no offence, the invocation continues, because the *adat*, the established order and code of agreement, is being followed. The offerings have been prepared. Pulang Gana is, accordingly, invited to attend: 'Come out here, uncle, Pulang Gana' (*nurun, aya, Pulang Gana*)—where 'uncle' is used not to indicate relationship but respect for an elder. The welcome of Pulang Gana is always central to the prayer. After Pulang Gana has been called, the omen birds are frequently invoked:

> *Udah aku ngangau ka Pulang Gana,*
> *Baru aku ngangau ka burong.*
> *Ni Nendak, bulu burak* . . . ?
> *Ni di Ketupong* . . . ?
> *Ni di Beragai* . . . ?
> *Ni di Papau* . . . ?

After calling upon Pulang Gana,
I call upon the birds.
Where are you, Nendak, the white-feathered . . .?
Where are you, Ketupong . . .?
Where are you, Beragai . . .?
Where are you, Papau . . .?

And after the birds, the Iban may summon the spirit of the wind:
'Now I call upon the Wind Spirit' (*baru aku ngangau ka bunsu ribut*). At last he addresses himself to the rice spirits:

> *Baru aku ngangau ka bunsu padi:*
> *Baru aku ngangau ka padi entayu tanam di munggu,*
> *Padi sangking tanam di tinting . . .,*
> *Padi putong tanam di darong.*

> Now I call upon the spirits of rice:
> I call upon entayu rice planted on hillsides,
> Sangking rice planted on the ridge . . .,
> Putong rice planted in the valley.[1]

The invocation concludes with the common prayer for a full life-span, health, and comfort (*gayu, guru, grai nyamai*).

Planting begins when the introductory rites are complete. If a member of the family is believed to be particularly 'green-fingered', to have 'healthy hands which make things grow' (*chelap jari, utai ka nyadi*), he or she is the one to begin. Normally the senior hereditary member of the *bilek* (*pun bilek*) or head of the family (*tuai bilek*) begins. The order of planting the various rices is important, but varies according to local tradition and conditions. If the planting is to be done in a day, the sacred rice (*padi pun*) is planted first, then the less sacred *padi sangking*, followed by the normal varieties (*padi taun*), the quick-ripening *padi muda*, and finally the sweet, glutinous *padi pulut*. When planting is spread over several days the order is: (1) *padi muda*, (2) *padi taun*, (3) *padi pun*, (4) *padi sangking*, and (5) *padi pulut*. Like the focal and sacred *padi pun*, these are not specific varieties. *Pulut* refers to the sweet, glutinous rices; *muda* are quick-growing; *taun*, average. *Sangking* is the name given to the particular variety which a *bilek* adopts as its own special rice. *Sangking* varieties may be acquired in more usual ways, but, ideally, they are associated with a spirit

---

[1] Individual names given to varieties of rice which are distinguished by the Iban, here used in a poetical manner, hence the usual 'puting' is replaced by 'putong' to rhyme with '*darong*'.

experience.[1] Lanchai's uncle, for example, experienced a serious flood during which he had a dream and was told by a spirit to gather rice seed from the base of a flooded clump of *aur* bamboo when the waters receded. He did this and named the rice *aur*. This was the origin of his particular *sangking*, a white *semambi* rice. Close to the sacred *padi pun* the Iban plant their 'magic' plants, known as *sengkenyang*. The mythical origins of *sengkenyang* are associated with Pulang Gana, and the plants are believed to watch over, protect, and serve the needs of the rice—hence they are known as *indu padi*, 'mother of the rice'. Several species of plants called *sengkenyang* by the Iban have been examined and identified by a member of the Sarawak forestry department; he considers the word a collective name for all *indu padi* varieties.[2] The existence

[1] A miraculous revelation of rice believed to be the gift of Pulang Gana occurred in 1955 and attracted widespread attention. For a full account see Jamuh, 1955.

[2] B. E. Smythies, quoted in Richards, 1963, 40–1: 'According to the Ibans in Sungei Bena (Sut) there are seven species of sacred plants associated with their padi cult and planted round the *padi pun*:—

(1) *Jungkal* (*Sengkual*) (Richards calls this *singkenyang* but in the Sungei Bena the Ibans use this as a collective name for all the *indu padi* species and do not use it for any individual species).

    Eurycles amboinensis, Loud., a bulbous herb of the family Amaryllidaceae. Found wild on the shores of Malaysia and cultivated by the Malays as a plant of magic. Sir Hugh Low (Sarawak, 1848, 273) calling it *bunga si-kudip* and *bunga si-kenyang*, states that the Dayaks plant it yearly with the rice, because they consider it ensures the success of the rice crop, and they dig it up at the end of the season. . .

(2) *Pantak* [Richards calls this *jungkal*]

    Sansevieria trifasciata, Prain. An African plant of the family Liliaceae, introduced to Malaya many years ago. Several species of the genus were at one time the chief fibre-plants in some parts of Africa, and the fibre was known as Bowstring Hemp.

    The recorded Malay name is *lidah buaya*, a curious name for Malays to use, as they believe that the crocodile has no tongue.

    The Ibans say that this plant has the magical power of blinding anyone who trespasses on a farm and attempts to steal something.

    A striking plant, easily recognized by the long narrow soft leaves banded dark and light green. Commonly grown in pots in Kuching.

(3) *Seli-lali Cymbopogon citratus*, Stapf.

    A genus of aromatic grasses. This species is known as Lemon Grass or Citronella grass. Easily recognized by the strong smell of mint or citronella from the crushed leaf. A graceful tufted grass, leaves 3′–4′ long, narrow, saw-edged, dropping over gracefully to the ground.

    It very rarely produces flowers. The Ibans credit the flowers with the magical property of conferring great strength on anyone who wears them on his body as a *pengaroh*.

[Note 2 continued opposite]

of *sengkenyang* was mentioned already by Low (1848, 274). He writes that

the order Amaryllideae . . . is only represented by one species of Crinum, which is found on the muddy banks of the river. By the Sibooyoh Sea Dyaks, this plant is called Si-kenyang. By the Dyaks of the southern river, the roots of this bulbous plant are preserved with jealous care, being always taken up when the padi is ripe, to be planted again with the seed padi in the following season. . . . These and other Dyaks assert that the padi will not grow unless a plant of the Si-kudip (as called by Dyaks of the southern branch of the Sarawak river) be in the field. . . .

Among Iban hill rice farmers this is still true.

Basoh Arang

When all families in the longhouse have completed the planting of their farms, the rite which terminates the planting prohibitions takes place. This is known as *basoh arang*. A little burnt wood, charcoal (*arang*), is taken from the farm and mixed with a few grains of rice which have been set aside while planting the *padi pun*. The *tuai burong* leads the proceedings, and, as soon as all families have prepared *piring* sacrifices (which may be anything

Its origin cannot be traced to any known wild species of grass, but it is believed to have originated in Malaysia, where it has been grown for a very long time. Skeat recorded in 1898 that Malays plant it in a corner of the rice field to protect the crop. . .

(4) *Entemu Curcuma zedoaria*, Rosc.

A genus of rhizomatous herbs of the family Zingiberaceae, found in Asia and throughout Malaysia.

Best-known is *C. domestica*, the Turmeric. *C. zedoaria* is known as Long Zedoary or Round Zedoary, and is considered to be a native of north-eastern India. . .

(5) *Chekur Kaempferia galanga*, Linn.

A genus of herbs of the family Zingiberaceae, found in the tropics of the Old World.

Chekur is a herb of India, cultivated throughout Malaysia. It is a small plant with short stem and flat, spreading, plain green leaves, 3 to 6 inches across.

The rhizome is aromatic and is an article of trade. It is also medicinal (prescribed for chills in elephants!!). . .

(6) *Japar*

Looks like a small ginger. Not yet identified.

(7) *Tapak antu gergasi*

Not seen, but from the description a species of cactus, or a spiny Euphorbia.'

from three to ninefold), he waves a fowl in the *biau* ceremony and
says:

> *Nyadi kami tu basoh arang*
> *Udah tembu nugal.*
> *Nyadi lelaki tau manchak, tau nimbak,*
> *Tau ngarut, tau ngelibut,*
> *Tau munoh urar, matah akar,*
> *Mayong engkalong.*
> *Nyadi ke indu tau ngikat, tau ngebat. . . .*
> *Rumput mati, padi nyadi,*
> *Padi bauh, rumput mansoh.*
> *Kami tu bulih padi sakayu rumah nyentok ka tisi spiak.*

We are here to wash charcoal
Having completed the planting.
Now may men spear, and may men shoot,
Plait rottan handles, stop up holes,
Kill creeping snakes, and cut down creepers,
Clear and cut bark.
Women may tie and weave *kebat*. . . .
Death to grass-weeds, growth to rice,
Rice flourish, grass-weeds perish!
May there be plentiful rice for all the longhouse from
    one end to the other.

He washes his own hands symbolically in a bowl of water which
also contains the charcoal and rice seed. First he throws water
against the wall that 'the rice may be close and thick like the wall'
(*ngambi ka padi rapit baka dinding*), then against the posts of the
longhouse that 'the rice stems may grow to the size of a post'
(*ngambi ka pun padi besai tiang*). While his hands are still wet he
should not touch his head lest the rice be small like the individual
hairs (*takut ka padi mit rambar baka rambar bok*). After the *tuai
burong*, other members of the longhouse wash their hands in the
charcoal water.

Stages in the Growth of Rice

The growth of rice is observed and expressed with meticulous
attention: a great many stages are recognized and named (as mentioned above, p. 152):

(1) *Jelimut, mansang kadiri ari lubang tugal*: nasal hairs, just
    showing from the planting hole.

(2) *Nyarum, baru merekah, pansut baka jarum*: as a needle, just splitting and growing out like (the point of) a needle.

(3) *Nyangkoh, ngerembai daun ujong*: as a spear head, the end of the leaf opening out.

(4) *Ngiku pipit, leboh daun iya udah nipah tanah*: as a sparrow's tail, when the leaf touches the ground.

(5) *Ngelanggai, daun nyau chuit, nyau ka rebah*: as a cock's tail-feathers, the leaf sticks up and (the end) droops.

(6) *Bayam ribut*: plaything of the winds.

(7) *Tungkat daun diri; daun nyau nipah tanah, pagi hari lemai hari bediri ga iya*: standing up like a prop; the leaf touches the ground but morning and evening it stands up straight.

(8) *Ngelamun batang anak, batang iya nyau dibalut daun iya empu*: hiding the stalks of the sprouts, the stem is wrapped about by its own leaves.

(9) *Basah kain dandong, enti bejalai seblah padi ngena kain simpul baroh, samoa puting iya basah*: tall enough to wet a sarong, if you wear a long sarong and hitch it up as you walk in the rice (still below the knee) the end of it will be wet.

(10) *Basah kain chaput, enti bejalai kena kain pandak, samoa puting iya basah*: tall enough to wet a short skirt, if you wear a short (knee-length) skirt the edge of it will be wet.

(11) *Baru bebuku, kena iya maia tu enda tau ditinjau*: just growing joints; at this time the rice may not be looked at (?).

(12) *Ngerempong, samoa daun bla-bla betumpu pun*: bunching, all the leaves are opposite each other at the base.

(13) *Ngijap bubu, ngasur iya udah ngerempong*: like the cone of sharp points inside a fish-trap, when the leaf points are all bunched together.

(14) *Dara tuai*: an older, unmarried girl.

(15) *Kandong lelaki, lunchik daun enggau batang*: male fruiting, the stem and leaves all taper together.

(16) *Kandong indu, batang iya besai, endang baka orang indu ngandong*: female fruiting or with child, with swollen stem just like a pregnant woman.

(17) *Blah buloh*: splitting open like a bamboo shoot; the panicle begins to emerge.

(18) *Ngetup dilah*: like a tongue protruding; i.e., the panicle.

(19) *Murai, sapemeda*: ripening (into ear), as may be plainly seen.

(20) *Ngerichau, baru baka tukak, betumbok-tumbok*: confused, like ground-spikes (set against an enemy) pointing in all directions.

(21) *Baru bekangau*: newly calling from afar; the rice spirits are thought of as calling to each other.

(22) *Napur murai, leboh nyau selampur murai nyau buah*: in ear, when all the rice is in ear it forms the fruit (grain).

(23) *Mansau, leboh baru iya nyau mansau ujong*: ripe, when the tips of the ears are ripe.

(24) *Sumba lesau, leboh iya baru mansau betampok bedau sajarit*: early in the first stage of reaping, when the ripeness shows but is not yet even or widespread.

(25) *Sumba tisir, leboh iya mansau sajarit, nyau tau diketau samoa, enda ditinggal*: well on for reaping, when the rice seems evenly ripe and all can be reaped without leaving any.

(26) *Matah padi, awak ka tau diketau, tujoh tau ka lima batang*: 'Snapping the rice', a rite inaugurating the harvest (see below, pp. 189 seq.).

(27) *Ninggal umai, ngetau mimit, satangkin satengah hari*: leaving the farm; harvest a little, half a day's work only.

(28) *Ngetau, ngiga ulih*: reaping, working towards a good rice harvest.

These are simply Iban ways of describing the growth cycle in personal, human terms, and using Iban analogies. There is no obligation to employ a particular description, although most of those listed are widely used. Freeman[1] gives other descriptions for certain stages:

(1) *Baru baka chuit*: newly fully out.

(2) *Tebai murai*: thickly mature.

(3) *Brat dan*: heavy branches.

(4) *Tuai buah*: mature fruits.

(5) *Mansau mulut*: ripe lips.

(6) *Betengan tangkai*: half ripe panicles.

(7) *Rapus tangkai indu*: the panicle of the main plant of each rice clump is fully ripe.

(8) *Nyau ngankong*: hanging down with ripeness; i.e., the height of the harvest.

(9) *Nyau patah patong*: the panicles are broken at a nodule and hanging down with ripeness.

[1] 1955a, 57, n. 1.

Rites to Foster Growth

Just as the stages in its growth are described in terms of human experience, so rice is said to suffer from 'illnesses' like a human being: a headache (called *pedra*), a cold (*renga*), or even warts (*butir*)! But the most tangible manifestations of rice suffering are the pests, in particular the rice bug (*empangau*), locusts and grasshoppers (*buntak*), rats, mice, and other vermin (*chit*).

There are many rites designed to protect the rice and foster its growth. As early as 1865 Boyle (1865, 205) observed a life-size 'male and female alligator, shaped of mud and bristling with sharp wooden spines . . . on enquiry we were told with much laughter, that the figures were expected to roam about at night and devour the antus, malignantly destroying the produce of the padi field'. Ribai, the spirit associated with rivers and water, sometimes appears to men as a crocodile. The crocodile is credited with a *samengat* and held in considerable awe; the Iban only venture to kill a crocodile (as is the case also with cobras and other venomous snakes) in self-defence or retribution for an Iban life. The earthen figure of the crocodile, Ribai, is moulded by a *tuai* who is noted for his success in rice cultivation. After the ceremony, which is associated with extensive rites in the longhouse, prohibitions take effect for a period of seven days, during which no outsider may enter the longhouse, and none of the members of the community may work. At the end of the seven-day period, offerings, which include the usual *piring* items, are made to Ribai, a *biau* is performed, and a pig is killed. The ground surrounding the site of the crocodile image remains sacred for three years afterwards; were this final restriction not to be observed, it is thought that the community as a whole would have continually poor harvests.

This ritual, however, is performed only when the more usual *paung padi* rites have proved ineffective. These in practice are commoner and perhaps to that extent more important. If only one farm is seriously affected by pests, the *bilek* concerned may conduct its own propitiatory rite. In this event the other families of the longhouse are not directly involved and the prohibition against work lasts only one day (*diau sahari*). During the propitiatory rite the farm is subject to special restrictions—the rite is often called *mali umai*—and no one may walk in or through it. When many or all farms suffer from pests, and if one has pests it is usual for others to have them, the rites are more elaborate. The Iban take auguries (*beburong*) beforehand, and a portion of sacred rice (*padi pun*) is brought to the longhouse. *Piring* sacrifices are offered and a *biau* ceremony is performed accompanied by an invocation cursing all manner of pests and invoking good growth and a plentiful harvest. At evening the sacred rice is the object of a long incantation (*timang paung padi*) similar to those used in *gawai* festivals (see below, pp. 200 seq.). In these circumstances, the prohibition against work affects the whole longhouse and lasts for three days (*diau tiga hari sakayu rumah*); access to the farms is prohibited.

Small figures, properly called *agum*, but also known as *pentik*, are placed as a sign at the farm. These are made of wood and may be anything from less than one foot to well over two feet high; they vary from very crude to quite ornate carvings. The commonest represent human beings (*pentik Iban*) and are associated with rites to ward off rice bugs (*empangau*), but others are carved to represent a cat (*pentik mayau*) if the farm is plagued by vermin, or the Kite (*pentik Lang*) if there are locusts and grasshoppers.

Minta Ujan

Various other minor rites may take place during the growing season, especially if the weather is not ideal. In case of drought (*kamarau*) there are rites to ask for rain (*minta ujan*). These rites are based, as is usual in Iban religion, on the principle of analogy.[1] As the hollow blow-pipe set beside a tree in the felling ritual is thought to make the tree as easy to fell as if it too were hollow, so the Iban believe that the *minta ujan* rites will make rain likely. Three bamboo shoots are planted in the river with *tekuyong* snails on top of them (perhaps symbolizing heavy ears of rice). A trophy head (*antu pala*) from the longhouse is sprinkled with water while the Iban implore the spirits for rain to drench the rice. The three bamboo shoots are then submerged in the river.

The Ripening Rice

Ritual top-spinning (*mangka padi*) is thought to speed the ripening process. And when the rice begins to ripen (*belaboh murai*) the

[1] See above, p. 173 and n. 2: reference to Freeman, 1957b, 156.

ceremony of burning wax (*nunu lilin*) normally takes place. After a simple *piring* has been prepared and an omen-stick (*kayu burong*) has been suspended at the height of ripe ears of rice (*tuntun buah padi*), a small piece of wax is burned on top of the stump of a tree at the farm. This is accompanied by an invocation (*sampi*) and followed by further fivefold *piring* and a second wax burning.

> *Nyadi aku saharitu nunu lilin.*
> *Nyadi samoa ambun orang tau tepang, tau andang, . . .*
> *Nya buai kesai.*
> *Nyadi samoa ambun orang tau padi, tau puli, . . .*
> *Nya tama padi aku.*

> Now I today am burning wax.
> May the dew of those who curse, who work evil
> [and bring misfortune]
> Be cast away, flung away!
> And may the dew of those who harvest rice in plenty,
>   abundant sweet rice,
> [who have success, fame and wealth]
> Enter into my rice.[1]

The invocation follows the usual pattern of wishing ill away, summoning the benevolent spirits, and ends with a prayer for a good harvest and health. The rite is concluded with a sevenfold *piring*. Afterwards the farm is under restrictions (*mali*) for three nights.

The Rice Harvest

When the rice ripens and is nearly ready to harvest, the introductory rites of *matah padi* take place. The *tuai burong* and family heads sit on a mat (*tikai*) at a point on the farm track (*jalai umai*) not far from the farms. No one, not even the women back at the longhouse, may bathe (*nadai tau mandi*) lest the feathers of birds be wet (*basah bulu burong*)—similar to the restriction when the Iban are seeking auguries for new farm-land (see above, p. 159). Once seated, the *tuai burong* may not move (*nadai tau nginsit*); if he does, the rice will refuse to be harvested (*padi enggai diketau*). When they have heard seven Nendak calls on the left and seven

---

[1] This refers to the dew of those who were good and successful in life; having now turned to dew they are expected to confer prosperity. See above, p. 108.

on the right and the *tuai burong* has obtained an equivalent number of omen-sticks, a *piring* is prepared. This is sevenfold, corresponding to the number of calls, and arranged in two portions, according to the sides. Only if the community has decided to celebrate an elaborate festival which includes the *timang* incantation, are the *kayu burong* then carried back to the longhouse. Otherwise, they are taken to the farms.

At the farm further *piring* sacrifices are prepared by the place where the seed baskets were at planting: one on the ground, one on a raised support. The Iban calls first on evil-minded spirits not to interfere or make trouble and declares his intention:

> *Laban aku ka ngambi tangkai padi,*
> *Padi pun, padi remun, padi sangking, padi puting.*
>
> For I am here to gather the ears of rice,
> The sacred rice, remun rice, sangking rice, puting rice.

All *bilek* members are expected to be present, since, like *manggol*, the harvest concerns the family and the fortune of one is the fortune of all. The senior *bilek* member sits on the ground with three rice stalks (*tiga pun*) between his legs. Tied to them is a left-side Nendak omen-stick (*Nendak kiba*) and surrounding them a length of thread, dyed red (*ubong mansau*). The red thread also encircles the foot of a raised *piring*. There is a second *piring* on the ground. With his fingers the Iban breaks off seven ears of rice immediately to his right. He may not use the reaping instrument (*ketap*) during the *matah padi* ritual and he must not separate the rice ears from the surrounding leaf lest the rice be embarrassed at its nakedness (*malu telanjai*). The rice is placed with the *pulut* rice in the *piring*. Opposite the Iban sits a woman, usually his wife, neither up-river (*ulu*) nor down-river (*ili*), and she plucks seven heads of rice to his left. Both must remain in the same position throughout the rite.[1]

The premature reaping of a little rice follows *matah padi*. This is called by the special word *nyumba*. On the first occasion only one basketful (*sasintong*) may be harvested and this, the first of the new rice (*padi baru*), is eaten the same evening. The freshly cooked rice (*asi*) is placed on a Nendak omen-stick; a short prayer often precedes the offering of a little of the rice at the hearth (*dapur*),

---

[1] Comparable elaborate harvest rites, designed to safeguard the 'soul of the rice' survive among the Malays from their pre-Islamic past; see Skeat, 1900, 225 seq.

and a portion is also set aside for the dogs 'for it is believed that any deleterious influences which may have become associated with the padi . . . will thus be visited upon the dogs' (Freeman, 1955a, 62, para. 138). Finally, the family members, in order of seniority, eat the new rice (*asi baru*), and this is invariably an enjoyable, cheerful occasion (as Freeman also remarks, ibid.). The extent of subsequent *nyumba* depends on two factors: first, whether or not rice stocks from the previous season have been exhausted, and, secondly, the speed with which the new rice ripens fully.

The harvest proper is preceded by another ritual called *nganjong ka penyedai* (literally 'carry to the mat'), although when the rice ripens early the distinction between *matah padi* and *nganjong ka penyedai* is less clear. *Penyedai* is the name given to a plaited mat which is placed under the carrying baskets (*lanji*) when the rice is being transferred from harvesting-baskets (*sintong*). After the appropriate omens (Nendak, Beragai) have been heard, the ritual begins. Two *piring* are prepared: one is offered to the spirit of the earth, one is placed in a raised support. At the same time the Iban calls on the prosperous rice spirits to ensure a good harvest:

> *Antu padi, orang maioh, orang banyak,*
> *Gempuru, geremu kitu.*
>
> . . . . .
>
> *Ngambi iya beranak ngelesak,*
> *Maioh bejumboh, betugang, bedurong.*

Spirits of rice, many and in multitude,
Gather and assemble here.
[List of guardian spirits of successful farmers]
Grant that our rice may multiply and increase,
Plentiful in heaps, in piles, in granaries.[1]

---

[1] A more elaborate prayer for plenty and increase is recorded by Geddes, 1954, 79, from the Land Dayaks as part of their pre-harvest ceremony:
May the rice return in a host, in a swarm, like the small ants and like the big ants;
May it become coiled together, intertwined, pressed together, inside the reaping basket, inside the carrying basket,

. . . . . .

May each stalk make one reaping basketful, may each sheaf become one carrying basketful;
May it bear fruit like the Nchuah grass, like the young betel-nut, like the Mangis padi, like the onion plant, like Langah flowers.
May they find the rice thick to get through, may they be unable to move fast, may they not get along too quickly—
Those who reap the rice this day and afterwards.

Then before spreading out the *penyedai* mat the Iban shakes it and wishes away undesirable, evil-minded spirits:

> *Antu tabar, antu lapar,*
> *Rari ambis, rari lengih.*
>
> Insipid spirits, hungry spirits,
> Be off entirely, clear away!

asking that they not interfere with his crop.

Underneath the *penyedai* are left-side Nendak omen-sticks (*Nendak kiba*) to help 'pitch up' (*nyagu*) the rice from below, and, in the support at the side, right-hand Nendak sticks (*Nendak kanan*) to 'hold the rice on the surface' (*ngatong*). The *penyedai* not only serves the practical purpose of catching rice grains which might fall when these are poured from *sintong* to *lanji*, but it is also the spirit assembly place for the rice spirits. The rite is designed to encourage the prosperous rice spirits to make this, in particular, their home and not to stray elsewhere. Throughout the harvest, it is thought vital that the *samengat padi* should have access to and from the *penyedai*. Reaping must be done in such a way that the *samengat* can retreat through standing plants to the *penyedai*, or at least never find itself cut off and stranded in a clearing. A path through the farm must remain as a 'bridge' for the *samengat padi*, and no one is allowed to cross this at critical times.

The initial reaping which follows the introductory rites is often called *nangkal* (lit., to cut a notch in a tree—as in rubber tapping; or to make a treaty) and should be done by a woman. She approaches with a *piring* on her *sintong* and begins by harvesting three stalks which are then bent over and knotted. Three *sintong* are filled on the first occasion. During *nangkal*, as on the first day of planting (*nugal*), it is forbidden to ask (*mali ditanya*) what the Iban are doing. The next day no one may work (*sahari diau*) in propitiation for any offence inadvertently caused, and on the first days following, when the harvest proper starts (*ketau*; verb *ngetau*), a *piring* is brought to the farm and offered at the *penyedai*; according to Freeman (1955a, 63, para. 141) only cooked rice (*asi*) is presented, but practice evidently varies. On the third day five *sintong* are filled, on the fourth, seven; after this *ngetau* is unrestricted.

During *ngetau* there are various *pemali/penti* prohibitions: for example, it is a *pemali* for the basket-string to break (*mali tali sintong putus*) lest the rice refuse to be harvested (*padi enggai diketau*); nor may small ears of rice be left (*enda tau ninggal ka tangkai anak*) lest they cry (*nyabak*) like abandoned children and curse the Iban. Should a barking deer (*kijang*) come into the farm-clearing during harvest, it must not be killed; a reaping tool (*ketap*) and basket (*sintong*) are placed before it, because it is believed to have been sent by Pulang Gana to assist, and next day a sacrifice is offered at the trees where it emerged. There are also a number of individual *bilek* prohibitions: some families are firmly forbidden to bring pigs to the farm (except for augury and sacrifice), others to urinate in a standing position (*kemi bediri*), and so forth.

Carrying Home the Rice

Before the full baskets (*lanji*) are carried back (*berangkut*) to the longhouse, the Iban listen for five Nendak calls on the left and three on the right. As each basket is lifted to the foot of the steps, a leading *tuai* of the community performs a *biau* ceremony and prays:

> *Niki meh nuan antu padi, antu puli,*
> *Padi pun, padi remun, padi puting, padi sangking,*
> *Niki tu tangga tekam, tangga keladan, . . .*
> *Sampal ambis, sampal lengih.*

> Come on up, spirit of rice, spirit of sweet rice,
> Sacred rice, remun rice, puting rice and sangking,
> Come up the hardwood steps, the steps of camphor wood, . . .
> All of you, every one, to the very end.

In the longhouse each *bilek* places one full *lanji* on the *ruai*. A *piring* is offered and again a fowl is waved in *biau* accompanied by an invocation:

> *Asoh maioh, asoh belaloh,*
> *Asoh melumpa, asoh melua;*
> *Saleka nyadi saratus,*
> *Saratus nyadi saribu,*
> *Ampa nyadi isi,*
> *Beranak dua, beranak tiga.*

> Make it much, make it more than enough,
> Make it dribble, overflowing, like an overfed child;
> A single seed become a hundred,
> A hundred become a thousand,
> Chaff become grain;
> May it multiply twofold, multiply threefold.

The fowl is killed and the rice touched with its blood. The *piring* is arranged in two portions: the one, fivefold, is placed together with the rice and has the five left-side Nendak sticks with it; the other, threefold, has the three right-side Nendak sticks with it and is suspended from the loft. The one below is intended to support the rice spirits, the one above to give them a hand up. This may be followed at evening by a *timang* incantation (see below, pp. 200 seq.).

Storing the Rice

Before the rice is stored (*besimpan* or *nyimpan*) in the bark bins[1] (*tibang, gentong,* or sometimes simply *kulit kayu,* meaning 'bark') kept in the loft, there is a final ceremony. One *piring* is placed below (*dibaroh*); another prepared for the open top (*moa*) of the bark bin. The senior hereditary member of the *bilek* (*pun bilek*), or a distinguished visitor if one happens to be present, picks up from the *lanji* several handfuls (*genggam*) of rice; the handfuls correspond to the number of persons in the *bilek*, but are made up to an uneven figure: five, seven, nine, as the case may be. While he does this, his eyes must be closed (*pejam mata*) and he prays:

> *Nyadi aku ka saharitu aku nyimpan padi.*
> *Ngaroh nuan ka tukau, ka sadau,*
> *Tibang penampang.*
> *Ditu nuan tindok, nuan dudok.*
> *Nyadi tibang awak ka mit, awak ka ngerupit,*
> *Nuan penoh, nuan belaloh,*
> *Beranak dua, beranak tiga.*

> Now I today am storing rice.
> I lead you to the vessel, to the loft,
> To the bark bin of increase.
> May this be where you sleep and where you sit,
> May the bin prove too small, be too tight,
> May you be full and fill to overflowing;
> May you multiply twofold, multiply threefold.

Although it is permissible for others to contribute their handful during the rite, actual filling of the first bin is done personally by the senior hereditary *bilek* member. To honour the occasion a feast (*gawai*) or celebration follows.

[1] See above, p. 152, n. 1, giving list and classification of rice bins.

5. Iban *tuai* finishing a hornbill effigy for the *Gawai Kenyalang*

XIII. *GAWAI* FESTIVALS

Types of *Gawai*

GAWA, which means any activity or work, is used by the Iban in a special sense. The common expression *bisi gawa mimit* can be translated 'we are having a small celebration' and is applied to the many minor rites of the Iban year. *Gawai*, the same word etymologically, is reserved for more important feasts and festivals. *Gawai* and *gawa* vary enormously in scope and significance, from the minor celebrations of individual families to the *gawai kenyalang* which takes an entire community many months of intensive preparation. They fall roughly into four categories.

The first are incidental celebrations, which are generally confined to one or two families and are not significant in the wider context. These may be occasioned by sickness, recovery from sickness, fear of sickness (for example, cholera, when the rumour of an epidemic is current), a dream, an omen, setting off on an expedition (*bejalai*), enlisting in the police or armed forces, returning from military service, or simply because someone 'feels like a party' (*rindu*) and offers an appropriate pretext. The second category consists of the specifically agricultural *gawai* which are directly associated with the ritual inauguration of the new season and, therefore, occur normally during the fifth Iban month (June). The most important of these are the *gawai batu* and *gawai benih* (whetstone and seed festivals) and Pulang Gana is the principal spirit concerned. The third group comprises festivals which used also to be bound up with head-hunting and warfare but continue to have general reference to community and individual prosperity and all forms of material success. These take longer to prepare and generally occur in the seventh Iban month (August). The *gawai kenyalang*, 'hornbill festival', also called *gawai burong*, 'bird festival', is the most important (certainly in the Lupar and Ulu Ai), and Sengalang Burong is the principal spirit. Finally, there is the *gawai antu*, festival of the dead, which is the Saribas-Krian group's greatest festival[1] but occurs only in

[1] See above, p. 58. For an account of the *gawai antu*, see Sandin, 1961.

a modified form elsewhere. This has as its focus the fate in Sebayan of prominent and other Iban no longer living.

Although each festival varies and has a different emphasis and aim, the general pattern remains the same. This structure is mainly ascribed to the teachings of Sengalang Burong, when, according to the myth, he revealed himself at Dempi's celebration for Maripat (see above, pp. 91–2). Auguries (*beburong*), cock-fighting (*sabong*), expiation (*ginselan*), sacrificial offerings (*piring*), *biau* ceremonies, divination by entrails (*ati jani*), and, in most cases, long incantations are the key features. In the *gawai antu* a wailer intones the *sabak* mourning chant, which describes a journey to Sebayan,[1] but in all other major *gawai*, the incantation describes a journey to the *menoa* of Pulang Gana, Sengalang Burong, or whoever the principal spirit guest may be, and is called *pengap* or, less specifically, *timang*[2] (see above, pp. 64–5).

However, *gawai* referred to as *pulai hari* ('return home the same day') do not include the *pengap* incantation, and since major festivals are not annual events in all communities, minor *gawai* such as these are a common substitute. For although all *gawai* are based on the same principle, the scope varies considerably.

Minor Celebrations

As an example of a small 'family' *gawai*, lasting till midday (*sandau hari*) and involving only members of the *bilek* itself and their relatives within the longhouse community, there was a festival in March 1965 at Nanga Delok for Medan who was about to enlist in the Sarawak Rangers.

After killing a pig and finding the liver satisfactory, a *piring* sacrifice was prepared on the *tanju* under the shelter of a woven *pua* —and a parachute. Medan himself was seated in the middle, surrounded by a basin filled with water, charcoal, spears (standing on their point), *ilang* knives and two gongs (*tawak*). There were seven plates each of *pulut* (glutinous rice), *rendai* (puffed rice),

[1] Harrisson, 1965a, bases his account of 'Borneo Writing' on a *sabak* text, part of which he quotes and translates.

[2] Maceda, 1962, 491, says that 'The term used in Batang Ai . . . is *timang*, and in the Saribas, it is *pengap*', which is not strictly true. The verb *nimang* means literally 'to praise' or 'to sing' and is commonly used of intoning the *pengap*, particularly among non-Saribas Iban, but *mengap* (the verbal form) and *pengap* also occur. In practice the words are interchangeable.

and *tumpih* (rice cakes), in addition to a large plate containing other *piring* ingredients. The officiants (three senior members of the longhouse: one was in fact a *tuai burong*, another a *lemambang*) put on their right wrists a ring of brass or iron (*selong* or *sengkrong*) to steel their spirits and, at the same time, giving their actions and words the 'strength of iron', and began to prepare a sevenfold *piring*.

In the centre was a plate supporting Medan's *bilek pengaroh* charms, designed to ensure his safety and give him courage, health, and success. Around the *pengaroh*, the officiants prepared, in sevens, the customary *piring*. When the *piring* was complete the senior officiant took a fowl by the legs and performed a *biau* over the *piring* and *pengaroh* as well as Medan and all those assembled on the *tanju*. As he waved it he invoked the blessing of the spirits:

> *Oha, oha, oha!*
> *Aku ngangau, aku mesau*
>
> . . . . .
>
> *Minta tulong, minta pandong,*
> *Minta peda, minta telah.*
> *Aku ngangau ukai ngangau ngapa,*
> *Ukai ngangau ngapa ngangau saja;*
> *Aku nyadi sandau hari*
> *Gawa begelah.*
> *Piring penoh, piring belaloh,*
> *Nyadi kami ngangau kami mesau*
> *Laban Medan betampah bulu saharitu.*
> *Kami ngambi enda busong enda lunggong,*
> *Ngambi brani, ngambi mensali,*
> *Ngambi enda telih,*
> *Bulih brita, ngambi raja,*
> *Tang enti orang nyerang, alah iya;*
> *Enti iya mungkal nanjal alah stungah iya,*
> *Ari nya ngambi iya lus ngambi iya mugus.*
> *Kami ngambi chelap, ngambi lindap,*
> *Ngambi grai nyamai.*

I call and I summon
[names of spirits].
I ask for aid and ritual presence,
I ask you to look and to observe.
I call, not calling in vain,

Not calling in vain or merely calling out;
I am celebrating till midday
A festival.
The sacrifice is full, is overflowing,
So we call and we summon
Because Medan is celebrating today—
That he may not suffer from a curse or from weakness,
That he may have true courage,
And be afflicted by no wounds;
Becoming famous and prosperous.
If any come against him—let him lose,
Made barren—without issue or purpose.
May we all live untroubled and content,
In health and in comfort.

After this he killed the fowl by cutting its throat, and, dipping a bunch of feathers in the blood, he touched first the *pengaroh*, then placed the bloody feathers on top of the *piring*. The severed head was used to touch the hands of the officiants and Medan. Medan remained seated with a woven *pua* over his legs containing a *piring*, while the women fixed short lengths of red thread into his clothing and head-cloth as a symbolic memento of the *gawai* and the blessings it was hoped to confer.

Subsequently, one *piring* was left on the *ruai* covered by a gong (*tawak*) and another was suspended from the *sadau*. A third *piring* was arranged above the steps leading into the longhouse.

Major *Gawai*

Major *gawai* are infinitely more elaborate and take much longer to prepare, but the basic pattern changes little. The event which initiates the proceedings is invariably the preliminary meeting (*baum begawai*), at which the longhouse community decides to hold a *gawai*, and agrees on an appropriate date. It is not necessarily all *bileks* which participate in all *gawai* on an equal scale.

For most *gawai* it is necessary not only to prepare food and drink, notably *tuak*, for offerings, as well as food and drink for guests, but also to assemble the relevant ritual objects. For example, in the case of the *gawai batu*, whetstone festival, those *bileks* which, because they are the result of recent partition or for some other reason, do not already possess ritual whetstones must first acquire suitable stones. The actual stone should have whetstone properties although it is used only ritually as a whetstone. After the festival it is regarded as having its origin in Ningkoh, the *menoa* of Raja Jembu (honoured as the father of Pulang Gana) who is the guardian spirit of whetstones. Having been blessed, it becomes a treasured ritual object and heirloom, surrounded by restrictions, and is carefully preserved between seasons.

Shortly before the *gawai* is due to take place, the invitations are sent out: this is known as *ngambi ngabang*. The number of guests depends on the size and importance of the festival. For major festivals many communities in the area may be asked—up to a day's walk away. It is usual to invite an entire longhouse community. Unmarried men and women like to take advantage of this, but apart from specially distinguished individuals, members of the older generation usually attend only if they have relatives in the longhouse concerned. The invitation is accompanied by a length of (bark) string, called *temuku tali*, which has been tied with a number of knots corresponding to the number of days before the *gawai*. One knot is untied daily (there are commonly six) and when the last knot has been undone, it is the day of the *gawai*.

The preliminary rites begin a day before the *gawai* itself. The first important event in the whetstone festival is the expiation (*ginselan*) of the spirits whose *menoa* may be affected by the new farm. There are also general propitiatory offerings to spirits who might have taken offence for some unknown reason and prophylactic offerings to ward off the potential ill unwittingly introduced by the guests.

The festival begins with a cockfight in which both hosts and guests participate.[1] Afterwards, to prepare the longhouse itself for the *gawai* proper, the *tuai* unrolls his own mats (*beranchau*) and waves a fowl the length of the *ruai*. From the *tuai*'s *bilek* two men walk carrying a winnowing tray (*chapan*) along the *tempuan* passage, one to each end of the longhouse. These winnowing trays are filled with old, worn-out items which are then thrown away as an offering to *antu rua*, spirits of extravagance and

---

[1] Cock-fighting in connection with a *gawai* is traditional and mythically sanctioned; see above, p. 92. It is more than a pastime; Sandin, 1959, calls it 'the Dayak National Game' and stresses its importance in the Iban tradition and way of life.

wastefulness. The *antu rua* are invited to remove the objects to their own *menoa* and not to ask for more.

In the *gawai batu*[1] the next event of importance is the reception of the whetstones which have been deposited just outside the longhouse in a shelter especially constructed for the purpose. The *tuai* leads a procession carrying a flag; behind him come two men, one with a fowl, one with a *piring*, then a woman who has a bowl of puffed rice, other *tuai bileks*, *lemambang*, and, finally, drums and gongs. After a brief prayer that the whetstones prove efficacious and produce a good harvest, the stones are carried, ceremonially wrapped in *pua*, back to the longhouse, where every *bilek* offers *tuak*. The procession goes up and down the *ruai* three times.

The whetstones are all washed on the *ruai* of the *tuai*. Before washing them, the officiant bites a knife for spirit strength, touches a *tepayan* jar to keep his own spirit in safety, and covers himself with a woven cloth for spirit protection. The stones are 'washed' in water which also contains the traditional Iban valuables: armlets, beads, bells, gold, and silver coins, as well as *kepayang* fruit (used for its oil), *langgir* skins (which serve as a kind of soap), scented *tepus* leaves, flowers, plants, and blood from the pig and chicken which have been sacrificed at the farm. The officiant concludes by preparing a sevenfold *piring*. While this is being done, the special rhythm of *gendang raya* is beaten on a drum seven times as a summons to the spirits.[2]

Pengap Incantations

The *pengap* (or *timang*) which may last from sunset to near sunrise the following morning or several mornings later, is intoned by a *lemambang*[3] accompanied by a chorus (*ngelembong*). It leads from the introductory ritual to the culmination of the *gawai* when the

[1] This version agrees in all essentials with the full account found in Sandin, 1962a.

[2] Not all drum rhythms are thought to attract the spirits. The special summoning beat is used only when a 'welcome' has been prepared for the spirit who is liable to appear (as, for example, the *sepepat* during *nampok*, see above, p. 123). The rising, insistent rhythm, is quite unlike that used during dancing and ordinary festivities. Maceda, 1962, discusses some Iban varieties and use of drum beats, but he does not mention their special function. For a general discussion of the role of percussion instruments in communicating with the spirits see Needham, 1967.

[3] See above, pp. 61 seq.

principal spirit guest gives his blessing, and simultaneously provides the *gawai* with its mythical context.

During the actual incantation, the *lemambang* wears a long cloak (*baju mengap*) to protect himself symbolically against hairs and bristles which might cause irritation on his journey through spirit *menoa*. He has also a *labong* head cloth to shield him when encountering spirits and he carries a *tungkat mengap*, '*pengap* staff', with little bells (*grunong*), to use in beating away weeds and undergrowth from overgrown paths (*jalai repa*) met on his journey and to enable others to follow him—by the sound of the bells—in the spirit world. Because there he may become invisible and disappear from sight. The staff serves a secondary function in being used to stamp out the rhythm; this is especially important in the chorus sections of the *pengap* but applies also to the intoned recitative.

For his services the *lemambang* receives compensation (*upah*). Apart from a money payment of $2 which is nowadays the custom, this consists of at least four items, but may also include a fifth. The first, *kring samengat*, strength for the spirit, consists of a bush knife (*duku*) to be bitten before and after the chant. The second, *blachu sadepa*, one fathom of cloth, serves, in spirit terms, as the *lemambang*'s coat or cloak, which protects him in his encounters in the spirit world.[1] The third item is a fowl, *manok*, which is used for a *biau*. It is waved seven times but is not killed and the *lemambang* takes it away alive. The fourth is a *tepayan* jar. This is for the *lemambang*'s *kurong samengat*, the container or keeping-place for his *samengat* spirit, which might otherwise stray when summoned by the returning spirits after the feast. There is usually also a fifth, *chapak*, a plate, given by each *bilek* family in the longhouse participating in the *gawai*.

Although they may be more or less elaborate, the journeys of most *pengap* again follow a common pattern. The *lemambang* is encouraged to invite the principal guest, he seeks suitable messengers to convey the invitation, the messengers are dispatched and communicate the invitation to the Wind Spirit who alarms the slave of the principal spirit guest. At last the principal spirit is

---

[1] Harrisson and Sandin (1966, 197), speak of this as protection against the 'heat' of adversaries; but 'heat' to the Iban really signifies the misfortune, sickness, etc., which is the likely consequence of an undesirable spirit confrontation.

found; he prepares himself to attend the *gawai*, and journeys to the celebrating longhouse, which is identified by the flags. The spirit guest(s) of honour arrive. The outward journey passes the *menoa* of men, heroes, and spirits; the journey back to the longhouse passes the *menoa* of important charms. The spirit of honour varies from *gawai* to *gawai*, and so do the messengers. For example:

Gawai Festival	Principal Spirit Guest	Messengers
Batu (whetstone—farming)	Pulang Gana	Nendak assisted by Burong Malam (locust)
Kenyalang or *Burong* (hornbill—prosperity)	Sengalang Burong	Lalayang (swiftlet) and Kesulai (butterfly)
Sakit (sickness)	Menjaya Manang Raja	Entawai (small bat) and Kusing (large bat)

The details vary not only from *gawai* to *gawai* but from one *lemambang* to another. It is, however, typical for the *pengap* to begin by describing the arrival of the *lemambang* outside the longhouse and their entry.

> *Lalu niki tangga laka*
> *Ke bengkaramba burang orang.*[1]

Then they climb the ladder notches,
Carved into a human shape.

They look for the *ruai* of the *tuai* leading the celebrations.

> *Lemambang ke datai ngiga ruai*
> *Tu baru tetemu ka ruai orang*
> *Ke empu pengawa megai gawai.*

The *lemambang* have arrived and seek the *ruai*;
Now they find the *ruai* of the one
Who leads the celebration.

And they sit down.

> *Nya baru lentok lentok langgai manok,*
> *Lemambang ke datai bebai dudok.*

Now the feathers of the cock's tail fall,
The *lemambang* who have come are invited to sit.

Before setting off on their journey to the spirits, the *lemambang*

---

[1] These *pengap* quotations follow the sources used by Harrisson and Sandin, 1966, pp. 101 seq., although translation of the texts is not always identical.

invoke the particular spirit whom they individually consider their patron and guardian. For instance:

Nya baru aku ngading yiang aku lemambang Nendak
Nya baru aku ngading yiang aku lemambang Luong.

Now I welcome my patron spirit, *lemambang* Nendak,
Now I welcome my patron spirit, *lemambang* Luong.

They ensure that all is in readiness, the mats unrolled, the betel nut and other chewing ingredients prepared.

Rengai rengai, mendu ilai
Nyadoh ka tuboh branchau tikai

. . . .

Nyadoh ka tuboh nanggong baku
Sarang langgu buah pinang.

The birds make it clear,
Telling us to unroll mats and prepare.

. . . .

Telling us to make ready the betel box,
The box of fresh betel nuts.

And they protect themselves with charms against occult evil.

Lemambang ke mengap mai ubat.

The *lemambang* who intone bear charms.

The actual journey begins. It leads first to the *menoa* of human beings who live in 'real' places: famous Iban of the past, like Ambau who led a migration from the Kapuas and comes from Pangkalan Tabau, near the watershed and the present Sarawak–Indonesian border. The names are real, and used in the context of familiar localities like the Skrang or the Undup.

Ni tuai nama Langkup, tuai Undup,
Dudi jadi dulu satamang?
Ni tuai ke benama Sabungkok?

Where is the leader called Langkup, leader of the Undup,
He who married his namesake?
Where is the leader known as Sabungkok?

Slightly more remote from historical Iban territory come the Malays. The *pengap* sometimes calls to these in passing:

Ni nuan patinggi Datu Julak?
Ni nuan patinggi Datu Nuga?

Where are you, honourable Datu Julak?
Where are you, honourable Datu Nuga?

The legendary heroes and their associates follow. While these in one sense belong to the world they are also spirits.

Ni Nading Panas Kuning?

Nya apai Kling Aji.
Ni nuan Sempun Murun Api Neraka?

Nya apai nuan Laja.

Where is Nading Panas Kuning?

That is the father of Kling Aji.
Where is Sempun Murun Api Neraka?

That is your father, Laja.

As they are mentioned, the spirits are sometimes thought to join the party and can be considered present.

Meringai pen udah ga datai ditu.

Kling udah datai ditu
Datai ari Panggau Libau.

Meringai has already come here.

Kling is already here,
Arrived from Panggau Libau.

And after Kling and the others from Panggau Libau and Gelong have been included in the party, the journeying group reach the *menoa* of true spirits.

Nya menoa Siasi bekaki kuning,
Bujang Nendak Nendai berambai biring.

This is the country of yellow-legged Siasi,
Young Nendak Nendai with the red-plumed tail.

And

Nya menoa pangkang Gangga Ganggai.

The country of Gangga Ganggai who distributes good fortune.

As soon as Nendak—in this example which follows the scheme of a *gawai batu*—has conveyed the message to the Wind Spirit, Bunsu Ribut, Nendak's mission is complete and Bunsu Ribut assumes responsibility.

> *Lalu muput Bunsu Ribut*
> *Ke rumput rambut ubong.*

> And the Wind Spirit blows
> The grass like strands of cotton.

Or,

> *Nya baru ngelagua angin raya*
> *Baka baya pansut ari lubok.*

> Then the storm wind blows,
> Rising like a crocodile from the still pool.

With the exception of the messenger there is little variation up to this point from *gawai* to *gawai*, since the introductory journey follows much the same route. *Pengap* beginnings vary in relation to the skill of the *lemambang* and the importance of the occasion. Although the early messengers are not identical for different *gawai*, they all go to the Wind Spirit, Bunsu Ribut, (except in the case of a *gawai sakit*). After the Wind Spirit takes over, however, the direction of the journey varies according to the purpose of the *gawai* and the person of its principal guest.

In the whetstone festival, *gawai batu*, a principal guest is Pulang Gana and Pusai is his slave. Consequently:

> *Pusai ke ngibun kebun lalu ninga;*
> *Rari Pusai enda tetiki ka rumah diri*
> *Lalu niki rumah Endu Serentun Tanah Tumboh.*

> Pusai who attends the garden, hears;
> Pusai runs away, but not up to his own house,
> He goes to the house of Endu Serentun Tanah Tumboh.

In all *pengap*, a close and important relative (or relatives) of the principal guest is away from home when the invitation arrives and a drum is beaten to convey the message. Sengalang Burong has first to summon Ketupong. Pulang Gana announces that he will beat a drum to call his son, Sigai.

> *Pulang Gana nyadoh ka tuboh deka nutong*
> · · · · ·
> *Pending Sigai lansik ninga.*

Pulang Gana states that he will beat a drum.

. . . .

Sigai's ears are sharp of hearing.

Pulang Gana does not attend the festival empty-handed; he has first to collect the benefits which he is being asked to bestow. In the process of gathering charms, the *pengap* continues through spirit *menoa* and eventually passes Raja Jembu, father of Pulang Gana according to certain accounts, who is the spirit especially associated with whetstones. But first the *pengap* passes Pusai's father, although he does not join the group.

> *Nya menoa apai Pusai,*
> *Iya enda enggau ngabang.*

> That is the country of Pusai's father,
> Who is not taking part in the party.

It continues past, among others,

> *Nya pangkang Raja Jegedong*
> *Ke tau ngempong besi umat.*

> That is the place of Raja Jegedong,
> Who forges iron and welds it.

And,

> *Nya menoa Selampandai,*
> *Nempa mulai taing taing.*

> That is the country of Selampandai,
> Who hammers out, clang clang.

And, finally, arrives at

> *Nya menoa Raja Jembu*
> *Dudok di batu tinggi dinggai.*

> This is the country of Raja Jembu
> Seated on a high and lofty rock.

Pulang Gana and party, bearing the appropriate benefits, advance towards human territory; they have identified the celebrating long-house from afar by the flags seen outside. When they reach Kling's bathing place, the human/spirit meeting point, Pulang Gana rests.

Pandi Kling Nading brani
Ditu Pulang Gana ngetu.

. . . .

Mai pirak ke beberak mandang moa
Mai mas ke merempas ninggang dada.

The bathing place of Kling Nading the brave,
Here Pulang Gana rests.

. . . .

Bringing silver shining brightly from his face,
Bringing gold across his chest.

They pass Kuaong Kapong, chief of the non-spirit birds, and, at last,
noises from the longhouse tell them that they have virtually arrived.

Nya menoa Nira Raja Burong,
Menoa bujang Kuaong Kapong.
Ditu bala Pulang Gana ninga auh rumah
Orang ke begawai.

This is the country of Nira, king of birds,
The country of young Kuaong Kapong.
Here Pulang Gana's party hears the sounds
Of longhouse celebration.

Throughout the entire *pengap* the *lemambang* continue to walk
around the *pandong* which contain the *piring* and other offerings.
There is no specific signal to mark the concluding parts of the
incantation and no clear visible link between the *pengap* stages and
other aspects of the *gawai* apart from a procession on the 'arrival'
of the spirits. The *pengap* ends after the *lemambang* has intoned a
final passage in which Pulang Gana blesses the whetstones for
their symbolic use at the farm before both spirits and singers set
off home.

Although the *gawai* is a religious occasion and the ultimate Iban
rite, it is also a party, a time for eating and drinking, dancing,
jollification, and drunkenness. Occurring as it usually does after
the harvest is home and before the new cycle is under way, a
gawai can be said to be the social climax of one season and ritual
inauguration of the next. It provides a restatement of mythical
relationships and offers an occasion to affirm the harmony desired
between men and the spirit world, stressing their interdependence
and mutual concern. Both men and spirits participate in the rite
and in the celebration as in other aspects of Iban life.

XIV. CONCLUSION

For the necessities of existence the Iban depend on their environment, which they know from experience that they cannot control. They look, however, for some explanation of the phenomena of life and the fact of death, and on this basis they attempt to achieve constructive relations with the forces which surround them. Their thought and action, not least their religious ideas and practices, are all bound up with Nature as we know it, and the scope and limits of human activity and influence within their particular environment.[1]

The Iban objectives in life are common enough. At the end of almost every prayer, the Iban prays that he, his *bilek* and his community may be free from hunger and deprivation, from sickness and from early or sudden death:

> *gayu guru*
> *chelap lindap*
> *grai nyamai*

He asks to live 'a full life-span in a state of contentment, health and comfort' (see pp. 115 and 181). This life-span is not counted chronologically; it relates to the life of the *bilek* family unit. The Iban do not measure their lives in years, but they remember precisely the record of their own life-stages in comparison with the stages of others. Life begins as a child, passes through the states of young and unmarried man or woman, newly married and parent, and culminates as a grandparent. The Iban who has achieved grandparenthood and has seen his grandchildren growing well, has completed a full and satisfactory life. The continuity of the *bilek*, the family and social unit, is ensured and, not infrequently, after his death, the dead man's name will be passed on to his great-grandchild.[2]

The Iban seek sufficient food, health, and a full measure of life in the context of the tropical rain forest. According to their

---

[1] As Lienhardt says of the Dinka, 1961, 29.
[2] The ancestral tables and genealogical surveys offer many instances of the same name repeated after an interval of two generations.

traditions and to the best of their knowledge the Iban have always lived by the rivers which flow through the jungle. The Borneo jungle may not be an especially exacting environment, but it is unpredictable. Any alien who has walked alone in tropical rain forest and secondary jungle can testify to a heightened sensibility and wariness. The stillness and lack of movement are offset by an impression of vibrant life. Although an overgrown clearing or the state of a recently abandoned dwelling does not indicate that the jungle is neutral, the Iban do not share the European's view of the jungle as threatening. It is an environment with which they are familiar—although they rarely enjoy being alone in it. But the jungle's behaviour does appear to them intensely arbitrary and inconsistent. Hidden dangers and sudden change are but two aspects. In practice the more dramatic examples of attack by animals and reptiles matter less than the everyday impact of poisonous insects and the pests, which attack not human beings but crops. Finally, the rainfall, which to the traveller seems depressingly reliable, has been known to fail when most required. Or, more commonly, has fallen too heavily during the critical drying season before the burn when comparatively dry weather is of the utmost importance. But far the most alarming event in Iban experience is the occurrence of sickness and sudden death: the unexplained illness and death of an apparently healthy child or young person, death in childbirth, or accidental death.

The Iban do not have the western concern that everything must have an explanation.[1] They do not often ask why things have to happen or do not happen at all, but they would wish to know why they happen at one time and not at another, to one man or *bilek* and not to another. One man hunts and is regularly successful, another returns empty-handed; one man's fish-traps are always full, another's rarely; one man consistently harvests ample rice, another suffers frequent crop failures; one family is often sick, another invariably healthy.

Iban religion and mythology offer a world-view which enables them to make sense of events which would otherwise seem arbitrary, even capricious. It also makes it possible for the Iban to enter into a constructive relationship with the environment in which they live by taking appropriate action to forestall the

---

[1] Monberg, 1966, 118, for example, notes the same attitude among the people of Bellona Island. It occurs widely.

undesirable or to restore desirable conditions when circumstances require.

As described in the myths and legends, the motivating forces in the universe are spirits. Only those aspects of animal and vegetable life which are significant to the Iban for their lives or livelihood, or considered dangerous, are peopled with spirits, but all of these have spirits. In addition there are spirit beings whose existence is largely independent of the Iban universe but who impinge on Iban experience from time to time. Most of the spirits are anthropomorphically conceived. In 'person' they resemble human beings and they have human ways of thinking and emotions. Like men, they may experience jealousy, resentment, fear, and even hatred, but their positive feelings are uppermost. Like men they are also liable to caprice. But because they have human feelings and responses, the Iban is not only capable of understanding the spirits but also of entering into a meaningful relationship with them, not unlike the relations he establishes with his fellow men.

The mythology delineates the personalities of the principal spirits and shows how these are genealogically related and how they interact with each other as well as with men. It expresses in personified encounters the relations between spirit, human, animal, and vegetable life.[1] The myths, in Iban thought, record progressive stages in their understanding of the universal order and consequently in their own religious and social development. This is linked to improvements in hill rice cultivation. With difficulty the Iban first acquired rice seed, but the harvests were poor until they had been taught by the spirits to follow the constellations, to attend to bird augury and other omens and rites, to observe the regulations concerning incest, and to avoid using the names of their parents-in-law. Only then did they become fully 'Iban'. The myths explain the reasons for the rites and practices which the Iban believe are necessary to ensure the attainment of their objectives in life. Both myth and ritual are symbolic statements about the social order (see Leach, 1954, 13–14), if the wider social order is understood to encompass not merely living human society but the universal society of men and spirits.[2]

---

[1] To this extent Iban mythology orders and arranges phenomena and life in the universe; cf. Durkheim and Mauss, 1963, esp. 77–8.

[2] Cf. for example, Evans-Pritchard, 1965, 111, concerning the explanation of the 'facts of primitive religions'.

The spirits, like men, have their own concerns and interests which they watch over, for although spirit territory does not coincide fully with human territory, in some respects the two overlap. The physical-human and the spirit world are two facets of a complementary view of the universe which characterizes Iban thinking: both parts of life contribute to the whole. There is no real dichotomy between the sacred and the profane,[1] since these are two aspects of an integrated world-view. Just as human beings can be classified in two: men and women, each with separate and distinct characteristics but of comparable value,[2] so the spirit and physical members of the world have different modes of expression and different powers while belonging to the same universal order. The sexual division is reflected in the balanced distribution of rights and responsibilities in Iban society. Similarly, right and left have different values, but one does not invariably connote the desirable alternative: although right may be 'stronger' in augury, left makes the soil 'softer' and more fertile. The balance inherent in the complementary universe characterizes Iban thinking and underlies the total order.

The belief in a universe peopled by men and (anthropomorphic) spirits, whose interests from time to time come into conflict, provides the Iban with an explanation of events. Human nature suggests the key to spirit behaviour with its essentially human attributes and characteristics. But it is not a universe of conflict, since both men and spirits are subject to the same social code devised to ensure the well-being of all.

Adat governs both the Iban and the spirits; it expresses the 'true' ordered behaviour of all facets of the universe, animal, vegetable, human, and spirit, and it lays down the ideal behaviour patterns and relationships, rights, and responsibilities. When the Iban say *adat kami bumai* they summarize the essence and function of the code as it affects them: 'we farm (hill rice) and live according to the order made known by the spirits.' The rules and the ritual, designed to ensure adequate harvests, are central to the prosperity of the Iban whose fortunes, socially and individually, are governed by *adat*.

[1] Cf. Leach, 1954, 12, who says: 'I find Durkheim's emphasis on the absolute dichotomy between the sacred and the profane to be untenable.'

[2] According to a myth the unborn child is offered a spear or a weaving implement and in choosing to handle one or other of the two determines his or her sex. Neither choice is felt to be 'better' (cf. Jensen, 1967,167).

Like men–spirit relations social behaviour among men is closely regulated, and serious offences, such as incest, are believed to disturb the total order. Even minor offences, if left unresolved, are liable to have consequences not only for the individual and *bilek* concerned, but for the health and prosperity of the community as a whole. Poor harvests, barren soil, sickness, and early death, since they have spirit origins, are attributed to disturbances causing an imbalance in the universal order of behaviour; they should not occur but for a breach of *adat*.[1] While the routine rites and ritual take into account the possibility of unheeded transgressions, special ceremonies make provision for ritual action consciously designed to heal known breaches of *adat*.

The *adat* sums up the corpus of Iban experience. It comprises the guidance of the spirits offered over the generations to the Iban for their common advantage, and this is related to practical experience. It holds out to the *bilek* family within the wider longhouse community the hope of sufficient food, health, and a reasonable life span, and an explanation of failure to achieve these in whole or in part. *Adat* succeeds in turning dependence on the arbitrary course of events (and personal caprice) into an ordered pattern; it offers reasons for otherwise inexplicable events, and makes possible a response. It enables the Iban to maintain a constructive relationship with the forces of the universe which are beyond his immediate or apparent control, and allows men to influence the environment on which they depend for their existence.

Like the Iban themselves, the *adat* is pragmatic. It functions not as an end in itself, but to achieve certain desired practical results. *Adat* is a dynamic concept, and the proof of correct *adat* interpretation and observance is to be found in subsequent events. But where *adat* ostensibly fails to achieve the desired objectives, the Iban, like many other peoples,[2] do not reason that the *adat* itself is at fault, but rather their own understanding or acting out of it. They claim that *adat* has proved successful 'in the past', although life in the world as the Iban experience it is not a

---

[1] Even the phenomenon of human cursing (*tau tepang*) which produces highly undesirable situations is regarded as due to the influence of an *antu* spirit, whose agents the *tau tepang* persons became during a disturbance of *adat*.

[2] See, for example, the exposition of Polanyi, 1964, 287–8, which uses material from Evans-Pritchard, 1937. The same passage is used by Lienhardt, 1966, 126, to explain the 'fiduciary basis of knowledge'.

'fallen-state', nor is it a stage progressing towards perfection. The Iban are preoccupied with present life as they know it and they concentrate their attention on those activities where their own involvement and concern are most obvious.

The *adat* is not a system of normative ethical standards; nor can it be called a personal morality. Although the interpretation of behaviour is invariably pragmatic in the light of subsequent events, and to this extent the Iban are free to disregard or reinterpret spirit guidance at their own risk, the consequences of transgressing *adat* are not necessarily confined to the transgressor. Thus *adat* serves not only as the expression of a functional order which enables the Iban to understand and redress the balance when experience indicates that things are not as they should be, but also to regulate social behaviour. In all his acts the individual Iban remains responsible before *adat* since his own behaviour has implications not only for himself but for the community of which he is a part. This is important since misfortune is thus not necessarily the fault of a man himself. It may be another who has failed to observe *adat* correctly, and to this extent the Iban is relieved of direct personal responsibility for his fate.

The Iban are not concerned to convert others to their view of life. Nor does it matter to them that other peoples interpret human experience differently. To the Iban the proof of *adat* is that it works; the ordering of the community and the agricultural rituals have provided and continue to provide the Iban with the means of working towards their objectives and fulfilling their hopes. At least this was true until recently.

Since the Second World War, and especially in the 1960s, the Iban have been exposed to three major outside influences. The first of these has been the impact of a cash economy and settled agriculture based on the cultivation of rubber. This is already widespread. The second influence has been that of academic (western) education through local authority schools which have been established lately in most Iban areas. The third influence is that of religious conversion. This is confined almost exclusively to conversion to Christianity, since the Muslims do not proselytize actively among the Iban.

The nature of rubber cultivation and cash economics has such profound implications for Iban concepts of *bilek* membership and ownership, and, in particular, for land tenure and land use, that it effectively undermines the pattern of traditional agriculture and, consequently, the role of the rice cult as life's central activity. Education detaches Iban children from their traditional occupations and instils new values; it teaches them that the birds provide no reliable guidance and that dreams can be explained psychologically. A conservative Iban in the Lemanak, in opposing the introduction of schools, coined the phrase:

> *Duduk bangku enda bulih padi;*
> *Utai pinsil enda nyadi sangkoh babi.*

> Sitting on a school-bench doesn't grow rice;
> A pencil's no use for spearing a pig.

Conversion to Christianity effectively replaces the traditional religion and eliminates the special role and importance of rice cultivation. One result has been that Christian communities were among the first to plant rubber and other cash crops and to send their children to school. Where the conversion of individual members of a community occurs, this poses serious problems to the Iban, since the behaviour of any one person, whatever his religious persuasion, has implications for the entire community, as the *adat* makes clear. In many cases an entire longhouse decided to 'become Christian' (*masok Kristian*) and this was often associated with the introduction of settled agriculture based on cash crops and the establishment of schools.

Nothing demonstrates more clearly than these developments the extent to which the Iban themselves experience the interaction and interdependence of their traditional social organization, their religious beliefs and rice cult, and shifting hill rice cultivation.

BIBLIOGRAPHY

OF WORKS REFERRED TO IN THE TEXT

Although this is not intended as a comprehensive Borneo or even Sarawak bibliography, most important references to the Iban and their religion are included.

ANONYMOUS. 1963. Religious Rites of the Iban. *The Sea Dyaks and Other Races of Sarawak.* Borneo Literature Bureau. Kuching. 132–68.

ARNOLD, Guy. 1959. *Longhouse and Jungle: An Expedition to Sarawak.* London.

BAILEY, D. J. S. 1963. The Sru Dyaks. *The Sea Dyaks and Other Races of Sarawak.* Borneo Literature Bureau. Kuching. 251–8.

BEIDELMAN, T. O. 1963. Kaguru Omens: an East African People's Concepts of the Unusual, Unnatural and Supernormal. *Anthropological Quarterly,* **36,** 43–59.

BISCH, Jorgen. 1961. *Ulu: The World's End.* Trans. Reginald Spink. London.

BOCK, Carl. 1881. *The Head-Hunters of Borneo.* London.

BORNEO LITERATURE BUREAU. 1963. *The Sea Dyaks and Other Races of Sarawak.* Kuching.

BOYLE, Frederick. 1865. *Adventures Among the Dyaks of Borneo.* London.

BROOKE, Charles. 1866. *Ten Years in Sarawak.* (2 vols.) London.

CONKLIN, H. C. 1957. *Hanunóo Agriculture; A Report on an Integral System of Shifting Cultivation in the Philippines.* Rome.

COOK, O. 1924. *Borneo, The Stealer of Hearts.* London.

DE R., F. 1963. The Sru Dyaks. *The Sea Dyaks and Other Races of Sarawak.* Borneo Literature Bureau. 259–60.

DICKINSON, G. Lowes. 1958. *The Greek View of Life.* Michigan.

DUBOIS, J. A. 1959. *Hindu Manners, Customs and Ceremonies.* Trans. Henry K. Beauchamp. Oxford.

DUNN, Father. 1963. The Creation. *The Sea Dyaks and Other Races of Sarawak.* Borneo Literature Bureau. Kuching. 21–3.

DURKHEIM, Emile, and MAUSS, Marcel. 1963. *Primitive Classification.* Trans. and ed. Rodney Needham. London.

DURRELL, Lawrence. 1960. *Reflections on a Marine Venus.* London.

ELIADE, Mircea. 1958. *Patterns in Comparative Religion.* Trans. Rosemary Sheed. London and New York.

EVANS-PRITCHARD, E. E. 1937. *Witchcraft, Oracles and Magic Among the Azande.* Oxford.

—— 1956. *Nuer Religion.* Oxford.

—— 1965. *Theories of Primitive Religion.* Oxford.

FREEMAN, J. D. 1955a. *Iban Agriculture. A Report on the Shifting Cultivation of Hill Rice by the Iban of Sarawak.* London.

—— 1955b. *Report on the Iban of Sarawak.* Kuching.

—— 1957a. The Family System of the Iban of Borneo. For *Cambridge Papers in Social Anthropology.* Canberra (mimeo).

—— 1957b. Iban Pottery. *Sarawak Museum Journal,* 8, no. 10 (New Series), no. 25 (Old Series), 153–76.

—— 1958a. To Wake a Lexicographer. (Review article of N. C. Scott, *A Dictionary of Sea Dayak*). *Sarawak Museum Journal,* 8, no. 11 (New Series), no. 26 (Old Series), 409–21.

—— 1958b. The Iban. For *Social Structure in Southeast Asia.* ed. G. P. Murdock. Canberra (mimeo).

—— 1960a. Iban Augury. *The Birds of Borneo* by Bertram E. Smythies. Edinburgh, 73–98. (Also published in *Bijdragen,* 1961, **117,** 1, 141–67.)

—— 1960b. A Note on the Gawai Kenyalang, or Hornbill Ritual of the Iban of Sarawak. *The Birds of Borneo,* by Bertram E. Smythies. Edinburgh, 99–102.

FURNESS, William Henry. 1902. *The Home-Life of Borneo Head-Hunters.* Philadelphia.

GEDDES, W. R. 1954. *The Land Dayaks of Sarawak.* London.

—— 1961. *Nine Dayak Nights.* London.

GOMES, (Revd.) Edwin H. 1911. *Seventeen Years Among the Sea Dyaks of Borneo.* London.

—— 1917. *The Sea-Dyaks of Borneo.* With a Chapter on Missionary Work amongst the Dyaks by the Revd. A. F. Sharp. London.

GOODY, Jack. 1958. *The Developmental Cycle in Domestic Groups.* Cambridge Papers in Social Anthropology No. 1. Cambridge.

GRAVES, Robert. 1957. *The Greek Myths.* (2 vols.) New York.

HADDON, Alfred C. 1901. *Head-Hunters: Black, White, and Brown.* London.

—— and START, Laura E. 1936. *Iban or Sea Dayak Fabrics and Their Patterns.* Cambridge.

HALL, D. G. E. 1964. *A History of Southeast Asia.* London.

HARRISSON, Tom. 1938. *Borneo Jungle: An Account of the Oxford Expedition to Sarawak.* London.

—— 1959a. *World Within: A Borneo Story.* London.

—— 1959b. *The Peoples of Sarawak.* ed. Kuching.

—— 1960. Birds and Men in Borneo. *The Birds of Borneo,* by Bertram E. Smythies. Edinburgh. 20–61.

—— 1962. Borneo Death. *Bijdragen Tot de Taal-, Land- en Volkenkunde,* **118,** 1, 1–41.

—— 1965a. Borneo Writing. *Bijdragen Tot de Taal-, Land- en Volkenkunde,* **121,** 1, 1–57.

HARRISSON, Tom. 1965b. The Malohs of Kalimantan: Ethnological Notes. *Sarawak Museum Journal*, **12**, nos. 25–6 (New Series), 236–350.

—— and SANDIN, Benedict. 1966. Borneo Writing Boards. *Sarawak Museum Journal*, **13**, no. 27 (Special Monograph No. 1), 32–286.

—— —— 1968. Iban Writing Boards. Correspondence in *Man*, **3**, no. 1, 131

HERTZ, Robert. 1960a. A Contribution to the Study of the Collective Representation of Death. *Death and the Right Hand*. Trans. Rodney and Claudia Needham. London. 25–86.

—— 1960b. The Pre-eminence of the Right Hand. *Death and the Right Hand*. Trans. Rodney and Claudia Needham. London. 87–113.

HOSE, Charles. 1920. *The Field-Book of a Jungle-Wallah: being a Description of Shore, River and Forest Life in Sarawak*. London.

—— 1926. *Natural Man: A Record from Borneo*. London.

—— and McDOUGALL, William. 1912. *The Pagan Tribes of Borneo*. With an appendix by A. C. Haddon. (2 vols.) London.

HOWELL, William. 1900. see Howell, William and D. J. S. Bailey.

—— 1961. Supplement to Howell and Bailey's 'Sea Dyak Dictionary'. *Sarawak Museum Journal*, **10**, nos. 17–18 (New Series), 127–69.

—— 1963. The Creation. *The Sea Dyaks and Other Races of Sarawak*. Borneo Literature Bureau. Kuching. 19–20.

—— and BAILEY, D. J. S. 1900. *A Sea Dyak Dictionary*. Singapore. (Parts originally published 1900, 1901, 1902, and 1903.)

HOWES, P. H. H. 1960. Why Some of the Best People are not Christian. *Sarawak Museum Journal*, **9**, nos. 15–16 (New Series), 488–95.

IVANOFF, Pierre. 1958. *Headhunters of Borneo*. Trans. Edward Fitzgerald. London.

JAMES, E. O. 1950. Augury. *Chambers's Encyclopaedia*. London.

JAMUH, George. 1955. A Mass Excitement: 'Sacred Padi'. *Sarawak Museum Journal*, **6**, no. 6 (New Series), no. 21 (Old Series), 567–72.

JENSEN, Erik. 1964. Towards an Iban Fowler. *Sarawak Museum Journal*, **11**, nos. 23–4 (New Series), 544–52.

—— 1965. Hill Rice: An Introduction to the Hill Padi Cult of the Sarawak Iban. *Folk*, **7**, 43–88.

—— 1966. The Iban World. *Sarawak Museum Journal*, **13**, no. 27 (Special Monograph No. 1), 1–31.

—— 1967. Iban Birth. *Folk*, **8–9**, 165–78.

—— 1968. Some Iban Concepts. *Folk*, **10**, 45–60.

—— 1972. Sickness and the Iban Manang, *Folk*. **14–15**, 93–102.

JONES, L. W. 1962. *Report on the Census of Population taken on 15th June 1960*. Kuching.

KEPPEL, Henry. 1846. *The Expedition to Borneo of H.M.S. Dido for the Suppression of Piracy: With Extracts from the Journal of James Brooke, Esq. of Sarawak*. (2 vols.) London.

KEPPEL, Henry. 1853. *A Visit to the Indian Archipelago in H.M. Ship Maeander with Portions of the Private Journal of Sir James Brooke.* (2 vols.) London.

LANDON, Kenneth Perry. 1949. *Southeast Asia: Crossroad of Religions.* Chicago.

LEACH, E. R. 1950. *Social Science Research in Sarawak.* London.

—— 1954. *Political Systems of Highland Burma.* London.

LIENHARDT, Godfrey. 1961. *Divinity and Experience: The Religion of the Dinka.* Oxford.

—— 1966. *Social Anthropology.* London.

LING ROTH, Henry. 1896. *The Natives of Sarawak and British North Borneo.* (2 vols.) London.

LOW, Hugh. 1848. *Sarawak; Its Inhabitants and Productions.* London.

MACDONALD, Malcolm. 1956. *Borneo People.* London.

MACEDA, Jose. 1962. Field-Recording Sea Dayak Music. *Sarawak Museum Journal*, **10**, nos. 19–20 (New Series), 486–500.

MALINOWSKI, Bronislaw. 1963. *Sex, Culture, and Myth.* London.

MARRYAT, Frank S. 1848. *Borneo and the Indian Archipelago.* London.

MJÖBERG, Eric. 1927. *Borneo: Het Land der Koppensnellers.* (Place of publication not known.)

MONBERG, Torben. 1966. *The Religion of Bellona Island: the Concepts of Supernaturals.* Copenhagen.

MORRIS, H. S. 1953. *Report on a Melanau Sago Producing Community in Sarawak.* London.

—— 1967. Shamanism among the Oya Melanau. *Social Organization: Essays Presented to Raymond Firth*, ed. Maurice Freedman. London. 189–216.

MORRISON, Hedda. 1957. *Sarawak.* London.

—— 1962. *Life in a Longhouse.* Kuching.

MUNDY, R. 1848. *Narrative of Events in Borneo and Celebes, down to the Occupation of Labuan: from the Journals of James Brooke, Esq., Rajah of Sarawak, and Governor of Labuan.* (2 vols.) London.

NEEDHAM, Rodney. 1954a. The System of Teknonyms and Death-Names of the Penan. *Southwestern Journal of Anthropology*, **10**, no. 4, 416–31.

—— 1954b. A Penan Mourning-Usage. *Bijdragen Tot de Taal-, Land- en Volkenkunde*, **110**, 3, 263–7.

—— 1955. A Note on Ethnic Classification in Borneo. *Journal of the Malayan Branch of the Royal Asiatic Society*, **28**, Pt. 1, 167–71.

—— 1962. *Structure and Sentiment.* Chicago.

—— 1967. Percussion and Transition. *Man*, **2**, no. 4, 606–14.

NOAKES, J. L. 1950. *A Report on the 1947 Population Census.* Kuching/London.

POLANYI, Michael. 1964. *Personal Knowledge; towards a Post-critical Philosophy.* Chicago.

RICHARDS, A. J. N. 1959. The Ibans. *The Peoples of Sarawak*, ed. Tom Harrisson. Kuching. 9–25.

—— 1961a. *Sarawak Land Law and Adat.* Kuching.

—— 1961b. Priest and Poet. *Sarawak Gazette*, 87, no. 1242, 138–43.

—— 1962. Tibang, Tebang, Tilong and Mandai. *Sarawak Museum Journal*, 10, nos. 19–20 (New Series), 409–11.

—— 1963. *Dayak Adat Law in the Second Division.* Kuching.

—— 1967. Review of *Borneo Writing and Related Matters*, ed. Tom Harrisson. *Man*, 2, no. 3, 488–9.

—— 1968. Iban Writing Boards. Correspondence in *Man*, 3, no. 1, 132.

RUNCIMAN, Sir Steven. 1960. *The White Rajahs: A History of Sarawak from 1841 to 1946.* Cambridge.

ST. JOHN, Spenser. 1863. *Life in the Forests of the Far East; or, Travels in Northern Borneo.* (2 vols.) London.

—— 1879. *Life of Sir James Brooke, Rajah of Sarawak.* Edinburgh.

SANDIN, Benedict. 1956. The Westward Migration of the Sea Dayaks. *Sarawak Museum Journal*, 7, no. 7 (New Series), no. 22 (Old Series), 54–81.

—— 1957. Iban Movements: from the Deluge (and the Survival of Dayang Racha). *Sarawak Museum Journal*, 8, no. 10 (New Series), no. 25 (Old Series), 117–32.

—— 1959. Cock-fighting: the Dayak National Game. *Sarawak Museum Journal*, 9, nos. 13–14 (New Series), 25–32.

—— 1961. Gawai Antu: Sea Dayak Feast of the Departed Spirits. *Sarawak Museum Journal*, 10, nos. 17–18 (New Series), 170–90.

—— 1962a. Gawai Batu: the Iban Whetstone Feast. *Sarawak Museum Journal*, 10, nos. 19–20 (New Series), 392–408.

—— 1962b. *Sengalang Burong.* Kuching.

—— 1964. Descent of Some Saribas Malays (and Ibans)—II. *Sarawak Museum Journal*, 11, nos. 23–4 (New Series), 512–15.

—— 1967. *The Sea Dayaks of Borneo before White Rajah Rule.* London.

SARAWAK GAZETTE. Kuching.

SARAWAK GOVERNMENT GAZETTE. Kuching.

SCHÄRER, Hans. 1946. *Die Gottesidee der Ngadju Dajak in Süd-Borneo.* Leiden.

—— 1963. *Ngaju Religion. The Conception of God Among a South Borneo People.* Trans. Rodney Needham. The Hague.

SCOTT, N. C. 1956. *A Dictionary of Sea Dayak.* London.

SEA DAYAK (IBAN) FINES, THIRD DIVISION. 1940. Kuching.

SEAL, John. 1958. Rainfall and Sunshine in Sarawak. *Sarawak Museum Journal*, **8**, no. 11, 500–44.

SKEAT, Walter William. 1900. *Malay Magic*. London.

SMYTHIES, B. E. 1956. Review of Iban Agriculture by J. D. Freeman. *Sarawak Museum Journal*, **7**, no. 7 (New Series), no. 22 (Old Series), 240–3.

—— 1957. An Annotated Checklist of the Birds of Borneo. *Sarawak Museum Journal*, **7**, no. 9 (New Series), no. 24 (Old Series), xi–818.

—— 1960. *The Birds of Borneo*. Edinburgh (includes Smythies, 1957).

SPENCER, J. E. 1966. *Shifting Cultivation in Southeastern Asia*. Berkeley and Los Angeles.

STURTEVANT, William C. 1968. Categories, Percussion and Physiology. *Man*, **3**, no. 1, 133–4.

TARLING, Nicholas. 1966. *A Concise History of Southeast Asia*. New York/London.

TER HAAR, B. 1948. *Adat Law in Indonesia*. New York.

T'IEN, Ju-K'ang. 1953. *The Chinese of Sarawak: A Study of Social Structure*. London.

WALKER, H. Wilfred. 1910. *Wanderings Among South Sea Savages and in Borneo and the Philippines*. London.

WARD, A. B. 1961. Some Sea Dayak Customs and Fines, 1909–15. *Sarawak Museum Journal*, **10**, nos. 17–18 (New Series), 82–102.

WILKINSON, R. J. 1902. *A Malay–English Dictionary*. Part II (Sîn to Nya). Singapore.

—— n.d. *A Malay–English Dictionary*. (reprint, no date—1932 edition?) Tokyo.

WONG, K. F. 1960. *Pagan Innocence*. London.

WULFF, Inger. 1960. The So-called Priests of the Ngadju Dyaks. *Folk*, **2**, 121–32.

INDEX

222

Index